Private Censorship

Private Censorship

J.P. MESSINA

OXFORD
UNIVERSITY PRESS

OXFORD
UNIVERSITY PRESS

Oxford University Press is a department of the University of Oxford. It furthers
the University's objective of excellence in research, scholarship, and education
by publishing worldwide. Oxford is a registered trade mark of Oxford University
Press in the UK and certain other countries.

Published in the United States of America by Oxford University Press
198 Madison Avenue, New York, NY 10016, United States of America.

Library of Congress Cataloging-in-Publication Data
Names: Messina, J. P., 1989– author.
Title: Private censorship / J.P. Messina.
Description: New York, NY : Oxford Unviersity Press, [2024] |
Includes bibliographical references and index.
Identifiers: LCCN 2023019517 (print) | LCCN 2023019518 (ebook) |
ISBN 9780197581902 (hardback) | ISBN 9780197581919 (epub) | ISBN 9780197581933 (ebook)
Subjects: LCSH: Freedom of speech. | Censorship. | Freedom of the press. |
Intellectual freedom. | Social media—Political aspects.
Classification: LCC JC591 .M47 2024 (print) | LCC JC591 (ebook) |
DDC 323.44/5—dc23/eng/20230622
LC record available at https://lccn.loc.gov/2023019517
LC ebook record available at https://lccn.loc.gov/2023019518

DOI: 10.1093/oso/9780197581902.001.0001

Printed by Integrated Books International, United States of America

Contents

Preface

During a snowy week in January roughly three years ago, I presented some work-in-progress at an event sponsored by Wellesley College's *Freedom Project*. My talk was primarily about the grounds and extent of constitutional protections for free speech. The student audience wasn't much interested in this. But participants did have a lot to say about the topic of this book: private censorship, censorship carried out by non-state actors. They wanted to talk about social media deplatformings, online shaming campaigns, employee firings, and the kinds of corporate and social power that made non-state censorship possible. At the time, I hadn't thought much about private censorship, and it showed in my replies. Later, back in my office, I decided to think about it more. This book is the result of that thinking. It is also an illustration of the profound ways in which engaging with students drives my philosophical interests.

As it turns out, there are some benefits to this: students are often better able than we are to see the next big thing. Academic research (especially in my field of philosophy) often lags behind the trends. No surprise, then, that since I began work on this book, the news cycle has exploded with headlines detailing events central to its topic. In the past three years, we have seen news editors spike stories for politics or profit; allegations of search results disappearing when they cut against received wisdom; instances in which social media platforms remove content, sometimes in politically charged ways; situations in which people lose their jobs for things they said or the company they kept; and mass social pressure campaigns used to enforce ever narrower interpretations of norms like civility and political correctness. Debates over events like these have become a constant fixture of our public lives.

Stanley Fish once complained that others lacked the decency to stop writing about topics once he'd committed to writing about them.[1] I sympathize. Every time I turn away, some new important article or insight relevant to the politics and practice of non-state censorship comes to my attention.[2]

---

[1] (Fish 2013, 402).

[2] The most recent example surrounds Elon Musk's recent takeover of Twitter and the resulting "Twitter Files" on social media censorship. For brief discussion, see Chapter 5.

Or so it seems. And yet there remains, as far as I know, no philosophical treatment of the concept of private censorship (let alone a normative analysis of its practice). This seemed to me a fact in urgent need of changing, even if I was unlikely to get things exactly right.

In a characteristic moment of wisdom, the late philosopher Robert Nozick remarked that there was "room for words on subjects other than last words."[3] This has been my mantra while writing this book. Without it, I'd never have finished. And so I said to myself over and over again that it was okay to offer a treatment of these themes that stopped short of finality. It was okay to just get the ball rolling.

As it seemed to Nozick necessary to complement his original prefatory statement with an insistence that he did not mean by it to be taking back what he wrote in the pages that followed, so here too. Much as I expect that others' work on these topics will eventually supplant some of my own work here, nevertheless, after a sustained period of reflection, the arguments I offer in this book are as nearly right as I can manage. I would not waste your time if I didn't think they were worth taking seriously.

No, these words by way of preface are not my way of capitulating. They are rather an invitation to receive this book in the spirit of a fellow traveler trying to get things right. When I've seemed to you to fail, point it out. The issues are urgent and, if we are to deliver on the promise of a liberal environment conducive to individuality and the pursuit of the truth, we need to get to the bottom of them. This is not, at the end of the day, one person's work.

Already I've had more help from others across many academic disciplines than it would have been reasonable to expect at the outset. Not only are many of my arguments deeply indebted to other people's scholarship, I've also received a great deal of direct aid in editing and revising this manuscript. My former colleagues at the University of New Orleans, especially Danny Shahar and Jake Monaghan, have been invaluable springboards for thinking through these ideas. Danny in particular provided extensive written feedback on an earlier draft that resulted in many significant changes.

The Institute for Humane Studies (IHS) not only provided summer funding, which was used to get this project off the ground, but also sponsored a workshop on a previous draft. The participants of that workshop (Ryan Muldoon, Linda Radzik, Andrew Jason Cohen, Carson Young, Pamela Paresky, Erin Dolgoy, Lee Jussim, Brandon Warmke, Justin Tosi, Sean

---

[3] (Nozick 1974, xii).

Stevens, Luke Sheahan, Rebecca Tuvel, and Jonathan Zimmerman) pressed me in numerous ways that have resulted in a more readable, better argued work. Thanks so much to the IHS for organizing it. Thanks also to my editor at Oxford, Lucy Randall, who has been supportive throughout this process and to the reviewers at Oxford for feedback that led to significant rewriting. Thanks finally to audiences at Virginia Tech University, Tulane University, the University of New Orleans, the University of South Florida, the University of Manchester, the University of British Columbia at Okanagan, and Purdue University for listening to early versions of some of these ideas.

In addition to the help I've had with the manuscript directly, I am lucky to enjoy support from my wife Lena Messina, my family (especially my brother Jeffrey and my parents Pete and Donna), and my friends across the world. Of special note are Crawford Crews, Cameron Cotton O'Brien, Brian Tracz, Sarah Mueller, Dan Burnston, Christina Machak, Claudi Brink, Max Edwards, David Ottlinger, Alex Stern, Carson Young, Danny Shahar, Jake Monaghan, my friends and neighbors in the 7th Ward (especially Willie, Sheila, Lou, and Gil), and my wonderful new colleagues at Purdue University. Thank you all so much for making my life exciting and for the many conversations we've had about this material and other things that inform my writing in ways I cannot quite know.

1

Free Speech and Non-State Censors

Complaints about censorship have once again reached a fever pitch across the liberal West. In other historical periods, such concerns may have marked reactions to book bans and burnings. Often, they followed prosecutions and subsequent jailtime for things spoken or written. During the red scare, they formed the hushed response to chilling state-sponsored watch-lists and employer-supported blacklists designed to ensure victory against communism. Against this history, complaints about the new censorship seem different. Here are some examples, to fix ideas:

- As they have ascended to prominence, social media providers like Facebook, YouTube, Reddit, and Patreon have made controversial moves to "deplatform" those whose speech violates their community standards. For example, Twitter and Facebook banned the accounts of former President Donald Trump, following concerns that his speech incited the January 6 Capitol Riot and risked inciting further violence. Deplatformings, especially when they appear politically motivated, have raised concerns about social media firms' powers to censor and control the information Americans can access. One journalist has it that Facebook (now Meta) operates "the largest system of censorship the world has ever known."[1]
- People worry about biased reporting in the news, aided by censorial editors eager to protect the integrity of their favored narratives or their bottom lines. New York Times editor Kathleen Kingsbury allegedly killed a Bret Stephens column commenting on an incident involving fellow Times reporter Donald McNeil Jr.[2] Bloomberg Business killed a positive story reporting on Fox Business that was months in the making.[3] Many others may decline to report newsworthy information that cuts against their editorial angle.

[1] (Benesch 2020, 86).
[2] (Bryant 2021).
[3] (Flood 2017).

Private Censorship. J.P. Messina, Oxford University Press. © Oxford University Press 2024.
DOI: 10.1093/oso/9780197581902.003.0001

- Prominent persons in leadership roles have had to step down from their posts following pressure on Twitter and other social media platforms. For example, *Teen Vogue* editor Alexi McCammond resigned weeks into her post after racist tweets from her college days surfaced;[4] Mozilla co-founder Brandon Eich stepped down following mounting pressure after revelations that he'd contributed some years earlier to an anti-gay marriage campaign.[5] Policy Analyst Will Wilkinson was fired from the Niskanen Center following conservative outrage in response to a tongue-in-cheek suggestion that the best way for Biden to unify the country was to lynch Mike Pence.[6] Many others have reportedly shut up in fear of meeting with a similar fate.
- Independent of any social media outcry, company employees face sanctions from their employers for their on- or off-the job political speech, raising concerns about employer domination. For instance, Google fired James Damore after he issued a controversial memo on matters of gender and technology.[7] NFL owners have been accused of colluding to keep Colin Kaepernick out of a job because he refuses to kneel for the national anthem before NFL games.[8] Since, the NFL has issued a memo to force players to "stand and show respect for the flag and the [national] anthem."[9]

With respect to the new censorship, there are no books burnings, no prosecutions, no laws or committees. Indeed, there is no state involvement *at all*.[10] And yet there are congressional hearings and executive orders and wonkish proposals to address it, and things are moving quickly.

---

[4] (Kelly 2021).
[5] (Barr 2014).
[6] (Shephard 2021).
[7] (Damore 2017).
[8] (C. Robinson 2020).
[9] (Seifert and Graziano 2018).
[10] A notable exception to the current focus on private speech restrictions is a number of laws currently under discussion in state legislatures that would ban discussion of and teaching of Critical Race Theory in schools. For discussion, see: (Sachs 2021). Additionally, republicans have moved to remove certain books from school libraries; Florida Governor Ron Desantis has attempted to stop faculty from testifying in courts and has sponsored the "Parental Rights in Education" bill, which bars age-inappropriate teaching on gender identity and sexual orientation in grades K-3. For discussion, see: (Diaz 2022). An anonymous referee suggests that one way of understanding these trends is as a kind of backlash: "Because the right has less power in the tech world and in popular culture, they are using state censorship to resist the left's use of private censorship."

My goal in this book is to slow down and ask some basic questions: What is censorship and why does it strike us as a grave problem? Is censorship the right concept for thinking about the above phenomena, or are complaints couched in the language of censorship confused, perhaps conceptually? Supposing that there is no confusion, what rights do the new censors have and do they act within those rights when they act in the ways described above? Supposing that they do act within their rights, is their behavior beyond reproach? And if it isn't, what exactly is wrong with it? Answering these questions is crucial for addressing a further question: What should be done about all of this? Do existing executive and legislative proposals represent a wise course of action? Or are they hastily drawn and likely to make matters worse?

In addressing these questions, I'll begin at the beginning, with an account of censorship and the reasons it is morally and politically troubling. With this account on the table, we'll see that thinking of the cases above in terms of censorship is perfectly above board. Next, I argue that it is sensible to be concerned about these forms of censorship. This is because, among other things, private censorship can threaten our ability to realize an intellectual environment we have reason to value, if we value free speech. Despite this, questions about the proper response to private censorship are far from straightforward. For although private parties and states can both act as censors, states and private actors enjoy distinct sets of rights and duties. Beyond this, their censorship affects others in importantly different ways. And those differences matter for determining how citizens, executives, and legislators should respond when they censor.

Before we begin, it is worth flagging a methodological point. In the remainder of this chapter, I will be asking you to consider various examples in the service of clarifying concepts or eliciting normative judgments. In discussing these examples, I will be making normative judgments of my own: things like, "such and such is clearly wrong" or "so and so is clearly permissible." It is a background supposition of this work that such judgments can be true or false and that they are no mere matters of opinion. But I will often be unable to argue for the judgments on which I rely. Rather, I invite you to think about the cases yourself and exercise your own judgment. If it departs from mine, think about why that is. If you come up with a compelling explanation, great! That's how valuable philosophical exchanges are born.

Now, let's begin.

1.1 What Censorship Is

Broadly speaking and intuitively, censorship involves stopping someone from expressing or accessing some content (be it a statement, a work of art, a song or video, or an image). But it must also involve more than this. The doctor that removes your tonsils stops you from speaking (and stops me from hearing you). Yet it would be odd to refer to the surgery as an instance of censorship, even if there's something you'd really like to say after the operation. Similarly: I may stop you from speaking by persuading you that it's a bad idea to say what you were going to say. Still, because you are ultimately responding to the strength of my reasons, rather than a threat, it is unnatural to speak of my censoring you. You've simply changed your mind.

Some believe that censorship is inherently a creature of state. The reason that neither tonsillectomy nor rational persuasion counts is the same reason that describing the above phenomena in terms of censorship is loose talk. Although you have been stopped from expressing your ideas, this has happened without the exercise of state power. Absent state power, talk of censorship only muddies the waters.

For others, censorship is all around us.[11] Not only do newspaper editors, social media platforms, teachers, judges, lawyers, and parents engage in censorship, you do too. Here's the thought: meaningful communication presupposes censorship. If we said everything that it crossed our minds to say, we would fail to get our true point across. So successful communication requires us to censor *ourselves*. If there were not significant filtering by experts, we would find ourselves drowning in a sea of barely comprehensible information. So successful communication requires *some* to censor *others*. On such an account, we should see the regularity of censorship as a "good thing." It is, after all, what enables us to communicate with one another and to piece the world together.

The truth about censorship is more nuanced than either of these pictures suggests. Sometimes non-state agents censor us and sometimes we censor ourselves, but censorship neither pervades our lives nor is it something for which we should be overly grateful. Censorship is often gravely wrong—especially when conducted by states—but it can also be justified in various circumstances (and is easier to justify for non-state agents).

---

[11] (Fish 1994, 2019). See also (Butler 1998) and (Schauer 1998).

What, then, is censorship? As a first pass, we might say that A censors B when A (1) intentionally prevents B from expressing or accessing an idea or representation in some context or (2) imposes some cost upon B to discourage her from doing so. Unfortunately, this definition generates hard cases.

A professor who docks student-participation grades for those who fail to raise their hands before speaking certainly intentionally imposes a cost on certain kinds of speech to discourage that speech. Still, it would be unnatural to speak here of censorship. Similarly, editors of various publications reject more written content than they accept. And yet it seems to be the exception rather than the rule to categorize exercises of editorial authority as censorship. In most cases, editors do not act censoriously (even though it is often within their power to do so).

It is possible, of course, to respond by accepting that our linguistic intuitions are wrong and the definition is right. Certainly, Fish would have no qualms about finding censorship in these examples.[12] But allowing any kind of restraint on speech to count as censorship makes it mysterious why anyone would care to talk about it. At least on its face, censorship is a special kind of thing. When we specify that a constraint involves censorship, we mean to be identifying something more specific than the kinds of speech norms and editorial practices that help us get on in the world. For this reason, it would be better to take these cases as an opportunity for revision and to try to come up with a definition that rules them out. We should, in other words, seek a conception of censorship according to which it is distinct from: self-restraint in the service of being understood, ordinary exercises of editorial authority, and rules of order that enable our (e.g., educational) institutions to function as designed.

To get a sense of what more censorship might require censor, it is helpful to look at paradigm cases of censorship—cases where it is natural to speak of censorship—and ask what they share. Consider, then, a few circumstances in which nobody (at least nobody not already in the grips of a theory) would deny that censorship is occurring:

---

[12] Though more restrained than Fish's account, Cohen and Cohen (2022, 14–15) argue that censorship occurs anytime one agent intentionally stops another from speaking or hearing. On their account, things like keeping a queue are expressly counted in. This too strikes me as too broad for the reasons I emphasize in the main text.

1. In North Korea, subjects receive nearly all their information from the government, under the heading of The Central News Agency. The press is under tight state control, and the internet is inaccessible for most individuals. Additionally, the state produces propaganda to ensure that subjects' attitudes toward subversive content are sufficiently hostile to prevent uptake. Here, there is a regime of state censorship which aims to ensure that opinions are kept within a narrow range in the service of maintaining power.

2. In the 20th-century United States, the Espionage Act prohibited conveying information that officials deemed detrimental to the US military's operations, or helpful to the success of its enemies. In a landmark case, plaintiff Charles Schenck (then general secretary of the American Socialist Party), distributed a pamphlet to draftees, encouraging them to claim their 13th Amendment rights against enslavement and evade the draft. He appealed his conviction. The court rejected the appeal, holding that Schenck's document, circulated as it was in wartime, intended as it was to obstruct the draft, constituted an attempt to incite to illegal activity. Like many other leftists during the same general historical period, Schenck was locked in a cage for what he wrote. Here, a single law functions as a locus of censorship, largely of left-wing political views, although the regime in question purports to protect free speech in other domains.

3. Broadcasting networks have censored speech that is inimical to their corporate interests. Recently, for instance, CBS censored a musical short in *The Good Fight* which was—ironically—critical of Chinese censorship.[13] Viewers of the show witnessed the words, "CBS has censored this content" flashing across their screens. Here, we have a private party protecting its material interests by ensuring that certain of its financial stakeholders will not be put off by the content that it broadcasts. More troublingly, news organizations dependent on advertising revenues from certain companies have suppressed syndicated stories (e.g., home recipes for soaps) that would, in theory, allow consumers to do without advertisers' products.

4. In 1933, hundreds of university students in several different cities publicly burned works of literature, history, and philosophy deemed to be anti-German (read: subversive to the National Socialist agenda),

---

[13] (Nussbaum 2019).

for the purpose of signaling to others that certain ideas would not be publicly tolerated. While the Third Reich had, no doubt, initiated an aggressive program of state censorship, the book burnings themselves (undertaken independently by the students) seem to be paradigm acts of censorship, even without the background conditions of state censorship. The students wished to send a powerful public signal that certain ideas would not be publicly tolerated. In doing so, they increased the costs for public profession of those views in a way that was experienced as censorious.[14]

Notice that censors target expressive content *for a reason*. Some seek to suppress ideas or works because they deem those works dangerous (this was the case with the instances of censorship under the Espionage Act). Others (e.g., North Korea) sense a threat to perceived (political, religious, moral) orthodoxy. Still others (e.g., CBS) censor to protect their material interests. Moreover, censors target expression with tools intended to bypass the ordinary channels of rational persuasion. They seek to *prevent* some audience from engaging with the expressed content. Often, they achieve this by means of threats. Schenck was imprisoned for violating a rule intended to stop speakers from undermining the war effort. Dissidents in North Korea can be executed. When censorship is not achieved by sanction or threat of sanction, it is achieved by withholding certain material from the public view, destroying it, or otherwise expressing that the ideas are not to be tolerated (the relevant scene in *The Good Fight* was removed from view; book burners try to create a climate of fear around certain ideas).[15]

I suggest, then, that we understand censorship as *the attempted suppression of expressive content*[16] *on the grounds that it is dangerous, threatening to (moral, political, or religious) orthodoxy, or inimical to the material interests of the agent aiming to suppress it*. This definition has several advantages over the one with which we began.

---

[14] (Berkowitz 2021, 186–87).

[15] Attention to these cases shows that censorship is not a success term. What I mean is that to act as a censor, you need not prevent uptake or expression, only to try. As (Berkowitz 2021) points out, *most* censorship is unsuccessful. Schenck's argument has been read by far more people given his imprisonment than it would have been otherwise. CBS censored a scene from *The Good Fight* despite the fact that the content of the scene is accessible elsewhere. And many of the books banned by church and state authorities have achieved a kind of permanence for the experience.

[16] I refer to expressive content rather than speech to capture the full range of media that can find itself within the censor's crosshairs. This might include speech, writing, works of art (even that which seeks to avoid expression), and so on.

First, it explains why ordinary rules of order (e.g., the rule to raise one's hand before speaking in class) are not cases of censorship. These kinds of procedural rules are not aimed at suppressing content at all, much less because it is judged dangerous (etc.). They are aimed instead at ensuring that the conversation proceeds without chaos.

The definition also explains why the biology professor is not engaged in censorship when she requires that questions in class be relevant to the subject matter at hand. She might have no interest whatsoever in suppressing speech surrounding the military industrial complex and nevertheless put a stop to my diatribe about the same.[17]

Finally, this account explains the difference between editorial censorship and ordinary exercises of editorial authority. As an editor of a newspaper or an executive at a broadcasting corporation, I must necessarily make myriad decisions about how to fill a scarce number of pages or hours. These decisions will result in disappointment for writers and other people with things to say. In the ordinary course of doing things, I will need to reject pilots and stories and op-eds. And yet as the above case with CBS shows, sometimes I will do so not because I face space constraints, but instead because I deem the content inimical to my financial or political interests. When I block the content in *these* instances, I do so for reasons other than simply making space for content that I deem better. Accordingly, I act as a censor.

One might object that the above definition fails to capture very well the behavior of real-world professional censors in the places and times that they were employed. For example, the historian Robert Darnton points out that those who were actually employed under the title "censor" often thought of themselves as men of letters and intellectuals. Real, historical censors were often just as eager to approve and certify brilliant works they thought the public would appreciate and to spare the public from reading poorly written drivel as they were to prevent the publication of works offensive to religion, morality, or state. Authors and censors often "worked together . . . they shared the same assumptions and values;" indeed, "most censors were authors themselves," while others were professors and enlightenment thinkers enthusiastic about ideas, not fearful of them.[18] In short, a good bit of the work of the censor consisted precisely in acting as an editor.

---

[17] This does not mean of course that teachers *cannot* censor their students. They can, namely by preventing students from raising points that are appropriate within the classroom. For instance, a teacher that requires that politically controversial viewpoints be kept out of a discussion to which they are relevant is recognizably acting to censor the students that wish to raise those points.

[18] (Darnton 2014, 36).

The history Darnton tells is illuminating, but I do not think it reveals any deficiency in the definition above. Instead, it shows clearly that, in addition to censoring, those who held the office and title "censor" did a whole lot more. They were state-appointed editors and literary critics who felt a responsibility to help their fellow readers determine what was worth their time. Given the proliferation of written material the printing press enabled, they performed valuable functions in this regard. But officials *also* assigned to them the work of suppressing publications offensive to religion, morality, and state. Such suppression was achieved not merely through state laws prohibiting works with those characteristics, but also by means of threats that those who would publish or print them would be punished. Censors did, in short, censor in the sense defined above, even if they acted in other capacities, too. Censors censored even though censorship was, paradoxically, a mere part of their job description.

Importantly, our definition makes no reference to states. This means that it can readily accommodate the new worries about censorship with which we began this chapter. Still, the definition is not without an explanation for why we so strongly associate censorship with states. After all, states need to coordinate collective action and maintain power. Such needs confer upon them extraordinarily strong interests in restricting and sanctioning expression. And their centralized power and wide authority to punish confers upon them an impressive capacity to effectively block speech.

But private parties, too, have interests in suppressing speech and powers to do so. In my view, when they exercise these powers in pursuit of these interests, private parties act as censors. They do so in exactly the ways that are fueling today's concerns about censorship. Social media companies prevent, sanction, and remove expressive content from their platforms, often because they judge the content dangerous (or harmful), sometimes in pursuit of a kind of community they hope to realize (sometimes for financial reasons). Media organizations seek to suppress ideas that threaten their monetary and political interests. Ordinary citizens mount social pressure campaigns to stamp out deviant speech. And our employers protect their interests by monitoring and sometimes punishing us for the things we say. In each case, I will say that they engage in *private censorship*—by which I just mean censorship by private (non-state) actors.

Now that we have a clearer idea about what talk of private censorship *means*, it will help to ask distinct questions about its normative status. Astute readers will have noticed that the definition I have offered is *descriptive*. It is no part of the definition that censors must act wrongly or badly in suppressing speech. There are, at any rate, two questions, and it aids clarity to keep them separate. The first question is whether some party is engaged in censorship. The second question is whether she acts well or justifiably.[19]

To see that the questions come apart, consider a variant of the CBS case. Rather than a scene critical of Chinese censorship, executives are considering a scene in which the characters walk through an accurate, step-by-step construction of a bomb from easily accessible household goods. The bomb is then detonated at a political rally designed to refer to an upcoming real-world event about which tensions are high. Worried about inspiring viewers to violence in a politically delicate moment, the executives remove the scene when the episode airs. Note that their action continues to satisfy our definition of censorship. Executives suppress the scene because they judge that it is dangerous. Still, provided they are correct about the dangers (suppose there is, in fact, a .99 probability that, if they run the segment, violence will result), they act permissibly and arguably under a duty of due care. Identifying a case of censorship is one thing. Showing that it is wrong requires further steps.

In the next section, I offer an account of the importance of free speech. This will allow us to better understand under what conditions censorship is wrongful, which is the first step toward understanding how to wisely respond to concerns about it.

1.2 Why Censorship Is (Often) Wrong

Censorship has long been an attractive tool for powerful governing bodies to achieve their goals. It is easier for states to act with the veneer of legitimacy and to retain power despite horrific behavior when they can quiet dissent. What's more is that states' track record when it comes to determining what speech warrants suppression is remarkably poor.[20] For these reasons, there is now a powerful consensus that state censorship needs to be kept within extremely tight bounds. According to John Stuart Mill, such a consensus had already solidified as early as 1859. "No argument," Mill wrote in *On Liberty*, "can now be needed, against permitting a legislature or an executive, not

---

[19] Strictly speaking, things are more complicated. One could hold the view that censorship is always pro tanto wrong, but that it can be justified, and sometimes the justification is so strong that we cease noticing the negative valence inherent in acts of censorship.
[20] (Berkowitz 2021).

identified with the people, to prescribe opinions to them, and determine what doctrines or what arguments they shall be allowed to hear."[21]

The consensus Mill observed left two crucial questions wide open: First, may the government ban expression or prevent the spread of dangerous ideas when it is asked to do so by the people? Second, may the people—acting independently of the government—permissibly exercise social pressure to censor their peers? Mill famously answered these still-open questions in the negative. In short, he held that the "complete liberty" of thought and opinion was so crucial to the progressive development of humankind that it could not be permissibly restricted by states, even if citizens voted (even unanimously) for the restrictions. So crucial was this value that citizens ought not to restrict the expression of opinions even through informal social pressure.

These broad pronouncements stand in need of justification. What exactly is so bad about censorship? Here's Mill:

> the peculiar evil of silencing the expression of an opinion is, that it is rob-bing the human race; posterity as well as the existing generation; those who dissent from the opinion, still more than those who hold it. If the opinion is right, they are deprived of the opportunity of exchanging error for truth: if wrong, they lose, what is almost as great a benefit, the clearer perception and livelier impression of truth, produced by its collision with error.[22]

With a flair for the dramatic, Mill characterizes the suppression of opinions as a kind of *robbery*. As he sees it, there are really just two options with re-spect to any given act of suppression: Either the opinion suppressed contains some truth or it doesn't. In the first case, the would-be censor robs humanity (or some part of it) of the opportunity to appreciate the truth in it. In the second, she robs humanity (or some part of it) of the opportunity to under-stand what's really true more fully, in the view of its contrast with error. But if so, then genuine truths can quickly become "dead dogmas," empty husks of ideas that contain no motive force. In short, Mill thought that censorship was bad news for us as *epistemic agents*. It compromises our access to true propositions and stops us from fully understanding what justifies them. To this general argument, Mill adds three considerations.

---

[21] (Mill 2003, 86).
[22] (Mill 2003, 87).

The first is that human beings are fallible—and massively so. We are, in other words, likely to be overconfident in our judgment that the opinions that we wish to restrict are mistaken. Thus, even if you're skeptical that collision with error is really anything so valuable, you should worry—as a censor—that you'll have gotten things wrong.

The second hinges on the ways limited creatures like us can be justified in holding beliefs in the first place. For us, to be warranted to believe requires remaining open to criticism from others. Since suppressing others' views walls our own off from criticism, such suppression can only reduce our justification for believing what we believe.[23] Put differently, if others can't challenge our views by offering us reasons to go a different way, we are, in a real sense, left acting and reasoning in the dark.

The third is that, in addition to its relationship to the truth, freedom of thought and expression are important for allowing us to envision and enact experiments in living, by which we depart from the common ways of doing things and carve out our own paths. The ways in which censorship can impede the development of these experiments is not merely bad news for our autonomous self-development and capacity to develop as individuals, it can also stop us from discovering problems in our local culture and better ways of doing things. But if so, then suppressing opinions impedes the progress of humankind and impedes democratic decision-making.

Along with these Millian arguments that free expression promotes the pursuit of truth, the development of individuality, and the quality of collective decision-making, theorists have found other reasons for protecting the freedom of expression. For instance, for some, freedom of expression is important for accommodating diversity.[24] For others, it is important for enabling persons to autonomously choose a course of life.[25] And for yet others, allowing states to silence opinions gives governments powers we have reason to fear will be turned against us.[26]

In my view, these defenses of free speech present so many perfectly good reasons to be concerned about the suppression of ideas. The freedom to speak unmolested is constitutive of autonomy; without it, our development as individuals would be very difficult. In atmospheres where expression is suppressed, our understanding withers in darkness. And when

---

[23] (Joshi forthcoming).
[24] (Schauer 1982).
[25] See (Scanlon 1972), though see also (Scanlon 2011).
[26] (Messina 2020).

we're reasoning together about what to do, it is just as important that we are exposed in our deliberations to dissent as it is to ensure that it is as difficult as possible for those in charge to stamp it out. We need not choose between these grounds. If we refuse to do so, then we accept a kind of pluralism about why just states enshrine rights to free speech, and we reject that free expression needs to maximize or invariably advance any single value for it to be worthy of strong protection.

Legal and political developments in the roughly 150 years following the publication of *On Liberty* have been good news for those sympathetic with these arguments against government censorship. Constitutions in most Western democracies recognize that individuals have rights to free speech that most forms of state censorship violate. What's more is that when those constitutions have been read and interpreted by judges, those judges have found ever more kinds of speech to lie beyond the scope of permissible state interference (especially in the United States). The result is that state suppression of opinions is these days rare.[27] If the freedom of expression is threatened in the West now, it is not, in the main, threatened by governments, at least not so far as they regulate in a direct manner what their citizens can say.

But Mill's argument against censorship does not apply only to states. He saw that social groups and private organizations could also act as censors, and that their censorship could result in a "tyranny more formidable than many kinds of political oppression."[28] Although private censors have less severe sanctions at their disposal than states, they often leave "fewer means of escape, penetrating much more deeply into the details of life, and enslaving the soul itself."[29] For this reason, a free society cannot stop at protecting against state censorship. It must also offer "protection against the tyranny of the prevailing opinion and feeling; against the tendency of society to impose, by other means than civil penalties, its own ideas and practices as rules of conduct on those who dissent from them."[30]

And yet our constitutions, most of them, offer no protection of this kind. Laws, especially in the United States, protect our rights to speak *only* against

---

[27] In a certain narrow sense, legally permissible state censorship in the United States is limited to incitement (narrowly construed), defamation, obscenity, fraud, true threats, and other forms of unprotected speech. Beyond categories of unprotected speech, it is generally acknowledged that schools must teach certain things and that they might be restricted from teaching others and that states can regulate here. When they do so within reasonable limits and for the reasons laid out in our definition, it can be sensible to talk of permissible censorship here, too.

[28] (Mill 2003, 76).

[29] (Mill 2003, 76).

[30] (Mill 2003, 76).

state interference. They offer virtually no protection against social and corporate tyranny. They tolerate wide powers of censorship on the part of private parties. Those who worry about the new censorship sometimes argue that this fact stands in urgent need of correction. If we value free speech, we must bar private censorship in the same way we bar state censorship.

1.3 Do State and Non-State Censorship Merit the Same Response?

Worries that our current legal environment inadequately protects against private censorship are widespread. Those on the political left observe that private corporations often possess substantially more power than ordinary individuals. Such power can distort public discourse by allowing the wealthy and powerful an outsized influence in our political conversations. Moreover, employers are often in a position to punish vulnerable persons for their speech and will be motivated to do so when that speech mobilizes for political change that cuts against the employers' interests.[31] Those on the political right worry that, when public discourse takes place on platforms controlled by those who share a certain narrow set of viewpoints (like Silicon Valley executives seem to), opinions inconsistent with those viewpoints are likely to be suppressed, resulting in an atmosphere of uniformity that impedes the pursuit of the truth.[32] We respond to worries about state censorship by enshrining rights against it. So perhaps we should do the same with respect to private censorship.

Proponents of the position that state and private censorship ought to receive similar treatment argue by analogy.

(1) State censorship ought to be prohibited because it inhibits free speech values (e.g., autonomy, individuality, the pursuit of the truth, and democratic deliberation).

(2) Private censorship also inhibits these values.

(3) So, private censorship ought to be prohibited, too.

---

[31] See: (Anderson 2017). Such appeared to be the motivation behind efforts by South Carolina and Louisiana to ban "discrimination against most private employees based on 'political opinion'" (Volokh 2012, 42).

[32] See: (Carl 2017).

Because state and private censorship both inhibit free speech values, and because we know that state censorship merits prohibition on this basis, we may infer that private censorship likely merits prohibition as well. The trouble with the argument is threefold.

First, there is a problem with the first premise. For although it's true that state censorship is troubling insofar as it makes it difficult to realize these positive values, this isn't the only reason it is worthy of condemnation. Another major reason is that we have historically well-grounded fears concerning what politicians specifically will do when we provide them with even narrow powers for censoring speech.[33]

Oliver-Wendell Holmes's early decisions under the Espionage Act are a case in point. In upholding convictions under this act, Holmes perpetuated an unjust censorship regime in which persons were prohibited from expressing their political beliefs to the extreme advantage of state orthodoxy. Such persons were disproportionately punished with jailtime when they failed to comply. Their convictions impeded political progress.

Consider, again, Schenck's conviction for distributing pamphlets urging men to evade the draft. Conscription, he had argued, was inconsistent with the constitutional right against enslavement. For simply making this argument, he was jailed. Given the chance to overturn, the court instead upheld the punishment. There was, Holmes argued, no constitutionally protected right to shout fire in a crowded theater. And that's effectively what Schenck had done.

Schenck's conviction demonstrates the importance of restraining the state from engaging in even what seems like uncontroversially acceptable censorship. *Everyone* agrees that there's no good reason to protect the right to shout *fire!* in a crowded theater. The problem is that public officials (even those whose vocation is to curb legislative excess) will often read even reasonable constraints on speech as justification for quelling political dissent. Schenck's pamphlet was nothing like shouting fire in a crowded theatre. But the rule that states might regulate such speech nevertheless created extensive powers that led to severe abuse. The process of disempowering states from acting in this way would take decades.

If these worries about the abuse of power apply to non-state censors, they are here apparently much less weighty. Consider that extensive private powers of censorship are commonplace. Newspaper editors and publishers

---

[33] (Cass 1987)

get to decide what gets printed and in what form; TV networks decide what goes on the air (and what doesn't); professors can decide which views are heard in their classrooms. Ordinarily, when things are going well, those occupying these roles do not censor much. But the roles do create *powers* to censor. And yet when these powers are abused and wrongful censorship is the result, no one winds up in jail and the truth has a chance to find its way out (often in other publications or on other networks or in other classrooms). Thus the first premise occludes the fact that one of the most powerful reasons for prohibiting state censorship does not apply as strongly to private parties, if it applies to them at all.

Beyond this, it's reasonable to worry that a state prohibition on private censorship itself grants to the state new powers that it might well abuse in ways that conflict with the common good. Consider: if private organizations are barred by law from censoring, the state acquires a new power over the editorial authority of newspapers and broadcasters and publishers and over the content management of social media companies. It doesn't take much imagination (and history helps it along) to envision how these new powers might serve the interests of the already powerful, at the expense of the rest of us.

Perhaps this sounds a bit paranoid to you. (It doesn't to me.) Or perhaps you think it undersells the degree to which we have reasons to fear private powers. Even so, the argument by analogy fails. For there are problems as well with the second premise. To see this, notice that, although Facebook, Twitter, and YouTube govern their platforms in ways that prohibit certain kinds of speech, it is nevertheless plausible that—on net—their existence has democratized speech and resulted in a more inclusive marketplace of ideas.

Before these platforms existed, the class of persons who had access to an audience for their political views extending beyond their immediate social circle was remarkably small, including those influential and well-educated enough to obtain publication in print media or in television or radio broadcast.[34] "Tech giants" have given a voice and audience to literally billions of people whose speech would have otherwise been confined to a soap box in a local park, if it made it that far.[35] Moreover, when Facebook censors me,

---

[34] For this reason, it strikes me as not quite fair to say that social media moderation compromises persons' "fair opportunity to participate" in discourse on matters of concern to them (Klonick 2018, 1603).

[35] As of 2020, Facebook had 2.85 billion daily active users. Every minute, 510,000 comments are posted, 293,000 statuses are updated, and 136,000 photos are added. This is all content that would not previously have received any audience at all. Photos are relegated to dusty photo albums; comments are kept to oneself; one's "status" is shared with those who can observe it or hear stories about it. See: https://kinsta.com/blog/facebook-statistics/. For similar statistics on YouTube and Twitter, see

the options that were available to me for expressing myself before Facebook existed remain available: I can start a website or a blog or try to place an op-ed, or speak at local meetings, and so on. The audience's attention might have shifted, but these kinds of shifts are the ordinary stuff of social and technological change. The same is true when someone starts a new publication: The editor creates additional space for the expression of views, and this needs to be factored into the equation when assessing its practice of turning down some speech. Whether, then, private powers are a net boon or net cost to the marketplace of ideas is at least questionable.

Things are worse yet: for even if we grant both the argument's premises, there are relevant dissimilarities between states and private parties that suggest that they merit different moral responses, similarities notwithstanding.

The chief dissimilarity is that one can typically avoid private censorship at a reasonably low cost, say, by using a different platform (or none at all), by seeking information from non-corporate sources (public radio, public libraries, universities, etc.), or by seeking another employer.[36] By contrast, it is very difficult to avoid sanctions for violating laws that impose prior restraints on speech.[37] Exiting states is notoriously difficult. In addition to the various costs (financial and otherwise) involved with leaving one's home (including expatriation taxes), one must find a willing state to accept your residence, and indeed one that does not impose the relevant restrictions on speech. Escaping state censorship may be practically impossible.

By contrast, where it is hardest to avoid private censorship—in the long-term effects of social shaming campaigns which can be so damaging to an individual's social standing—legal remedies would themselves restrict people's most basic freedoms of speech and association. Indeed, prohibiting private censorship often introduces a conflict between the First Amendment freedoms of expression and association.[38] If employers cannot fire employees

https://www.omnicoreagency.com/youtube-statistics/ and https://www.omnicoreagency.com/twit ter-statistics/.

[36] According to the 2016 Census, there are 5.6 million firms in the United States alone, and many of these are struggling to fill their posts, with available jobs outnumbering jobseekers (see: https:// www.bls.gov/charts/job-openings-and-labor-turnover/unemp-per-job-opening.htm). In July alone, 3.7 million workers quit their jobs—and more voluntarily left their posts than were fired. These numbers are, of course, only suggestive. But what they suggest is that the labor market is sufficiently competitive as to give employees robust exit options. The pandemic has only increased workers' bargaining power, as firms struggle to find help.
[37] The notion of prior restraint is central to constitutional law. A prior restraint is a legislative effort to prohibit speech before it happens.
[38] On the connection between these freedoms, see: (Emerson 1964).

for their political speech, if platforms must host speech that they loathe, if editors must publish opposing views, the state is effectively forcing persons to associate with persons and amplify positions they may reasonably prefer to avoid. Similarly, requiring platforms to host content they'd prefer not to host effectively forces them to deploy resources to serve persons and viewpoints they might reasonably prefer not to serve. Thus whether we should prohibit private censorship in the way that we prohibit state censorship depends on its being true that the improvements to the marketplace of ideas achieved by the prohibitions justify infringing the similar rights of others.

I suggest that this is a difficult case to make. First, forcing people to associate with those they loathe seems an especially strong violation of their rights. Second, it is difficult to show that limited spheres of censorship, freely entered into, are not beneficial. To see the latter point, notice that some degree of non-state content moderation might help weed out hatred and false speech, leaving our discourse healthier than it would be if every conversational space mirrored the public square. When people opt into content moderation of this kind, it makes sense to let them. They sometimes have good reasons, and even when they don't, the choice is properly theirs to make.

A third dissimilarity is that firms plausibly have a duty to ensure that their corporate culture functions well. But accommodating political disagreement of certain kinds in line with the First Amendment may compromise their ability to discharge these duties.[39] Consider the following case for illustration.

Good Boss: Lucky Dogs hotdog outfit serves a diverse body of hotdog lovers and consists in a diverse group of employees. One of its employees, Ignatius Riley, takes to Twitter to post a racist manifesto, which the customers and other employees see. Lucky's staff descends into disorder and customers head for the exits. In response, Lucky Dogs informs Ignatius that, if he does not remove the tweets and issue a public apology, he will be let go.

Management at Lucky's, it seems to me, acts appropriately. Even if you don't think that Lucky's has a duty to ensure an atmosphere of equal respect between its workers, she is clearly *permitted* to pursue such an atmosphere.

[39] Indeed, there are statutes that expressly forbid employer discrimination on the grounds of protected political speech that occurs outside the workplace (Volokh 2012). But since the courts have held that hate speech is protected speech, this seems to imply that an employee cannot be let go after uttering racist speech. But consider the costs in terms of corporate culture that might attend keeping such a person on a diverse staff that includes members targeted by the speech.

Tolerating Ignatius's behavior is at odds with that goal. Sanctioning his behavior is an attractive remedy. This is so even if Ignatius is stopped from
speaking as he wishes, even if he is censored thereby.

Fourth (and relatedly), for-profit companies have fiduciary duties to their
investors, co-owners, and shareholders to keep patrons coming back to
maintain profitability. This is—to be sure—not their only duty. But it does
confer upon them a legitimate interest in regulating content accordingly—
one that states lack. If censors often suppress speech to protect their material
interests, duties to shareholders might justify them in engaging in some content suppression. It might be, for example, that users of a platform will not
continue to return if they encounter too much pornography or hate speech.
If so, these kinds of firms should be empowered to act accordingly, even if
doing so results in censorship.

Finally, companies that began with private investment have a right to operate to realize a creative vision, whereas states lack such duties and such
interests. Consider the case of Rightbook to illustrate the latter point:

> *Rightbook*: A new social media company aims to cultivate a space for right-
> wing political views and so has an explicitly politicized set of community
> standards. It instructs its team of content-moderators to ensure that con-
> tent posted to Rightbook is politically appropriate, and within the bounds
> of conservative thought.

Despite the fact that Rightbook suppresses speech due to its inconsistency
with a certain political orthodoxy (censoring left-wing views), private organizations ought to be able to carve out spaces for partisan purposes. Barring
private censorship would mean disallowing this kind of thing.

The above arguments have all challenged the strength of the analogy
above. They have done so either by suggesting that private censorship is less
concerning than public or state censorship or by suggesting that states have
fewer compelling reasons to censor than private parties. One might object,
however, that there are conditions under which many of these disanalogies
between states and private parties look less stark. This appears especially true
when private parties enjoy monopoly (or near-monopoly) power.

Consider the share of the market for search engine advertisement
controlled by Google, which has recently been sued by Tulsi Gabbard for violation of her First Amendment rights for "censoring" her campaign contribution page. Ignore for now that Gabbard lacks legal standing and that her

claims appear to be unsubstantiated. Still, when a firm enjoys dominance like Google does (capturing nearly 90% of search engine hits), and consumers face high costs of exit (doing without Google is unimaginable for many), we might think that they should be treated like states and barred from censoring content. I offer a deeper analysis of the case to regulate Google and other alleged monopolies in later chapters. For now, it suffices to note that there are traditionally two responses to the existence of monopoly power.

The first response is to leverage the state's anti-trust powers to constrain firms from attaining monopoly status and from engaging in anti-competitive practice. But this supports, rather than undermines, the point that state censorship and private censorship require different approaches. For it is just not true that we respond to concerns about state censorship by breaking up the state's monopoly on, say, force. And, recall: my point here is only that the well-studied response to state censorship does not apply straightforwardly to private censors. Generally, private censorship warrants a separate treatment.

The second response—most useful when we have reason to suspect the existence of a natural monopoly—is to regulate the monopoly according to public principles. If we anticipate that the market in which the monopoly firm operates is one in which a single provider will emerge (or is one in which we have reason to think that additional firms would introduce waste), then we might choose to simply enshrine the existing firm and subject it to regulations such that it cannot exercise its market position to the detriment of citizens and consumers. In doing so, government might shield the firm from competition in exchange for legal assurance, e.g., that it does not overcharge or discriminate against consumers. When such monopoly affects speech, perhaps it can be regulated to ensure that it does so without compromising citizens' interests in free expression.

But notice that even in the quite special case of private censors that are natural monopolies, it is plausible that the regulations we will want to subject them to will differ from the restrictions we place upon the state. (Indeed, as I argue in Chapter 6, is not at all obvious what the First Amendment regulation of Google would even look like.) Thus, recognizing the existence of natural monopolies does not straightforwardly entail that private censors are to be treated analogously with state censors.

If what I've argued for so far is correct, we should accept a kind of institutional pluralism.[40] It is false as a general matter that the norms appropriate

[40] (Levy 2015).

to the state are appropriate to the norms of other institutions within its jurisdiction, even when these other institutions act in similar ways. As I argue throughout this book, the appropriate response to state censorship is distinct from the appropriate response to private censorship. This is partially, we have seen, because private parties will often have moral rights to engage in the kinds of activities associated with their censorship, whereas states will not.

1.4 (When) Is Private Censorship Wrong?

Some will take the last section's arguments to mean that Mill was wrong to worry about private censorship. After all, if private parties have rights to act as censors, then their conduct is beyond reproach. Minimally, any reproach should be directed at the instrumental rationality of their behavior.[41]

As above, this conclusion has appealed to partisans on both sides of the political aisle. Those on the left have argued that, because there is no right to a platform, conservative antagonists who are deplatformed are not mistreated thereby.[42] On the right, those who are consistent in supporting whatever follows from persons' private property rights have sometimes accepted the argument's conclusion as a genuine (if sometimes unwelcome) implication of their foundational principles.

Consider one way of supporting this conclusion:

(1) Private parties have rights to (a) associate with (and dissociate from) others as they see fit, (b) direct their resources in pursuit of their creative visions and pecuniary interests, (c) speak, and (d) blame as they see fit.

---

[41] For Stanley Fish, for instance, an organization may censor speech just in case doing so advances its goals better than toleration (Fish 1994, 108). But this is false. More is required to gain a permission to censor than simply efficiency in pursuing one's goals. After all, my only hope of securing a zoning regulation that helps my business might be to threaten to fire you if you publish your devastating op-ed against it. Surely, however, this would be morally wrong. Additionally, it isn't *necessary* to permit one to censor that one is thereby doing better at realizing one's goals than one could through toleration. One might, in contexts of deep injustice, profit more by tolerating some racist or sexist speech among one's workforce than by disciplining it. Yet it is clear that, in ordinary contexts, and for sufficiently bad speech, weeding it out is the right course. Thus, non-state institutions may censor permissibly—indeed, might be required to censor—*even when their goals would be better advanced by toleration.*

[42] Though he is speaking specifically to the legal question of whether Facebook's community standards violate First Amendment freedoms, the tone of Aria Waldmon's recent testimony seem to be in this vein: https://www.nyls.edu/news-and-events/nyls-news/professor-ari-waldmans-capitol-hill-testimony-makes-news/.

(2) Private censors typically suppress speech by exercising rights (a)–(d).

(3) Thus, when private parties censor, they typically act within their rights.

(4) If one has the right to do something, then it is permissible to do it.

(5) So, private censors typically act permissibly.

The crucial premise is (4), which implies, in effect, that rights do not protect wrongful behavior. But this premise is false.[43]

To see why, consider a pair of stories.

Bad Citizen: Vincenzo is a well-off citizen of the United States about to cast his vote for president. Throughout her campaign, Vincenzo has felt like he could have a beer with candidate A. Aware that this would be a poor reason to help someone gain political power, he has plans to research her policies the evening before the polls close. On his way to the library, however, he runs into an old friend. They catch up, drinking late into the evening. The next day, he wakes up just in time to make it to the polls. His time for research has run out. Nevertheless, he casts his vote for A.

Family Business: Bethany owns an Italian restaurant and advertises for a new assistant manager position. She receives 10 applications, one of whom is her cousin Michael. Of the applicants, Michael is the least well-qualified, having a demonstrated history of unreliability and theft. Despite this, she hires him, blood being thicker than water.

Vincenzo and Bethany remain well within the boundaries of their rights, at least in the sense that it would be ludicrous to suggest that anyone is permitted to stop them from acting as they do. Still, each commits a serious wrong. The sort of right that makes premise (1) true is the sort of right that implies that no one can prevent you by force of law from behaving in certain ways. But such rights do not imply freedom from moral criticism. And they do not imply freedom from social pressure and other sanctions that are available to agents but stop short of state power. Thus, premise (4) is too general, and the argument fails to generate the conclusion that private censorship is permissible by default. To secure the argument's conclusion in the face of the right to do wrong, one needs to show that there's some special reason for

[43] (Waldron 1981).

thinking that private censorship is ordinarily permissible. How might one establish such a conclusion?

One strategy begins by noting that censorship constitutes a wrong insofar as it violates the right to free speech. Proponents of this strategy will then note that the right to free speech is a specific kind of thing that can be violated only by a specific kind of agent (namely a state agent). As Stanley Fish notes, for instance, free speech is "a right you hold against the government's efforts to curb it; it is not a right you hold against nongovernmental actors who may wish, for a variety of reasons, to silence you."[44] Notably, Fish does not deny that nongovernmental agents can silence and censor. His claim is not conceptual but normative: though nongovernmental agents might censor, they do not violate any right that you have when they do so.

But although the right to free speech may be held against states, still, one can commit a wrong (or act badly) without violating any right that a person has. Consider: no one has a right against the bad voting practices of others. In a democracy committed to equal representation, we tolerate behavior like Vincenzo's, even if Vincenzo wrongs us by subjecting us to incompetently exercised political power. Likewise, none of the better-qualified candidates at Bethany's restaurant have a right to the job her cousin Michael was offered. But in passing them over for a dunce, Bethany surely treats the more deserving candidates badly.

Mill's remarks on social tyranny suggest that private censorship can wrong others by compromising their ability to live as individuals. Even if we do not want to say that persons' free speech rights are violated when they are the targets of censorship, it does seem plausible that they can find themselves dominated as speakers, and this might suffice to wrong them. Consider another example to illustrate.

Bad Boss: Ignatius Riley, an employee of Lucky's hotdog outfit, has recently begun advocating for a zoning restriction that would bar Lucky's from placing its distinctive carts anywhere in the French Quarter. The owner of Lucky's threatens to fire Ignatius if he carries on.

Although the owner of Lucky's pursues a legitimate interest in opposing the new zoning, it strikes me that he wrongs Ignatius by using his economic power over him to suppress his political activism. Even if we want to suppose

[44] (Fish 2019, 12).

that Ignatius's *right* to free speech was not violated by his boss, surely his interest in expression and political agency are compromised. If so, perhaps this is because it is wrong to wield private power to intimidate others into supporting your causes. If so, that's the sort of thing that can be wrong even if there's no assignable right that makes it wrong.

Moreover, sometimes rights other than the right to free speech make private censorship wrong. Consider a variant on the Rightbook case considered in Section 1.3.

> *Partisanbook*: Despite paying lip service to the goal of creating an open community, a social media company develops vague community standards and instructs its moderators that these are to be interpreted such that those advocating positions outside those included in the Republican party platform are to be removed.

Partisanbook behaves badly. It is wrong to lead people to believe that they are participating in an open forum while covertly pursuing personal political ends that they might not share. Members of Partisanbook might reasonably object that the platform uses them as a mere means, provides a fraudulent description of its services, and so on, without appealing to their right to free speech. And plausibly, there is a right against being used as a mere means or being defrauded.

These cases demonstrate clearly that the wrongs of censorship need not begin and end with the ways in which censorship inhibits the right to free speech. But Mill's worries about social tyranny were not reducible to worries about fraud or other kinds of misconduct. Instead, he was worried specifically about the ways in which private powers could compromise individuality by making inquiry and experimentation difficult. Keeping this in mind, I want to suggest that, when private censorship is a distinctive wrong (reducible neither to the violation of a person's political right to free speech nor to some other right), it is because it compromises the kind of *intellectual atmosphere* we have reason to value, if we value free speech.[45]

Those committed to a basically Millian view about the value of open dialogue seek more than rights to free speech guaranteed against state authorities. They seek, in addition, an atmosphere in which political minorities, not just political majorities, are empowered to discuss their views, to present and

---

[45] This way of framing the issue is not new. See e.g. (Chartier 2018).

respond to the evidence as they understand it, free of (undue) social pressure from their peers.

Part of what ensures such an atmosphere, Mill called the *real morality of public discussion*. The real morality of public discussion triumphs when arguments are assessed on their merits and vices are not inferred "from the side which a person takes."[46] It requires giving "merited honour to every one, whatever opinion he may hold," as well as the "calmness to see and honesty to state" what our opponent's "opinions really are, exaggerating nothing to their discredit, keeping nothing back which tells, or can be supposed to tell, in their favor."[47] When private parties exercise their rights in ways that vilify persons for the views they hold in good faith before giving them the benefit of the doubt, this unduly raises the costs of holding and airing views that are held without any vice. When organizations exercise their rights in ways that stop people from expressing their opinions, this can result in those opinions not receiving a fair hearing. This is a problem, in part, because the benefits of free speech in helping to realize the truth cannot be realized if people are not willing to state their views in the public sphere or if those views cannot get out in the first place.

Of course, vilifying good-faith speakers for their views or explicitly censoring content are just two ways of compromising an open environment for discourse. As critics of laissez-faire interpretations of free speech have spent decades pointing out, simply enshrining the formal freedom to speak can yield a situation that is not optimal for discourse. For example, feminists argue that enshrining formal rights to speak where many will use such rights to spout misogyny can silence women.[48] Marxists and critical theorists have argued that enshrining such rights in contexts of material inequality predictably allows the rich and powerful an outsized voice.[49] Others argue that laissez-faire approaches to discourse allow nonsense and misinformation to drown out reason.[50] Finally, liberal perfectionists fear that merely formal freedoms of thought and opinion do not suffice to guarantee against free-riding in the epistemic commons: faced with social stigma for speaking our minds, many prefer to leave the hard work of saying it like it is to others.[51]

---

[46] (Mill 2003, 119).
[47] (Mill 2003, 119–20).
[48] (MacKinnon 1994); (Langton 1993); (McGowan 2009, 2014).
[49] (Marcuse 1965).
[50] (Leiter 2014; Sunstein 2021).
[51] (Joshi 2021).

Many such theorists urge that we replace a negative understanding of free speech that merely bars state censorship with a material understanding, according to which some censorship (e.g., bans on certain kinds of pornography, hate speech, or certain kinds of corporate speech) better realizes free speech values than laissez-faire. I've argued elsewhere that such positions are too quick in rejecting the importance of formal freedoms from state censorship.[52] But they're also onto something crucial: a healthy atmosphere for discussion—one which conduces to truth, allows for diverse experiments in living, and befits free adult persons—is not guaranteed simply by means of constitutional provisions against government interference.[53] Rather than seeking some general principle capable of capturing all the cases of censorship that might arise, then, we should ask how private powers to censor affect our speech environment.

We might wonder, for example, how various different institutions can combine to ensure that there is adequate space not just for the exchange of opinions, but also for the genuine exchange of reasons. One helpful way of thinking about the issue involves accepting a division of labor between state and non-state bodies. The state secures the kind of formal freedom that is a necessary condition for individuals and communities to speak without threat of imprisonment or state interference. At the same time, social norms and intermediate institutions structure discourse in ways that put participants in a good position to exchange ideas productively.[54] Having the ability to structure discourse in this way implies the power to censor, and some non-state agents will *exercise* those powers. When they do, we need to ask: to what effect? On this front, there are both individual and systemic effects to consider.

On the individual level, we can ask whether an individual's interest in free expression was compromised by an act of censorship. On the systemic level, we can ask whether the overall atmosphere for discourse was enhanced or degraded by an instance of censorship or a pattern thereof.

[52] (Messina 2020).
[53] This is the truth—and it is a limited truth—in Stanley Fish's claim (widely represented among free speech scholars) that "[A]ny celebration of [the value of free speech] typically includes a list of the benefits free speech provides . . . But if these are the goals the First Amendment helps us to realize, there must be some forms of speech that impede rather than aid their realization . . . If you have any answer at all to the question "What is the First Amendment for?," you are logically committed to censorship somewhere down the line because your understanding of the amendment's purpose will lead you to regulate or suppress speech which serves to undermine that purpose" (Fish 2019, 24–25). As a claim about the First Amendment, this is far too quick. But as a claim about censorship—considered as something that private parties may engage in (and we may engage in with respect to ourselves)—Fish's is the right view.
[54] Compare (Balkin 2020, 6–7).

This is the strategy I pursue in this book. We will look at the ways in which private parties can restrict speech and ask in each instance: are they contributing to or detracting from a healthy speech environment? In the course of surveying the landscape in this way, we will want to keep in mind several of the questions raised already in this first chapter.

1. Is the censoring party pursuing a legitimate aim (e.g., ensuring they satisfy their fiduciary duties to shareholders, pursuing a creative vision, or acting to give voice to the vulnerable)?
2. Is the censoring party pursuing that aim transparently or covertly?
3. Does the censoring party enjoy de facto monopoly power?
4. Are the sanctions for undesired speech proportionate, where they exist?
5. Is the censoring party acting in a way that promotes or maintains an atmosphere in which people feel free to express their unpopular views or an atmosphere of uniformity?

I do not mean to pretend that this is an exhaustive list, and I want to caution against thinking that the answer to any of these questions is straightforward. In any given case, delivering answers will be a difficult matter that requires interpretation and considerable care and effort.

Difficulties aside, attempting answers matters. It matters, in part, because the answers determine our duties with respect to parties that engage in private censorship. If the relevant entities act inappropriately, they may be subject to blame, boycott, regulation, or other kinds of sanctions. Whether such sanctions are wise is a further question, depending for its answer on how likely they are to deter bad behavior, how likely they are to be in line with norms of proportionality, and what unintended effects they might have.

1.5 Summing Up and Looking Ahead

We've covered a lot of ground. It's worth taking stock. We've seen, first, that there is a core concept unifying various paradigm instances of censorship. Moreover, this core concept allows that it is possible for non-state entities to act censoriously. We've seen, second, that, though censorship is not necessarily wrong, concerns about censorship are grounded in a plurality of values—values which seem to take no account of whether the censor is a state or private entity. Finally, we have seen that private censorship requires a different treatment than state censorship. While some exercises of non-state power that make the air of our intellectual atmosphere hard to breathe and frustrate persons' individuality, other exercises are perfectly above board, and some even aim to improve the same atmosphere. For this reason, it is not at all obvious what to do about private censorship. Simply adopting our well-studied response to state censorship risks running roughshod over private parties' rights to expression and association. What's more is that sometimes those parties exercise those rights in response to genuine wrongdoing by unscrupulous speakers.

In what follows, I will often stress the degree to which the ills in our speech environment (including incivility, polarization, misinformation, and hate speech) are in us. To some substantial degree, we can't fix the problems we face without becoming better than we are at present. In practice (and less in the mode of self-help), this means making investments to ensure that people are capable of and interested in assessing information and arguments without being sucked in by the allure of partisan spin and misinformation. This is not easy work. But nor am I optimistic that regulatory fixes or better oversight by corporate bodies are promising ways of avoiding it. Such fixes tend to leave the core underlying issues unaddressed. They also risk making things worse long term by entrenching new powers more subject to abuse than is wise to tolerate.

The plan for the rest of the book is to move beyond the stylized cases considered here in this first chapter—cases, which, however useful for evaluating matters of general principle, are too unmoored from the messiness of the real world to help guide our thinking about the kinds of private censorship we confront in our daily lives. Since this censorship takes so many different forms, I focus on five crucial areas in which the notion of private censorship is helpful for thinking through the kind of atmosphere for deliberation that we live in.

I begin in Chapter 2 with an extended discussion of the values that support a healthy public sphere and the various ways in which certain kinds of bad speech compromises its realization. I argue that there are strong reasons for us as individuals to hold back in conversation. Still, too much of our discourse now involves policing how others participate in discourse and too little concerns frank and honest talk about the issues that shape our lives. Our failures as speakers generate reasons for non-state institutions to step in to clean up the mess we've made.

Chapter 3 picks up on informal attempts by employers to police their employees' speech. In this chapter, I develop more fully the relationship between freedom of association and freedom of speech. I argue that limiting firms' freedom to associate is no surefire way of better realizing an atmosphere of freedom for expression. Still, there are strong moral and prudential reasons for firms to avoid playing censor.

Chapter 4 begins a series of three chapters on speech intermediaries by treating general issues of press freedom and editorial authority. In this chapter, I examine how television networks, broadcasting companies, publishers, and newspapers censor content. In addition to making clear how professional journalism helps to fill an epistemic need—one which facilitates a healthy atmosphere for discourse when it goes well—the chapter lays the ground for the discussions of social media and search which follow it. We will see in this chapter that the concerns raised by critics of new technologies have in fact plagued us before today's bells and whistles were even imaginable.

Chapter 5 undertakes a similar exercise with respect to various new media forms, particularly social media platforms, which have been at the center of recent controversies regarding private censorship. I distinguish between various kinds of platforms and think through their rights and duties, in view of the place they occupy in our lives. I also indicate where they might do better and the limits of proposals to regulate them.

Finally, in Chapter 6, I consider the unique case of search censorship. Since the major player in that space is currently being charged with anticompetitive practice, I offer a brief history of antitrust law and indicate how we should approach companies that enjoy the kind of dominance that Google enjoys. While our approach is sure to differ in certain respects from our approach with respect to state censorship, the case for sweeping regulation is strongest here.

The concluding chapter brings the various lessons from these case studies together, emphasizing the liberal view that emerges therefrom. I try to give voice to the anxieties that this view causes reasonable people and why we should not respond to these anxieties by rejecting the view. By the end of this last chapter, I hope to have provided enough real-world legal, social scientific evidence for my conclusions to eliminate any concerns that my analysis benefits from trafficking in abstraction. What I will not have been able to do is advance these arguments in a way that will satisfy everyone beyond a reasonable doubt. For that, I'll have to wait for others to articulate objections that I cannot yet see clearly.

2

Self-Censorship, Self-Restraint, and the Ethics of Conversation

I've argued that censorship is the suppression of expressive content premised on the judgment that the content is dangerous, threatening to perceived orthodoxy, or inimical to the material interests of the censor. When censorship is widespread, speech is regularly subjected to scrutiny, sanctioned, and removed from public view. Insofar as this is so, the battleground of ideas is waged in the space of causes, rather than reasons.[1]

Of course, even well-motivated censors can't catch everything. It is difficult to reach into people's homes and private conversations. Censors must often therefore rely on a background climate of fear and uncertainty to induce people to refrain from speaking "voluntarily." This is easier to achieve when some members of the public accept that the targeted content is worthy of suppression. In conversations, it is hard to know the orientation of the audience: does it share the censor's view? If so, then speaking up risks having expression thought deviant drawn to the attention of the relevant authorities (and perhaps subsequent sanction). Minimally, say the wrong thing to the wrong person, and you risk significant reputational damage. Faced with such risks, people may keep quiet, even when what they have to say is valuable.[2] When they do so, they self-censor.

It is important to distinguish such self-censorship from a different kind of self-restraint, though the difference is not always clear and obvious in practice. Whereas self-censorship is grounded in fears of bearing personal costs for expression, what we might call *mere self-restraint* is based on the authentic[3] judgment that what one wants to express is for some reason

---

[1] As (Thomason 2021) worries, such a shift from reasons to causes can undermine our very effort to determine which norms are authoritative through a process of co-deliberation.

[2] Thanks to Linda Radzik for pressing me to clarify the relationship between censorship and self-censorship and to Sean Stevens for a helpful suggestion.

[3] It is important that such a judgment be authentic, i.e., deeply your own. No doubt many living in censorious regimes come to identify the bounds of appropriate speech with the censor's view. If the judgment that things are better left unsaid is the result of the exercise of censorial power itself, then talk of self-censorship remains appropriate.

Private Censorship. J.P. Messina, Oxford University Press. © Oxford University Press 2024.
DOI: 10.1093/oso/9780197581902.003.0002

inapt.[4] In a way, self-censorship is to self-restraint as censorship is to rational persuasion.[5] Just as my rationally persuading you can help you recognize that your speech would be unproductive or worse, so too can thinking through the effects of your speech yourself. Reflection can yield the judgment that it is more appropriate to remain quiet, even if you expect to be able to speak with impunity.

Judgment, even authentic judgment, is imperfect. Sometimes we judge that speech is inapt[6] (and so restrain ourselves) when in fact it is precisely what the situation calls for. This results in self-restraint where expression would be better. Other times, we wrongly judge some expression to be apt while correctly apprehending that saying it would elicit censure from peers or authorities. When so, we self-censor when self-restraint would demonstrate better judgment. Sometimes we refrain from saying something in anticipation of bearing costs that we would not in fact bear. If so, we self-censor unnecessarily. If what we wanted to say was inapt, self-censorship does work that self-restraint should've done.

Self-censorship and self-restraint, in short, are both ways of *holding back*. What distinguishes the one from the other are the *reasons* for which we hold back. This chapter develops two simple ideas: First, sometimes, holding back is the right thing to do. As John Locke reminds us, liberty is not license. Just as well, second, sometimes we should speak our minds: aspects of our intellectual atmosphere can induce us to hold back where we should not.

I begin in Section 2.1 with an account of the kind of atmosphere we have reason to value, if we value free speech. In Section 2.2, I argue that realizing this kind of atmosphere requires some measure of self-restraint on the part of speakers. When we fail to exercise the required self-restraint, this generates defeasible reason for others to intervene, either through rational persuasion or, where this fails, by applying sanctions aimed in part at suppressing the speech and discouraging future speakers. Section 2.3 takes seriously the

---

[4] Naturally, those who find censorship everywhere (e.g., (Fish 1994; 2019); (Schauer 1998)) will deny any important distinction here.

[5] If there is a sense in which rational persuasion stops you from speaking, it is usually by convincing you to exercise self-restraint. There is also a special sense of rational persuasion, common in censorious environments, in which one party convinces another that the costs to her of expressing something apt are not worth it on instrumental grounds: you will suffer if you say that!.

[6] I have in mind here an all-things-considered, objective conception of when speech is apt. As Mary Kate McGowan and others have convincingly argued, there is a meaningful sense in which pornography and hate speech enact conversational norms that make apt further discriminatory speech against women and racialized groups. But since these norms are non-authoritative, the appropriate thing to do in response is to refuse to play the game. For discriminatory speech also makes apt liberating counter-speech, and it does so by enacting authoritative norms.

defeaters for these reasons: I argue that reasons to engage rationally and especially to socially punish bad speech are subject to an effectiveness constraint. If attempting to rationally persuade is likely to make things worse, better to sanction or disengage. If sanctions are likely to encourage further bad speech, or radicalize targets, then it is better to attempt rational persuasion or else disengage.[7] Because there are systematic reasons to doubt our effectiveness as social censors, we should be cautious about taking up that role. Section 2.4 takes stock.

2.1 Air We Can Breathe

In broad outlines, we want an environment in which people can say the things that they think need saying without having reason to fear censure for saying them. A social context in which people fear speaking about certain important topics because certain positions are so well entrenched as to be beyond questioning is one that will predictably fail to uncover, properly diagnose, and adequately respond to social problems.[8]

In broad outlines we want an environment that encourages wide participation across social groups. A social context so replete with derogatory speech against women or minorities that they check out of the conversation or are not heard when they attempt to participate is one that will likewise fail to uncover, properly diagnose, and adequately respond to social problems.[9]

In broad outlines, we want an environment in which people can attempt to defend controversial ideas vigorously. A social context in which everyone advances only the moment's best supported theories is one that will struggle to come up with better ones.[10] One that confuses spiritedness in conversation for incivility is unlikely to hear hard truths about the current status of its institutions.[11]

In broad outlines, we want an environment in which the best-supported theories guide our actions. A social context in which it is impossible to

---

[7] For example, recent studies suggest that online political hostility is driven by individuals who view hostile political speech as a cheap way of attaining status (Bor and Petersen 2022). Attempting to censor such individuals will likely draw attention to them, which may result in their getting the very thing they came for. But nor will rational persuasion exert any great effect. In these cases, disengaging is plausibly the best course.

[8] (Rauch 2021).

[9] (Fricker 2011).

[10] (Kitcher 1990).

[11] (Bejan 2019b).

undertake necessary action due to misinformed disagreement fails to respond well to the problems it faces.[12]

In broad outlines, we want a public sphere in which "citizens listen to one another's concerns, examine each other's ideas, and engage together in inclusive and accessible collective reasoning" and in which citizens are vulnerable to "their fellow citizens' arguments, ideas, and experiences."[13] A social context so dominated by uncivil and irrational responses to the arguments, ideas, and experiences of others is unlikely, as Robert Talisse puts it, to sustain democracy.

The tensions are obvious. Some things that people think need saying will lead others to check out or prevent the uptake of what they say. Sound concern for inclusiveness will lead well-meaning people to attempt to punish speech perceived to threaten (or that actually threatens) minority participation. Fallible as they are, these social censors will overreach, targeting apt speech. When they do, others will complain about social censorship. As more people enter the conversation, those who previously dominated can find their views criticized in sometimes harsh ways and with a frequency that can feel stifling, even when the freedom to speak has never guaranteed a large platform or deference on the part of listeners.[14] This will generate spurious complaints about censorship, which will have some believing that worries about censorship are advanced in bad faith. And so on, in an all-too-familiar pattern.

Although many of the claims and counterclaims that arise when discussing how best to realize this kind of environment are unproductive, there is wisdom all around. Both bad speech and censorship make our intellectual atmosphere heavy. Both compromise our ability to discover the truth and realize flourishing lives as individuals and communities. When censorship is a response to bad speech, it can seem to support, rather than undermine, our interest in a healthy intellectual atmosphere. Other times, censorship targets or discourages speech that is perfectly above board. When it does, it compromises free speech values in just the ways that Mill suggests.

If everyone exercised self-restraint when tempted to express something that would be better left unsaid, there would hardly be a problem of censorship. All of it would be bad and in just the way that Mill suggested it was.

---

[12] (Sunstein 2021).
[13] (Talisse 2019, 94).
[14] (Muldoon 2018a).

When we exercise our political rights responsibly, others have no good reason to interfere. When they *do* interfere under such conditions, their interference is easy to appraise.[15]

Likewise, if everyone who set out to sanction speech targeted all and only bad speech (and this had no chilling effects on good speech), there would be few problems. In circumstances like ours, where bad speech is widespread and those who would seek to sanction it are often incompetent, things are murkier.

The overall dynamic is like this: When we exercise our speech rights irresponsibly, this generates pro tanto reason for others to intervene in ways authorized by their own rights. Such interventions can themselves be effective or not. Attention to the goal-directed reasons of censorship hints at defeaters for reasons to intervene. When attempts to censor speech are unlikely to be effective, then there is a pro tanto reason not to intervene. By getting clear on this dynamic at the level of the reasons that we have, we better understand the challenges of our current political moment.

2.2 Pollutants

Having described the kind of atmosphere we have reason to value in public life, I describe in the coming subsections several categories of speech that can threaten our ability to realize such an atmosphere. As J. L. Austin reminds us, we do more with words than communicate facts about the world with one another.[16] So far as what we do makes it more difficult to realize the

[15] There is a more general point here. When freedom imposes costs on others, they will try to restrict it and their attempts can leave us worse off. This is why the Nobel Prize winning economist James Buchanan said that liberty's survival requires "orderly anarchy." We minimize coercive interference by following rules that keep freedom from being too costly to others (Buchanan 2000, 7–9). Consider: There are no laws (much less police enforcing them) that keep you from standing the wrong way around in the elevator, and yet most people wouldn't dream of doing it. Prior to the coronavirus pandemic, it has not been a political matter to determine the appropriate distance to keep from another person during conversation, and yet Seinfeld's famous complaint about rule-violating "close-talkers" is familiar to most of us. While many of us sometimes have problems speaking over others, most recognize a rule against that sort of thing. In short, our lives—and our conversations— are governed by hundreds of informal rules that help us form stable expectations and allow us to avoid stepping on one another's toes. But for our willing adherence to these norms, we would need to greatly expand the sphere of explicit social regulation.

[16] (Austin 1962). As a legal matter, there is a narrow range of cases in which speech is punishable under the criminal law (as with incitement, conspiracy to commit a crime, criminal libel, harassment, true threats, fraudulent advertising, and so on). Even where the criminal law is silent, individuals harmed by these kinds of speech can seek monetary relief through torts. When these categories of speech are at issue, speakers are often doing more than just expressing ideas. But the protection law offers is imperfect, and sometimes empowering officials to address the harms of speech would invite

benefits of free speech and good-faith disagreement, it undermines a kind of common resource, something we have reason to protect.[17] Our interests in protecting it demonstrate something of a paradox: censorship can under certain circumstances seem required for realizing the kinds of values that are often associated with free speech.

2.2.1 Defamation and Harassment

The ability to speak freely wouldn't amount to much if the things you said stood no chance of being heard. A society that allows each citizen to voice her opinions while isolated in a soundproof chamber is not well positioned to reap the benefits of open discourse. This shows that realizing the values of free speech and open discourse turns in part on the prospect that others will take it up, engage with it, and (minimally) hear it.[18] But my ability to be heard by others depends on more than it's being the case that they're around when I choose to speak. It also requires that I have a certain kind of standing in the community. If I speak on some matter of concern to an audience that does not hold me to be an epistemic peer, then in some real sense my words fall on deaf ears. This brings home how important the presumption of a good reputation is for a public sphere that is likely to realize the value of free speech.

The importance of a good reputation for our real ability to benefit from the exchange of ideas illustrates one reason responsible speakers will refrain from defamation, i.e., speech that expresses falsehoods about a person with the effect of damaging her reputation. Such speech not only imposes costs on others in ways that can damage their careers, relationships, and financial well-being. It also encourages those who hear the defamatory speech to lower their esteem for its target. When defamation concerns the target's intellect or moral character, this can result in their contributions being taken less seriously.

In recognition of the many costs of lost reputation, many jurisdictions offer legal remedies for those targeted by defamation. But not all victims are willing and able to seek remedies under the law, and not all cases rise to the

more problems than it would solve. These facts confer upon persons stringent duties to use speech rights responsibly.

[17] (Joshi 2021).
[18] (Scudder 2020).

evidentiary standards required to grant relief for plaintiffs. Among other things, this means that we cannot simply leave persons to defend their reputation in courts of law.[19]

Defamatory speech is often accompanied with a second sort of bad speech, namely harassment. Harassment subjects others to hostile or prejudicial remarks, often persistently. Victims of harassment may be taken less seriously, but more frequently the problem with this kind of speech is that it can lead victims to check out of important conversations or avoid places where they take place. Their rights might be perfectly protected against state encroachment. But if they are intimidated to keep silent by peers, the effect for our communities is the same: we are deprived of their perspectives.

Like defamation, harassment has negative effects beyond those it has on our speech environment. Unlike defamation, anti-harassment laws are often struck down as being overly broad and violating the U.S. Constitution's First Amendment. Irrespective of what the law allows, those who violate duties against defamation and harassment give third parties reasons to intervene and to censor.

2.2.2 Incitement and Failures of Due Care

The presumption of a good reputation is not the only precondition for a healthy speech environment. The ideal of free speech entails a commitment to work many problems out intellectually, rather than through force. And yet some speech calls precisely for violence against others. For example, after reading an anti-Islam manifesto by the mass murderer Anders Breivik, a man killed 51 people in a New Zealand mosque.[20]

While incitement is not protected speech in the United States, such a manifesto would likely not meet the relevant legal standards. According to current court doctrine, speech rises to the level of incitement only if it (1) directs its audience to perform some imminent illegal act and (2) is likely to incite or produce such action. If advocacy fails to rise to that standard, if it abstractly

---

[19] As we will see in Chapter 5, technological developments have made it easier than ever for speakers to damage others' reputations. While libel remedies remain available, tort reform has made it near impossible to seek relief from the intermediaries that are often responsible for allowing the relevant speech to reach a wide audience. For discussion, see (Volokh 2021).

[20] (Howard 2019, 208).

recommends violence and does not steel some determinate individual or group to engage in it, states are not permitted to prohibit it.[21]

We might think here about Mill's famous example of telling an excited mob gathered outside a corn-dealer's house that corn-dealers are starvers of the poor. Speaking in this way with the expectation that the mob, already angry, will attack the dealer is directed to producing lawless action and likely to do so, as *Brandenburg* requires.[22] As Mill suggests, it is permissible to allow the anti-corn-dealers to circulate their opinions in the press.[23] Like violent manifestos, these are not likely to produce illegal action simply by themselves. Thus, at least in the United States, the right to free speech protects the freedom to write works like the one that inspired Breivik's lawless action.

Prior to *Brandenburg,* courts used other criteria to determine when governments might legitimately punish speakers for recommending illegality or compromising collective goals. The result, in a long range of cases, was court-sanctioned state punishment of speech that ranged from misguided to salutary. With *Brandenburg,* the court tied its hands, narrowing the definition of incitement considerably. In my view, rightly so. The predictable and unfortunate byproduct of this otherwise good decision is that state actors are now prohibited from policing much speech which is careless and, though not particularly likely to cause violence, might nevertheless cause violence. (Improbable events happen, after all.)

Despite being legally protected, it is a lousy use of the freedom of speech to encourage rights violations in the way that various manifestos do. As Jeffrey Howard argues, there is a duty against dangerously advocating or arguing for actions that violate others' uncontroversial rights.[24] To illustrate, he offers a simple example involving Adrian, Beatrice, and Cassandra.

> Adrian, addressing an audience including Beatrice, argues that members of Cassandra's religious group are vile scum who deserve to be killed. Beatrice subsequently attacks Cassandra. What has Adrian done wrong? The intuitive answer is that Adrian is failing to regulate his conduct by appropriate concern for the weighty, normatively significant interests of Cassandra (among others). Cassandra's weighty interest in life generates a moral duty

[21] *Brandenburg* v. *Ohio,* 395 U.S. 444 (1969).

[22] (Mill 2003, 121).

[23] (Mill 2003, 121).

[24] Howard thinks that this is a duty the state can enforce. In my view, the pro tanto reasons a state might have for enforcing this duty are swamped by a track record that shows its incompetence to get these matters right. See again (Messina 2020).

for Adrian to refrain from conduct that frustrates that interest—a duty corresponding to a moral right held by Cassandra.[25]

Adrian speaks in a way that intentionally encourages Beatrice to kill Cassandra. Facts about Beatrice (e.g., that she and other audience members are disposed to hate those with Cassandra's religious beliefs, that they are riled up, and so on) might make it the case that Adrian's speech rises to the level of incitement. But even if features of the context indicate that this is unlikely, still we can say that Adrian fails to exercise due care in speaking. Advocating in earnest for the violation of someone's right to life is not, legal standards aside, a wise and judicious (or even important) use of one's rights to speak. Even if the likelihood of fallout is low, such advocacy always courts danger. Advocacy of positions that court this kind of danger (even if indirectly) is acceptable only when the speech is high value, and even then, the duty of due care will impose constraints on *how* such advocacy proceeds.

Speech violates the duty to take care when exercising our rights, then, when it is either intended to motivate others to mistreat others or foreseeably motivates a third party to do so. (In this way, the duty to exercise due care is much more demanding than the duty not to incite.) When important issues are at stake (as they sometimes are with political manifestos), some probability of inspiring rights violations may be the cost of trying to get to the bottom of things or realizing greater justice. But if we are speaking loosely or joking or using casual language, or if we should know that our contribution is less than useless, we ought to exercise self-restraint. When we notice others speaking in ways that do not seem live to the high stakes, we have pro tanto reason to stop them. The fact that the state must restrain itself in the face of potentially dangerous (but non-inciting) speech does not mean that we must similarly do so. Instead, using our own rights to speech and association to make this kind of behavior costly appears to be perfectly admissible .

2.2.3 Misinformation

In 2016, unscrupulous sources reported a bunk theory that presidential candidate Hillary Clinton was running a child prostitution ring out of a pizza restaurant. Although the theory was spread widely on social media, one

[25] (Howard 2019, 216).

man took it particularly seriously. His name was Edgar Welch and he was a concerned father. His was a mission to save the children. When he arrived, heavily armed, he didn't find any. Fortunately, no one was hurt.

Misinformation, a third kind of pollutant, has long been with us. But many worry that features of our current environment are making the problem worse than ever.[26] It is clear that the rapid spread of falsehood can have devastating effects on civil society. While ordinary people are often unwitting participants in the spread of falsehood, their participation is often grounded in an ignorance of how to assess information. Because we should, in our ordinary lives, strive to stem the spread of falsehood, we also have a duty to learn to recognize it. We ought not to share sensational sounding stories before we've had occasion to look into their reliability. When we do not have time to do our own due diligence, we should share these stories only when the message they contain is urgent or (often and) the story has been reported by a reliable source.

However obvious this may seem, insisting on accuracy in the things we say to one another involves considerable self-restraint. We might miss out on the satisfaction of sharing something that has our sense of righteous indignation up; we may miss out on camaraderie with others; and we may lose out on having the first take on some breaking story. But we should bear those costs.

Restraining our first impulse to share until we've had a chance to verify (or hedging our reports with indications that we *haven't* verified) does more than allow us to avoid badly mistaken collective action. It also encourages us to develop information literacy and intellectual humility. We might find ourselves qualifying our reports: "I couldn't find a terribly good source for this claim, but I've heard it said that . . . ." This kind of humility makes us better interlocutors, because it encourages in us a kind of self-doubt, the natural complement of which is a healthy interest and curiosity about the views of those who see things differently. Hedges like this also quell swift, hopefully heroic, but often catastrophic action of the sort that can seem demanded by certain ungrounded theories and reports.

It is also worth noting that sentence-level accuracy isn't the only thing that matters in this direction. Although every aspect of a claim might be accurate, the overall picture it generates can be highly misleading. Consider a Breitbart headline that ran in 2015: "Jerry Brown Signs Bill Allowing Illegal Immigrants to Vote." At the sentence level, the story contained no falsehoods.

---

[26] (Sunstein 2021).

And yet the article created the misleading impression that allowing undocumented immigrants to vote was the intended result of Brown's legislative action. It was not. The legislative action simply registered all driver's license recipients automatically to vote. As Benkler, Faris, and Roberts have it:

> While the text of the article included factually correct statements—that Jerry Brown signed a law that automatically registered eligible voters when they obtained a driver's license, and that, if the secretary of state of California should fail to check the eligibility of registrants such a law could result in undocumented immigrants being registered—the gap between the chain of unlikely but possible events that would lead to such an outcome and the highly salient interpretation embedded in the distribution of the story suggests an effort of intentional manipulation.[27]

Spreading misinformation does not require saying anything false. Sometimes facts, irresponsibly framed and designed to elicit outrage, do better than misinformation at skewing political outcomes. The need to generate web traffic has made headlines like this a commonplace, even among more reputable outlets. Still, the outlets that aim to mislead (for the sake of eyeballs or clicks or political advantage) do not exercise their rights responsibly.

It is not merely spreading falsehood and misleading truths that is to be avoided. As Mill says in *On Liberty*: we should be sufficiently honest to state what our "opponents and their opinions really are, exaggerating nothing to their discredit, keeping nothing back which tells, or can be supposed to tell, in their favor." This is for two reasons.

First, when we misrepresent what someone says while criticizing them, we necessarily miss the mark. When we miss the mark in this way, we can fail to do justice to the positions we take to be correct.

Suppose, for instance, that someone rejects relaxing border restrictions. She argues that immigration will have negative effects on the local political culture. Imagine now that her interlocutor responds by saying (without evidence) that she only rejects open borders because she is a xenophobe and a racist. Observers (to say nothing of the original speaker) might reasonably take it that there is nothing at all to be said against the actual argument. ("If the best that can be said against this view requires misrepresenting it or

---

[27] (Benkler, Faris, and Roberts 2018, 35).

attributing to its author some wickedness that appears to be no necessary part of the view itself, perhaps it's not so bad after all."[28])

Second, when we misrepresent another person's view, we often fail to understand it. When we fail to understand why others believe the things that they do, we can find ourselves tempted to accept a cartoonish picture of the world in which everyone is either good or evil.[29] This can lead us further down the path of polarization and away from true understanding.

Accepting the demand not to misrepresent others' views takes one tool for getting what we want in the social-political world off the table. And it is often easier to say this than to do it in practice. But a social world in which much conversation sets out from the assumption of bad faith is bound to frustrate our interests more often than not. So we do best to begin with an assumption of good faith, relaxing that assumption as we learn that it is misplaced.

When misinformation about policies, courses of action, and people's positions proliferates, people vote and behave in ways that impose undue costs upon others. The higher the stakes, the weightier the reasons to impose some discipline on the flow of information and to stop the spread of falsehoods, caricatures, and misleading constellations of truths. Here too, irresponsible exercise of speech rights offers pro tanto grounds to intervene, rationally or otherwise.

2.2.4 Discriminatory Speech

Turn now to a fourth category of speech, discriminatory speech. Discriminatory speech targets persons due to their perceived characteristics (e.g., race, ethnicity, sex, sexual orientation, gender presentation, etc.) or religious beliefs. It aims to communicate that persons with certain of those traits occupy positions of subordinate social status. Accordingly, discriminatory speech predictably leads those it targets to check out of important conversations.[30]

Consider an example from Jeremy Waldron.

---

[28] This sort of strategy appears to play a role in some persons' radicalization. See: (Marantz 2019, 289).

[29] Lukianoff and Haidt characterize this as one of the most pernicious and influential untruths that plagues our current politics (Lukianoff and Haidt 2019, 53–80).

[30] (Nadim and Fladmoe 2021).

A man out walking with his seven-year-old son and his ten-year-old daughter turns a corner on a city street in New Jersey and is confronted with a sign. It says: "Muslims and 9/11! Don't serve them, don't speak to them, and don't let them in." The daughter says, "What does it mean, papa?" Her father, who is a Muslim—the whole family is Muslim—doesn't know what to say. He hurries the children on, hoping they will not come across any more of the signs. Other days he has seen them on the streets: a large photograph of Muslim children with the slogan "They are all called Osama," and a poster on the outside wall of his mosque which reads "Jihad Central."[31]

What kind of message does such signage send? To those (Muslim) persons targeted, the signs are meant to communicate the message that they are not welcome. To non-Muslim readers, the message is somewhat different: if you feel this way about our neighbors, you are not alone. This can embolden hateful persons to commit crimes against persons who share such characteristics (along the lines discussed in Section 2.2.2). But it might have further effects as well. For instance, scholars have pointed out that discriminatory speech can constitute harm by reinforcing the subordinate status of already disadvantaged groups.[32] We can get further effects by asking: what becomes of an atmosphere for discussion in which these kinds of messages are widespread?

We might notice several possible effects. First, targets of such messages have their interest in being treated as dignified equals set back. This is Waldron's concern. Though they might enjoy equal protection under the law, regularly confronting such speech can undermine their social standing and public reputation. But those effects in turn plausibly raise the costs for targets of speaking up in public and lower its benefits. Without a firm reputation as an equal to rest on, those targeted might anticipate being racially profiled or having their contributions dismissed as stemming from their social identities rather than the free exercise of their reason .

There are three distinct points, each of which is important. The first is that targets of discriminatory speech may be less likely to come to the table. The second is that, even when they do, their audience will tend to fail to hear them well.[33] The third is that there might be discernable setbacks to the

[31] (Waldron 2014, 1).
[32] See e.g. (McGowan 2019).
[33] On this point, see (Fricker 2011); (Langton 1993); (McGowan 2009); and (McGowan et al. 2011).

dignitary and other interests of the speech's targets.[34] The strong reasons that there are to avoid discriminatory speech explain much of the truth in calls to keep speech within the bounds of political correctness.

Liberating people to speak and be heard matters in part because their contributions aid us in our search for the truth and help us develop as individuals. For this reason, atmospheres characterized by too much discriminatory speech should concern us. Their predictable result is that some will stay quiet for no good reason. When they stay quiet, we lose their perspectives.

And yet, as with other pollutants discussed in previous sections, much discriminatory speech rightly receives constitutional protection, and there plenty of speakers are keen to take advantage of the law. Concern about the effects oof widespread discriminatory motivates people to do something to curb its spread to the degree that they can. These attempts can be understood as responsive to pro tanto reason to protect our speech environment from degradation.

2.2.5 Incivility

Discriminatory speech may well be a subtype of a broader category of speech, incivility. Civility demands that we keep the temperature of important conversations low (where appropriate). It also demands that if we choose to participate in the public sphere, we do so in a way that focuses on reasoning things out and refrains from gratuitous personal attacks.[35] Sometimes, of course, a person's character is relevant to a conversation. When someone with a demonstrated history of lying offers testimony to some facts that cannot be otherwise verified, others have reason to know these details of his biography. When a person says that she harbors hatred or resentment for this or that group (racial, religious, political, etc.) and goes on to advocate for policies that disadvantage the disfavored group, her character is relevant to the conversation.

Still, as Mill points out, we have an unfortunate tendency to treat mere disagreement as evidence of unsavory character. When we infer the latter

---

[34] For an argument that there are setbacks to the non-dignitary interests of targets of racist and sexist speech, see (M. C. Bell 2021, 169–71). For some doubts, see (Strossen 2018, ch. 6).

[35] For further detail, see (Messina 2022a).

from the former, we create an environment in which honest, good-faith disagreement is unnecessarily risky. As with discriminatory speech, a speech
environment characterized by too much incivility can lead to a shrinking
conversational tent and one in which people are less likely to try out ideas of
which they are not certain.

For example, some 62% of Americans (including 77% of conservatives and
23% of liberals) fear expressing certain of their considered views owing to
a hostile political climate.[36] Part of what explains this striking number is a
widespread sense that incivility has won the day: According to a 2019 survey,
93% of Americans believe that political discourse has a civility problem.
Nearly 70% claim that the problem is severe.[37] To many, today's partisanship
requires seeing those with whom we disagree as enemies, rather than persons with a different perspective, potentially valuable in our common pursuit
of truth and justice.[38] Civility's defenders argue that this adversarial attitude
toward our conversation partners is hostile to the kind of epistemic environment that is likely to facilitate the discovery of new truths.

Of course, not everyone is convinced. For many, calls for civility and a less
hostile climate for discourse are thinly veiled attempts to maintain the status
quo and quell revolutionary momentum. Defenders of this view often appeal,
plausibly, to the dark history of civility and the ways in which it is weaponized
against those vying for their rights. As Alex Zamalin puts the point, "the idea
of civility has been enlisted to treat black suffering with apathy or to maintain
an unjust status quo." "Worse," he continues, "it has been a tool for silencing
dissent, repressing political participation, enforcing economic inequality,
and justifying inequality."[39] Where the stakes are this high, civil engagement
with those who threaten those values is properly out of place.

A similar concern finds support in an essay by the great radical Marcuse,
which famously argues that, in contexts of inequality, universal toleration is likely to do little more than enshrine an unjust status quo. In such
contexts, "[s]uppression of the regressive [opinions] is a prerequisite for
the strengthening of the progressive ones."[40] From the right, politicians and
pundits regularly accuse democrats of trying to destroy the country. It is a
misguided toleration that does not square up to this fact. Rather than lay

---

[36] (Elkins 2020).
[37] ("Civility In America 2019: Solutions for Tomorrow" 2019).
[38] (Haidt 2013); (Iyengar et al. 2019).
[39] (Zamalin 2021, 6).
[40] (Marcuse 1965, 106).

down arms, such critics of civility argue that we should embrace mocking tactics and seize on populist economic discontent to restore balance.

Even these brief descriptions suggest that objections to civility can take a number of distinct forms. On some versions, agents have reasons to take a stand in response to injustice (perhaps because doing so is crucial for victims to maintain their integrity). On these views, expressing resentment and indignation is often necessary for conveying the gravity and significance of injustice and is sometimes a fitting response to it. But since language conveying resentment and indignation is often read as uncivil, there can be no fair or reasonable prohibition of incivility.[41] This is the thrust behind the oft-repeated line that "we can disagree and still love each other, unless your disagreement is rooted in my oppression and denial of my humanity and right to exist."[42]

There are questions of course about when disagreement is "rooted" in the oppression of others. Easy cases include literal affirmations (or insinuations) to the effect that certain persons or groups are subhuman, deserve to be oppressed. Things are substantially less clear when it suffices for speech to be rooted in a group's oppression for it to advocate policies which cause or exacerbate social inequities (regardless of whether the advocate knows this and views these outcomes as part of the reason for her advocacy).[43]

Difficulties of this sort aside, the proper reply is concessive. When confronting wrongdoing, toleration might require forbearance from retaliatory violence. But it does not require refraining from expressing fitting attitudes to wrongdoing. In circumstances like these, sanctions for speech do not necessarily compromise, but may even enhance, our understanding of the problems that we face. This is so even if they are wrongly perceived to involve violations of duties of civility. It is no part of my claim that incivility often counts as bad speech to deny as much.

---

[41] In this direction, see (Cherry 2021) and (Cooper 2017).

[42] This line was tweeted by Robert Jones Jr. but is often understandably misattributed to James Baldwin.

[43] Kendi for example defines a racist policy as "any measure that produces or sustains racial inequity between racial groups" (Kendi 2019, 18). On an intentionally capacious definition like this (which ensnares so many well-meaning persons who are merely mistaken about the empirics of public policy), many policies that are explicitly anti-racist in intent will count as racist and oppressive. As a result, advocacy for them may be read as disagreement grounded in the oppression of the groups on the losing end of the inequities. Kendi's is, after all, an objective criterion: it is not, accordingly, telling us to regard as racist those policies that we *think* or *believe* or *say* will sustain or produce racial inequity, but to regard those policies and their advocates as racist when they in fact do so. Therefore, which real-world advocacy satisfies the definition will be a substantive empirical question not settled by discerning an agent's motives or intentions and a significant matter of disagreement.

But there are others who recommend incivility not as an appropriate response to discriminatory speech or injustice, but on *strategic* grounds. On these versions, the reason to abandon civility is that doing so promises to better advance justice than the alternative.[44] As one commentator notes, such defenders of incivility reason this way: if "civility means showing respect for the opposition's views and the people who express them, it amounts to unilateral disarmament in the midst of an arms race that involves ever-more sophisticated propaganda apparatuses."[45] Such disarmament, understood this way, seems like a good way to lose a war.

In my view, we should reject these strategic defenses of incivility. This is for two reasons. First, strategic incivility is inherently disrespectful. It treats one's conversational partners as pawns on a chessboard to be manipulated more than persons to be reasoned with. Here, the idea is not to express indignation in response to wrongdoing, injustice, or ill will or to suppress discriminatory speech, but to express contempt to achieve some independent goal.[46] But second, incivility is not often the promising strategy it is made out to be, at least not in the long term. I focus here on the second reason, since it gets at the heart of the alleged justification for incivility.

It is helpful to first get clear on the basic argument in favor of strategic incivility. The argument begins by noting that are several areas in which we can be highly confident about how to eliminate injustice or realize justice. When we are confident in this way, the most important thing to do is encourage people to believe it and coordinate on the called-for practical measures. Especially when the wrong ideas are well entrenched, however, uncivil speech—speech that mocks others, calls them names, misrepresents their positions, and so on—can achieve both goals (coordination on true conclusions and on necessary practical measures) more efficiently than civil speech and rational engagement.

Let's begin with the goal of fostering true belief formation. By what mechanism does incivility effect this goal better than civility? Students of logic know well that the reasons that actually move us to act or believe and *good* reasons for action and belief are often different. We are deeply social creatures. When we are on the receiving end of moral condemnation—when people get up in our faces and call us out for wrong-thinking or wrongdoing—we

---

[44] (Jacquet 2016).

[45] (Gastil 2019, 163).

[46] Thanks to an anonymous reviewer for suggesting this way of expressing the point and for more generally encouraging me to be clearer in this subsection.

are likely to back off, to refrain from engaging in the conduct or speech that triggered the response in the first place. We may not have been given good reasons to revise the offending position or change the offending behavior (though such reasons might exist), but we are likely to try to change it, the thought goes, simply to avoid further sanctions.

The difference between being offered good reasons for adopting or revising a position and the pressures that incline real-world reasoners to do so has a long philosophical history. In his famous dialogue, *Gorgias*, Plato observes that we might come to hold a belief in two ways. On the one hand, someone might convince us to adopt or reject a belief by bringing us to knowledge. On the other, we might be convinced in a way that leaves us in ignorance. Rhetoricians achieve their goals, Plato argued, by producing pleasure or displeasure in their audiences, bypassing their listeners' rational faculties. In doing so, they leave listeners convinced of positions for which they have no justification.

For this reason, Plato was no great fan of rhetoric, characterizing it this way: "It's the counterpart in the soul to pastry baking, its counterpart in the body."[47] Moreover, just as consumers are likely to prefer a diet rich in pastries to one recommended by nutritionists, rhetoricians be more likely to gain adherents than those focused on rational persuasion.

Plato's analogy is apt. As the psychologist Jonathan Haidt tells us, our moral sensibilities are kind of like taste buds. The right kind of righteous indignation is likely to be more effective than cool, rational argument in producing our assent or prompting our dissent.[48] The more of these taste buds a speaker hits, the more likely we are to eat up what they're saying. But though pastry-baking and rhetoric might do better than nutrition and rationality at producing pleasure in us, they are *bad for us*. Just as a life of pastry consumption will lead to rapid physical decline, so too will a life in which we determine how to live and what to believe by responding to rhetoric make a shambles of our intellectual and spiritual lives. When speakers persuade audiences by bypassing their rational faculties, they purchase belief in the "right" conclusions at the cost of genuine understanding.

Still, a critic might point out, we should not pretend that knowledge grounded in understanding is all that matters. When issues of great practical importance are at stake, it matters also to produce the right beliefs. After all,

[47] (Plato 1997, 809).
[48] (Haidt 2013, 131–33).

if people only believe the right things, they are likely to act and vote better. In the long run, *of course* we want to make sure that people coordinate for the right reasons. But in the short run, uncivil rhetoric can help us achieve coordination on the right results, and that matters, too.

Even if we grant that there's a strong case to be made for rhetorical persuasion, notice that this does not itself prove that we ought to pursue our ends by publicly shaming our opponents. We need to know, additionally, that these measures are likely to hit the right taste buds (to stick to Haidt's metaphor). But there is reason to worry that uncivil rhetoric is not especially likely to change the beliefs of those who are targeted by it.

Although uncivil speech is highly pleasing to those who engage in it and to those antecedently inclined to agree with the speaker's message (allowing them to delight in the feeling of righteous indignation), it remains disagreeable to those who do not.[49] I may employ all sorts of rhetorical tools and logical fallacies to convince you of something you have no reason to believe. But I am not likely to be able to persuade to join my side you by yelling at you, calling you names, and refusing to take you at your word.[50] If I'm lucky, I may succeed in cowing you into self-censorship and presenting a false front. But that's compatible with me going on believing just as before.[51]

At this point, one might retreat to the second justification for strategic incivility: a false front is good enough. If what we really need is to ensure that people behave correctly, it is enough to discourage people from publicly stating their incompatible beliefs. This will, the argument goes, set the boundaries of acceptable belief, signaling to others what they should believe. Understanding this and reacting accordingly, much of the population comes, indirectly, to have the right beliefs.

---

[49] This may actually *overstate* the rhetorical value of incivility. To see this, notice that nasty political attack advertisements are not only ineffective in promoting the political interests of the attacker, but actually lead viewers to form negative views of the source of the attack. See: (Roese and Sande 1993). More recent research suggests, however, that "dirty" campaign measures are effective in increasing turnout for those campaigns that agitate against the status quo (whereas those that defend it are harmed by attacks). See (Nai 2013). As far as I can tell, however, the effects on turnout are ambiguous—attack campaigns might attract defenders of the status quo and advocates for change alike to the polls.

[50] Much uncivil speech is *dehumanizing*. Psychologists call one group's perception that another group dehumanizes them *metadehumanization*. This sense is frequently exaggerated, but its political effects (reduced support for democratic norms) are real (Landry et al. 2021; Moore-Berg et al. 2020). Insofar as uncivil speech increases our perception that the other side views us as less than human, we should worry that its costs will outweigh whatever benefits it might have.

[51] I also may succeed in generating a violent reaction. See: (Thomason 2018, ch. 2).

But this is (as we will see in our discussion of effectiveness) an empirical question. Moreover, in cases where voters make important decisions, even these benefits are counterbalanced by significant costs. After all, voting happens in private. Accordingly, I can simply vote my true preference while deceiving you into thinking that we agree. But this is likely to lead us to underestimate the challenges we face in pursuing our goals.[52]

Consider a simple example to illustrate the point. Imagine your local city council is about to vote on whether to allocate funds to a new park or to subsidize a new shopping center. If activists who (correctly, let's say) favor the park deride and insult anyone who supports the shopping center, such people might not voice their views. If they do not voice their views, the activists might take the mall to have less support than it does, taking it to be unnecessary to engage the opposition. They might find themselves surprised at the polls in a predictable and (recently) familiar way.

But what of the thought that incivility induces right beliefs in bystanders? First, notice that recent research suggests that incivility is likely to be ramped up on the extremes of the political spectrum. Both progressive activists and hyper-conservatives are likely to think it less important to compromise, more important to stick to one's guns, feel more pressure to adopt particular viewpoints, and so on. But these groups claim only 32% of the US population. And research suggests that the other 68% is getting tired of the behavior on the extreme ends of the spectrum.[53] Incivility appears to be leading these people to disengage from politics, to distrust the political process and their peers, and to feel that there is no place for their voices in the national conversation, not to adopt the views at the extreme ends of the spectrum.[54]

It appears that uncivil behavior leads moderates (the largest group of bystanders) and others to check out—not to march under any particular political banner. [55] Here's how one student at a university in Ohio expresses the point: "I have had encounters with students who have called me names and cursed me in e-mails as a result of speaking up, period. I have just blocked

---

[52] (Joshi 2021).

[53] (Hawkins et al. 2019).

[54] Incivility's effects in other domains are similarly concerning. In the work place, for example, civility is correlated with better outcomes and better relationships than incivility: (Porath, Gerbasi, and Schorch 2015).

[55] Tosi and Warmke point out research that suggests that moral grandstanding can lead moderates to check out. But since moral grandstanding is distinguished from strategic incivility based on whether the motivation for the speech is self- or other-regarding not on the outward behavior of the speaker, it is plausible that any effects of grandstanding are also effects of strategic incivility. For discussion, see (Tosi and Warmke 2020, 88–90).

them from all communication in order to avoid another confrontation."[56] Bystanders might sensibly simply avoid voicing their beliefs for fear of meeting with similar censure. When people disengage in this way, we lose their perspectives. When we lose their perspectives, we are likely to deliberate less effectively. Even if you are not sold on the deliberative value of having moderates in the conversation, you might care as someone with democratic leanings that so many of your compatriots are governed by rules that they take so little a part in shaping. And even if that's too romantic a view, you might worry about the legitimacy costs of having a population of frustrated and disengaged people ruled by exhausting fringe groups.

But let's allow that some will respond to incivility by acting in desirable ways. There are further problems. For instance, civility is typically taken to be a reciprocal norm of good behavior.[57] Research shows that if you are uncivil toward me, I am likely to respond in kind.[58] Thus incivility begets more incivility.[59] When we spend more time engaging with one another in dismissive ways that presuppose that our interlocutors are simply out to lunch, we spend less time finding common ground and less time improving the world. By contrast, civil engagement can induce pro-social behavior.[60]

It is easy to tell stories about the good that can be achieved by hurling insults at one's political opponents. But when the opportunity cost is missing out on engaging with someone who sees the world differently in a productive fashion, it is easier to see the wishful thinking in such stories.[61] Furthermore, because civility is a reciprocal norm, one ought to be reasonably sure of victory before one takes up arms in violation of it. Failing to do this, one might, after all, do little more than authorize one's opponents to use a weapon to the detriment of the truth that might have otherwise remained out of bounds.[62] In short, the more strategic value one finds in incivility, then, the more hesitant one should be to deploy it in cases where the balance of political power is constantly shifting.

---

[56] (Herbst 2010, 110).

[57] (Andersson and Pearson 1999); (Walker, van Jaarsveld, and Skarlicki 2017); (Han, Brazeal, and Pennington 2018).

[58] (Shmargad et al. 2022) find additionally that online comments are more likely to be uncivil when they occur nearby other uncivil online comments. (They also find that users respond to social rewards like upvotes and likes when deciding whether to be civil or uncivil.)

[59] For example (Stroud et al. 2015) find that having a reporter engage with commenters in the comments section of news articles reduces incivility. See also (Han, Brazeal, and Pennington 2018).

[60] (Leiter et al. 2011); (Gervais 2014, 2015).

[61] Some research suggests, e.g., that elites whose messaging civilly emphasizes disputants' common humanity reduces sectarian hate speech (Iyengar et al. 2019, 140; Siegel and Badaan 2020).

[62] See: (Aly and Sampson 2019, 141).

We've seen a number of reasons to be skeptical that incivility is good strategy. To recap:

1. Incivility can promote strong convictions at the expense of genuine understanding.
2. Incivility may not be particularly likely to change what people believe.[63]
3. Incivility can increase polarization by leading moderates to disengage, thereby reducing political autonomy and compromising democratic legitimacy.
4. Incivility can be strategically wielded by those in possession of the truth as well as by those peddling falsehood, and if it is effective, we take advantage at the risk of encouraging those who are wrong to do so as well.

Given that strategic incivility is disrespectful, these worries should give pause to those who think disrespect is simply the price of justice.[64] We should demand fuller accounts of its strategic virtues, and we should expect these

[63] Importantly, rational persuasion might also be unlikely to change what people believe (though see (Strossen 2018, ch. 8)). This is part of Haidt's point about our moral taste buds: if we do not engage the passions, we are unlikely to win hearts and minds. Two things: first, remember Plato's point. We ought to care about the evidence we're given, not merely how its packaging makes us feel. Second, the wisdom of engineering an effective rhetorical strategy depends very much on the justice of your cause. And the justice of your cause will depend on the reasons there are in support of it. Thus, rhetoric is important, but it is not all that is important.

[64] Defenders of incivility might insist all of this is rather obtuse. The idea isn't to change hearts or minds by means of incivility but to draw attention to issues that might otherwise be ignored—to force the comfortable and those endowed with power to consider issues they would rather ignore, and to force them to feel the urgency of those issues. Change, they observe, rarely happens when the powers that be can rest easy. Sit-ins and various other kinds of demonstrations are engines of progress: if civility means abandoning efforts that disrupt the ordinary course of things, then calls to civility exhibit an inevitable status-quo bias. And indeed, there is good empirical research that supports the idea that incivility catches our attention. We are more likely to engage with ideas and be able to recall arguments when they are presented in an uncivil manner (Mutz 2007, 2015). But even if we grant that uncivil speech is useful insofar as it is more likely to draw attention to an issue, it's important to see that this very feature of incivility—that it grabs our attention—cuts two ways. First, because uncivil discourse is more likely to catch our attention, we are more likely to proliferate it, not just when we agree, but also when we disagree. But if the uncivil message contains misinformation or other bad speech—as it often will—its attention-grabbing features can result in further damage to our information environment. What's more is that civil discourse is, whereas uncivil discourse is not, an antidote to misinformation spread on social media (Allcott, Gentzkow, and Yu 2019). Second, incivility draws our attention to the right issues only if the uncivil are picking up on the most urgent issues. But reporting my own sense of the matter, uncivil discourse often centers on the ways in which others are speaking about topics of genuine concern, including policing their tone. But this is seldom what's most important. In sum, attention-catching incivility is to be wielded carefully. It can just as easily draw our attention to urgent and neglected issues of serious concern as it can draw our attention away from these toward distracting side issues.

accounts to mark at best so many extreme circumstances in which it would be okay treat people in ways worse than they deserve.[65]

As with other pollutants, when our atmosphere for discussion becomes inundated with gratuitous incivility, there is pro tanto reason to intervene. After all, we have reason to believe that those engaging in conversation in these ways are compromising a vital common resource: an atmosphere in which good faith disagreement is not overly expensive.

2.3 Social Censorship

So far, I've characterized five distinct types of bad speech—speech which is frequently harmful in traditional ways, but which can also make our environment for discussing important public matters less healthy. Because we have reason to value a healthy environment for speech, we also have reason to want to root out these (and perhaps other) kinds of speech. We might attempt rational persuasion to deter those who speak in these ways, but if this doesn't work, we may wish to reach deeper into our war chests and look to censor these kinds of speech by means of social punishment. Because these forms of speech are pro tanto wrong, those who traffic in them make themselves liable to proportionate sanction aimed at making our intellectual environment a little healthier. As we noted in Chapter 1, censorship is a descriptive concept. Even if censorship is often wrong, it isn't necessarily so. And given the costs of these kinds of speech, it is far from nreasonnable for persons encountering it to see reasons to take up as the role of social censor.

In the rest of this chapter, I argue that despite the genuine reasons we have to engage in social censorship, there are also powerful defeaters of those reasons. The upshot is that we should be reluctant to play the censor, even when the situation seems clearly to call for it. In short, censorship is risky business, and its costs can quickly swamp its benefits (in ways that are

---

[65] Importantly, I mean only to be repudiating speech that is genuinely uncivil. Historically speaking, *of course* appeal to language of civility was used to keep the dominated in their place. On these old models, it might've been uncivil for a Black woman to speak up on some matter of public importance, regardless of her mode of engagement. Clearly, the conclusion to be drawn from this is not that we should abandon civility, only that we should beware of the ways in which it might be parochially invoked (more on which later). Also, I do not mean to be suggesting that all language must be civil in order to be acceptable. Indeed, much language is not aimed at persuasion at all: it is aimed to be satirical, expressive of one's commitments, and other things in the neighborhood. To insist that all speech regarding political topics must be civil would indicate a perverse obsession with the dispassionate exchange of reasons. .

difficult to predict and control). Before beginning, it's helpful to say a few words about what I mean here by social censorship.

In thinking about social censorship, it is crucial to differentiate between *stating* that some utterance falls into the above categories and providing an argument that it was inapt, on the one hand, and deploying sanctions to suppress the utterance, on the other. As Mill tells us in *On Liberty*, we owe it to one another to help each other "distinguish the better from the worse;" and "encouragement to choose the former rather than the latter."[66] We should, he continues, always press "each other to increased exercise of [our] higher faculties, and increased direction of [our] feelings and aims towards wise instead of foolish, elevating instead of degrading, objects and contemplations."[67] None of this involves censorship. It is not, after all, aimed primarily at suppressing dangerous or threatening speech by non-rational means. When people fall short and behave badly even after admonitions of this kind, it is natural to wish to quietly distance ourselves from them. But to punish them? That is a different matter—one that often perpetuates the "tyranny of the prevailing opinion."

Like Mill, when I speak of social censorship, I mean overt attempts to suppress speech by means of sanctions like naming, shaming, shunning, blaming, gloating dissociation, and so on.[68] The philosopher Linda Radzik helpfully classifies sanctions like these as forms of informal social punishment.[69] Informal social punishment intentionally imposes some social harm on a wrongdoer for her perceived wrongdoing.[70] For the purposes of this discussion, I will say that we engage in social censorship when we aim to suppress speech perceived to be dangerous, threatening to perceived orthodoxy, or inimical to our material interests by means of such informal social punishment. As we have seen above, social censorship is pro tanto justified

[66] (Mill 2003, 140).

[67] (Mill 2003, 140).

[68] Notice that ordinary persons and groups of persons cannot remove speech from view—they can at best respond with sanctions in hopes that these have a deterrent effect. For these reasons, they have fewer tools at their disposal than persons occupying institutional roles as moderators and intermediaries. Researchers have recently found that successfully removing speech from view can be more effective than counter-speech; if so, individuals outside institutional roles are likely to be fighting an uphill battle with respect to bad speech. For discussion, see (Shmargad et al. 2022). On the other hand, some research suggests that counter-speech can indeed productively change dynamics, especially when positive and constructive. See (Miškolci, Kováčová and Rigová 2020).

[69] Informal social punishment contrasts both with state punishment and formal social punishment. Much of the rest of this book will be occupied with issues of formal social punishment: social media deplatforming, pulling stories, firings, and so on.

[70] (Radzik 2020).

when it targets bad speech of the types just characterized in order to protect a common resource that we have reason to value.

Like censorship generally, social censorship is a *goal-oriented* activity. It is not merely backward-looking in the way that social punishment, undertaken for its own sake, may be. Censors aim to suppress the kinds of speech they target by associating that speech with a social cost. Goal-directed activity like this is constrained by more than mere propriety. Specifically, such goal-directed activity is irrational if it is unlikely to realize its goal. No big deal when we pursue irrational means to our ends or adopt bad ends when matters concern only ourselves. But when our behavior imposes costs on others for a purpose, as it does in the case of social censorship, things are otherwise. Then, it's plausible to think that the activity is governed by an *Effectiveness Constraint*.

> EC: use means that impose costs on others in pursuit of your goals only when (1) the means are likely to succeed in satisfying your goal (2) without causing comparable harm as a side effect.

If social censorship is unlikely to succeed in suppressing bad speech or it does so only at substantial social cost, this provides a powerful counterweight to our reasons to censor. I argue in this section that we should doubt that EC is normally satisfied for social censors, first by showing that social censorship often causes comparable harms as a side-effect (2.3.1), and then by raising doubts about social censorship's capacity to reduce the prevalence of bad speech (2.3.2).[71]

2.3.1 Side-Effects

To begin, notice that there is good empirical reason to think that, particularly in the case of misinformation, we will tend to overidentify conversational vice in those with whom we disagree and under-identify vice in those with whom we are sympathetic. Our cognitive biases can therefore lead us to inappropriately target certain speech for suppression.[72] This can have a distortionary

---

[71] These concerns about enforcing norms of good discourse are distinct from, but complementary to, concerns people have about enforcing norms more generally in online spaces. See e.g. (Norlock 2017; Billingham and Parr 2020).

[72] For an account of the ways in which our biases impact our information-seeking behavior, see (Williams 2022).

effect insofar as sympathies in a social context are distributed in an unbalanced way. When this is so, those who advocate minority positions will be punished for their offending speech, whereas those safely in the majority will get away with equal or worse offenses. If our efforts to censor convey higher order evidence about what to believe,[73] then our grounds for believing are thereby altered in a way unlikely to track the truth.

Additionally, our bias toward conformity is likely to lead us to identify bad speech in ways that are biased against eccentricity. To see the point more clearly, notice that for centuries, norms of acceptable speech were positively oppressive. Consider a virtue the philosopher Thomas Hobbes describes in his masterwork, *Leviathan*.

> A fifth law of nature is COMPLAISANCE, that is to say, *that every man strive to accommodate himself to the rest*. There is in men's aptness to society, a diversity of nature, rising from their diversity of affections; not unlike to that we see in stones brought together for building of an edifice. For as that stone which by the asperity, and irregularity of figure, takes more room from others, than itself fills; and for the hardness, cannot be easily made plain, and thereby hindereth the building, is by the builders cast away as unprofitable, and troublesome: so also, a man that by asperity of nature, will strive to retain those things which to himself are superfluous, and to others necessary; and for the stubbornness of his passions, cannot be corrected, is to be left, or cast out of society, as cumbersome thereunto. For seeing every man, not only by right, but also by necessity of nature, is supposed to endeavour all he can, to obtain that which is necessary for his conservation; he that shall oppose himself against it, for things superfluous, is guilty of the war that thereupon is to follow; and therefore doth that, which is contrary to the fundamental law of nature, which commandeth *to seek peace*.[74]

This is a dense passage. But Hobbes is expressing a simple idea: Human beings should do everything they can to be agreeable to one another. To achieve this, they must cast off any features of their personalities that might be upsetting to other people—whether those people have cause to be upset or not.

Hobbesian complaisance demands a kind of concealing of one's individuality that sounds to modern ears a lot like inauthenticity, but that would have

---

[73] (Levy 2020).
[74] (Hobbes 1994, 95).

been widely thought a fair demand in its time. As John Stuart Mill worried, good manners in Victorian England often required that persons strive "to be without any marked character; to maim by compression, like a Chinese lady's foot, every part of human nature which stands out prominently."[75] Although social censors are right to think that bad speech offers defeasible grounds for intervention, they should worry that attempts to pursue these grounds will result in punishing speech that is not genuinely bad, but that is merely strange.

Worse is the possibility that those simply advocating for their rights[76] and for fair treatment may find themselves silenced by appeal to norms of correct conversation.[77] This is how it was with calls to civility during the civil rights movement. And yet who could deny that, in the age of Jim Crow, it was the segregationists, rather than those who agitated against them, who posed the gravest threat to civility?

Nor is the problem isolated to policing incivility. Harshly punishing speech on the grounds that it is not supported by established sources can encourage excess reliance on existing thought on some issues—especially dangerous when existing thought is provisional and rough.

When we target speech for sanction, it is likely that we will target minority speech and that conversational vice will be allowed to flourish on the part of majorities. So far as our enforcement of these norms tends to pick out the behavior of social minorities for criticism, enforcing conversational norms itself risks damaging our speech environment by giving ever more influence to views already dominant.

These considerations are not meant to show merely that we will often fail to properly recognize speech worthy of suppression in practice (though this is true). Rather, even when we do pick up on genuinely bad speech, patterns of sympathy can lead to a distorted environment in which bad speech is unevenly punished. This uneven punishment can unfairly bias our environment for discourse against minority viewpoints that already take more courage to express. It can also generate a mistaken impression of where the best arguments lie.

Additionally, issues of fairness arise when we notice that the duty to speak responsibly does not equally burden all who are bound by it. For reasons just mentioned, it is easier if you're in the majority to respect these norms

---

[75] (Mill 2003, 134).
[76] (Thomason 2018, 190).
[77] See e.g. (Rasmussen and Yaouzis 2020).

and harder if your view or group is consistently marginalized. Punishing violations is—in practice—unlikely to be sensitive to these differential burdens and will likely in fact perpetuate them. This means that there is a substantial risk that punishment will target persons who have either an excuse or a justification for their bad speech, harming them unjustifiably.

For example, elites often effectively punish uneducated people who lack the tools for understanding why their behavior is irresponsible. This can lead to conversations being dominated by the well-educated, which can blind us to sensible (if imperfectly expressed) contributions from those with less of a handle on norms and language. Indeed, one of the more sensible complaints about the often shifting goalposts of political correctness is that it allows elites to decide that an ever-narrower range of expressive acts is acceptable. Those not sufficiently initiated into elite circles don't have a real chance to participate.[78] This is an issue because discourse is more productive when more people of diverse educational and socio-economic backgrounds contribute to it.

Further, when people regularly face social shame for the things they say, many will shut up for fear that their perfectly acceptable views will be thought deviant too. Michael Huemer calls this censorship's tendency to generate an indeterminate penumbra around acceptable speech.[79] This can happen irrespective of whether the social censorship they're responding to is well calibrated or not. As Glenn Loury puts the point:

> For every act of aberrant speech seen to be punished by "thought police," there are countless other critical arguments, dissents from received truth, unpleasant factual reports, or nonconformist deviations of thought that go unexpressed . . . because potential speakers rightly fear the consequences of a candid exposition of their views. As a result, the public discussion of vital issues can become dangerously impoverished.[80]

Loury is rightly worried that making even genuine deviance costly can impoverish our conversations. This is more likely in environments where social censorship is miscalibrated, targeting speech that resembles bad speech, but

---

[78] See e.g., the provocative piece by Columbia Linguist John McWhorter: https://www.theatlantic.com/ideas/archive/2021/03/nation-divided-language/618461/. See also this column by Conor Fridersdorf: https://www.theatlantic.com/politics/archive/2016/11/the-scourge-of-the-left-too-much-stigma-not-enough-persuasion/508961/.

[79] (Huemer forthcoming).

[80] (Loury 1994, 438).

is not in fact.[81] But it is a likely effect of censorship even when it is strictly limited to the proper targets.

Consider, moreover, that too-tightly enforced norms of responsible speech might reduce creativity. The psychologist Michele Gelfand points out that cultures can be sorted into those that enforce norms tightly and those that enforce norms more loosely.[82] Looser cultures tend to bring with them more creativity, more disorder, worse health outcomes, and so on. Cultures with tighter patterns of enforcement, by contrast, which tend to emerge in places where there are high degrees of external threats, tend to exhibit (predictably) more order, better health outcomes, but less creativity.

Although Gelfand is clear that which kind of culture to adopt depends on the kinds of problems the norms are introduced to solve, tight enforcement (and the creativity-losses that it brings) is difficult to countenance in domains where creativity in response to problems is crucial. Thus, even if we should in certain circumstances prefer our culture to enforce norms stringently, we should demand more evidence that doing so is necessary when the context is conversation, where creativity is a prized value. This is especially so when our very justification for believing that some claim is false turns on our having a sense that those who would question or challenge it would not be subject to severe costs and might be reasonably expected to come forward.[83]

Notice, finally, that policing bad speech can result in too much conversation about how conversation should take place. This can in turn distract from the real issues on the ground. Vigorously policing bad speech may paradoxically lead to evermore unproductive discourse, characterized by accusations of misconduct leveraged by partisans against one another, when, really, we should be addressing our common problems.

In sum, even if it is directed at genuinely bad speech, social censorship to better engineer our speech environment often risks distortions and harms of its own. These harms are comparable in severity to those that well-meaning censors attempt to avert.

---

[81] In this connection, consider the University of California's guidance on microaggressions. The guidance cautions that any appeal to the idea that deservingness should govern the distribution of benefits of burdens may violate its policies against creating a hostile environment for the vulnerable (University of California 1999). Yet the thought that deservingness matters for distributive justice retains traction among serious political philosophers.

[82] (Gelfand 2018).

[83] (Wright 2021).

2.3.2   Effectiveness

But there are good reasons to worry about ability to satisfy EC even beyond the its often-harmful side-effects. For such censorship also might not succeed in discouraging the targeted speech in the first place.

For instance, we must beware the Streisand effect: sometimes our zeal to suppress bad speech results in its reaching a much wider audience than it might otherwise have reached. The rational exchange of ideas rarely makes the news.[84] But outrage at bad speech can make it spread like wildfire, especially in certain media environments. Not only can this violate the proportionality principle (as more and more people rush to sanction the speech in ever harsher ways),[85] it can even increase exposure to speech that is ex hypothesi dangerous.

Similarly, we must consider a substantial risk that attempts at social censorship will trigger a well-studied psychological phenomenon known as *reactance*. Reactance occurs when persons are told that they are not allowed to do something, or that they shouldn't do something (or meet with sanctions for doing it),[86] and subsequently experience an increased attraction to do that thing (or a more extreme version thereof).[87] While explanations of the reactance effect vary, one credible hypothesis is that people resent having their freedom threatened and seek to reclaim it by engaging in the threatened behavior. For this reason, we might expect reactance to be especially prevalent in domains in which people believe they have a right to freedom from interference (as is surely true in the domain of expression). Moreover, researchers have explicitly linked censorship with an increased disposition to believe and express deviant speech.[88]

If our aim is to suppress speech because it is harmful to our speech environment, then we should avoid taking steps that increase its reach or encourage others to believe it. After all, this can lead to further expression of the idea that, by hypothesis, ought not be expressed, not to mention action informed by these new beliefs. As I argue elsewhere,[89] mechanisms like

---

[84] See e.g. (Jansen and Martin 2015) and (Hobbs and Roberts 2018).

[85] (Frye 2022, 188–89, 190–91, 194–95).

[86] Note that one can experience reactance without experiencing a sanction for a certain kind of behavior. Reactance requires only being aware that people sometimes do face such sanctions. For this reason, the reactance effects of punishing speech extend beyond the punished agent.

[87] See e.g. (Brehm 1966); (Powers and Altman 2022); (Rosenberg and Siegel 2018); (Steindl et al. 2015).

[88] See e.g. (Clark 1994); (Bushman and Stack 1996); (Conway et al. 2009); (Gläßel and Paula 2020); (Behrouzian et al. 2016); (Jansen and Martin 2003); (Worchel and Arnold 1973).

[89] (Messina 2022c).

psychological reactance and the Streisand effect suggest that those most concerned about the negative effects of bad speech should be especially alive to the dangers of worsening the situation through censorship.

Concerns about reactance are related to concerns about backlash.[90] Even if social censorship does not cause new people to believe the censored view or wish to express it as an assertion of freedom, there is a risk that the targets of the censorship will escalate. Instead of saying bad things that might've been corrected by open discussion, they may say worse things, or commit acts of violence. Instead of saying things in the public sphere, they may go underground and organize with likeminded others, insulating the relevant views from rational scrutiny, allowing them to flourish unchallenged. It's true that none of the worries I've raised about our ability to satisfy EC supports an absolute prohibition against social censorship. But each points to censorship's persistent dangers. Accordingly, we should often prefer rational engagement or strategic disengagement in responding to bad speech of various kinds. When thinking about how we can reward or punish behavior, it is better to withhold rewards than to dole out sanctions, at least as a general rule.

For all that, there will be clear cases where speech is so bad and the risks of sanction so low that censorship is the way to go. Cases involving harassing and defamatory speech will tend to more easily satisfy EC. Here, the speech is less likely to correlate with any particular outlook, and so the risk of disproportionate enforcement is lessened. Similarly, the speech tends to be low value, and so the costs of errant judgment are significantly lower. What's more is that they involve widely agreed upon notions of harm, making enforcement of these norms less likely to generate backlash and reactance. So far as they are likely to spread the negative speech by means of the Streisand effect, this is likely to result in sympathy for victims and so on.

Likewise, attempting to censor certain cases of discriminatory speech is likely to satisfy EC under certain conditions. Imagine happening upon a conversation in which a white man is yelling racial epithets at a black child on city streets or the online equivalent thereof. Clearly the appropriate thing to do here is to stand up to the man and to tell him to stop. Given the severity of the offense, it would be inappropriate to be overly gentle in this exchange. Depending on the details of the case, it would be perfectly

---

[90] For instance, Karen Adkins argues that the possibility of backlash makes enforcing feminist norms through public shaming risky (Adkins 2019).

reasonable to encourage others to take account of the man's tendencies and to withhold social benefits from him. Moreover, here the fact that the norms against this kind of speech are widespread, nearly universally adhered to, and widely endorsed drastically reduces the likelihood of negative unintended consequences. In this case and cases like it, the pro tanto reasons to sanction the speech win out. In many others, the better course of action is rational engagement or intentional disengagement.

To sum up the results of this chapter: There are many ways to exercise our rights to speech badly. When we do so, this will give others defeasible reason to intervene. And yet because intervention of various sorts is itself subject to EC, which it is difficult to satisfy in practice, rational persuasion and disengagement may be preferable strategies. When we recognize failures in others, we ought to help them reflect more clearly on the reasons they have to use the resource of speech wisely rather than punishing them for their irresponsible behavior.[91] Still, in any particular case, the wisdom of censorship depends on how the strength of the reasons to engage in it compare against the strength of the reasons to refrain from it, given our best alternatives.

2.4 Conclusion

An increased awareness of the effects and extent of bad speech leads almost mechanically to increased pressure to suppress it. In part, the pressure has its roots in reasons that we have to protect our speech environment from degradation. In turn, our well-meaning efforts in this domain can give rise to a harmful culture of self-censorship, and plenty of real-world cases where informal social punishment induces formal social punishment (e.g., firings, demotions, and other things of that sort). Both formal and informal social punishment rightly raise concerns about due process and proportionality.[92]

Despite these potential costs, some regard the widespread policing of speech with approval. More than ever before, we are now able to hold others accountable for their faults. Bigotry has become expensive, and it's a fine thing that these increased costs have resulted in people being less publicly

---

[91] Rewards like likes and shares appear to reinforce bad behavior, after all. See: (Brady et al. 2021). See also (Bail 2021).
[92] Applebaum (2021).

bigoted, even if for the wrong reasons. For others, the same developments induce concerns about an overly stifled atmosphere of discourse, where important truths must be left unsaid if one is to remain a member of the community in good standing. In writing this chapter, I've tried to indicate that both responses are sensible, if insufficiently nuanced.

On the one hand, there are genuine reasons—in public conversations regarding matters of public concern—to exercise self-restraint. Sometimes, we will face the temptation to share a story in advance of verification because it meshes perfectly with our priors or because verification is hard, often unpleasant work. Other times, it will seem alluring to lay into our argumentative opponents, failing to engage in good faith. Still others, we will wish to speak without considering the full impact of our words. Finally, sometimes we'll engage in dangerous or discriminatory speech that can make the conversational tent smaller than it ought to be.

On the other hand, there are ample reasons to be concerned about punishing others when they fail to speak responsibly. Such punishment is likely to target persons undeserving of it. It is likely to be disproportionately wielded against minorities. It is unlikely to be sufficiently attentive to differences in the burdens of keeping to the norms, which can conceal cases where the norm is justifiably or excusably violated. This can in turn yield further violations of the proportionality principle. Zealous punishment of bad speech can distract us from focusing on the issues at hand, policing bad behavior when what we should be doing is staying on track to get to the bottom of things.[93] Even when social censorship targets the right ideas, it can, paradoxically, amplify them and suppress good ones.

Despite social censorship's frequently being counterproductive, this chapter's arguments nevertheless serve as a proof of concept: censorship need not be bad news for our free speech environment. When it targets genuinely bad speech and satisfies EC, censorship can promote a healthy intellectual atmosphere.

In the chapters to come, we will leave behind discussion of informal social censorship and take up the issue of formal but still private censorship. Many of the themes raised in this chapter will continue to be relevant as our analysis continues. But institutions with the power to issue formal punishments in support of the norms they seek to support and that can to block content

---

[93] Some studies suggest, indeed, that talk about things like tone begets more conversations about tone, e.g. (Han, Brazeal, and Pennington 2018).

directly have different tools, competencies, and incentives than individuals or groups acting in an uncoordinated manner. Thus, the fact that groups and individuals often fail to satisfy EC does not imply that intermediaries do. Therefore, such intermediaries deserve a distinct treatment, to which we now turn.

3

Censorship and the Workplace

On May 28, 2020, David Shor—a young progressive data analyst—tweeted a
short summary of a paper by Princeton Professor Omar Wasow. The paper
reported results from a study of protest between 1960 and 1972. The study
distinguished between non-violent protests (especially those that were met
with repression by vigilantes or the police) and those including activist-
initiated violence. Wasow found that protests involving activist-initiated violence increased support for Republicans, whereas the former kinds increased
support for Democratic politicians friendlier to activists' aims.[1] Here's what
Shor had to say about the paper.

> Post-MLK-assassination race riots reduced Democratic vote share in sur-
> rounding counties by 2%, which was enough to tip the 1968 election to
> Nixon. Non-violent protests *increase* Dem vote, mainly by encouraging
> warm elite discourse and media coverage.[2]

Shor published his tweet days after the brutal police murder of George Floyd.
Given the timing of his tweet, peers, strangers, and co-workers alike piled
on to express condemnation for Shor. His tweet of the study was called tone-
deaf; he was called a racist; he was called other things beside. A day later,
pressures mounting, Shor issued an apology. His firm, Civis Analytics, undertook a review of the matter. Days later, he was fired.

Notice that Shor was speaking in a private capacity—he did not invoke his
position or the name of his firm when he tweeted the study. Moreover, his
gloss on the study (published by a respected scholar in a leading journal) was
about as accurate and devoid of sentiment as you could expect it to be, given
his chosen medium (and its famous character limit). There is little cause
for thinking that Shor was guilty of any kind of professional misconduct.

[1] (Wasow 2020).
[2] (Yglesias 2020).

Private Censorship. J.P. Messina, Oxford University Press. © Oxford University Press 2024.
DOI: 10.1093/oso/9780197581902.003.0003

Together, these points suggest that Shor was fired by his employer for his off-job political speech—speech that was arguably apt.[3]

In *Private Government*, Elizabeth Anderson laments that "only about half of U.S. workers enjoy even partial protection of their off-duty speech from employer meddling."[4] Only about half of employees, in other words, would be protected from the sort of treatment to which Shor was subjected. Fewer still enjoy protection for their political speech on the job. Such a legal regime allows employers to dominate their employees where it matters most: the exercise of their political liberties. In turn, this can exert a chilling effect on speech, leading people to hold back their views from public discussion, even when they have something to say,[5] for fear of losing their livelihoods.

The concern is not abstract. The mid-20th century United States witnessed massive coordination between employers across the entertainment industry to refuse employment to anyone suspected of communist sympathies. Doubtless, they were urged on in this by the government (and its House Un-American Activities Committee). But many of the worst offenses were perpetrated by trade unions, advertisers, and network producers. Those working in the industry could have their characters, reputations, and livelihoods destroyed for merely appearing in the wrong place at the wrong time.[6] The result was a chilling atmosphere for discourse in which those even suspected of communism had to engage in regular rituals of self-flagellation to prove their loyalty to American values.[7]

While this was some years ago in a time of war, worries that employers can contribute to a stifling atmosphere surrounding certain contested issues are bolstered by some empirical evidence that today's workplace is increasingly politicized. Researchers find that workplaces are more homogeneous than ever.[8] This appears to be in-part because hiring is already a partisan

---

[3] The firm denies that the firing was related to the tweet. Anonymous sources within the company, fearing reprisal, say otherwise. For a helpful analysis, see (Mounk 2020).

[4] (Anderson 2017, xi).

[5] This qualification is important, as many people choose to remain on the sidelines of political discussions not for any fear of what will happen to them if they participate, but instead because it is rational for them to remain ignorant of political matters (Downs 1957, 253). Encouraging those ignorant of politics to inveigh on complex matters of governance is likely to make our environment for speech worse, rather than better.

[6] This is what happened to John Henry Faulk, the entertainer whose horrible treatment led to the end of the practice of blacklisting. See the captivating retelling by his trial lawyer (Nizer 1968).

[7] (Nizer 1968, 379).

[8] (Mutz and Mondak 2006).

affair: Employers are looking not just at their employees' qualifications, but also at their values and political orientations.[9]

Some of this, we might expect, is for reasons downstream from employer preference: social media have made it easier than ever to cause a great deal of hardship for an enterprise by noting that it employs one unsavory type or another. Thus part of the reason that informal social censorship of the sort we have so far discussed (particularly that consisting in online naming, shaming, and call-outs) is dangerous is that it can occasion costly formal action against perceived deviants by employers seeking to protect their reputations. When faced with these kinds of external pressures, businesses have an incentive to ensure that their hires are "safe," meaning that they are unlikely to tarnish the firm's reputation. If they've hired someone who is in the throes of an informal censorship campaign, this can lead them (as it led Shor's employers) to take formal disciplinary action. If this sort of practice becomes sufficiently widespread, those with unpopular ideas are encouraged to conceal them, leaving our public conversations impoverished.

I argue in this chapter that, severe though these concerns are, laws prohibiting employers from firing employees for their speech are not the answer. This is principally because such legal remedies violate employer freedom of association. Of course, the idea that employers enjoy such freedoms is controversial. Accordingly, I begin by making that case. I argue that we should embrace a version of the freedom of association that extends not just to families, clubs, and leisurely organizations but also to for-profit enterprises (Section 3.1).[10] Of course, it is reasonable to object that the interest in association does not obtain equally for all firms. Plausibly, the strength of a firm's right to the freedom of association increases as it (1) is more intimate and (2) has a greater interest in expressing some determinate message (Section 3.2). Firms that are neither intimate nor have a strong interest in expression do not have very weighty rights to association. But even when firms do not have strong interests in association, legal remedies of the sort proposed may not deliver on their promise and may indeed make things worse. We are better served, I argue in Section 3.3, to help employers see

---

[9] (Gift and Gift 2015). More significantly, partisanship is becoming a litmus test for relationships of any kind (Iyengar 2016).

[10] What I say here stops short of a full-throated defense of at-will employment. I am not committed here to the view that *any* reason for dismissal ought to be upheld (though I think that many will be), only that firings for on- or off-job speech should be. For a defense of at-will employment, see (Epstein 1984). For several skeptical accounts, see (Dannin 2007); (Harcourt, Hannay, and Lam 2013); (Radin and Werhane 2003).

that they have moral duties to refrain from too tightly regulating employee speech. Section 3.4 sums up.

3.1 The Freedom to Dissociate

In *Anarchy, State, and Utopia,* the late philosopher Robert Nozick asks readers to imagine a woman who attracts four marriage proposals. Naturally, her decision about who to marry deeply affects each of the lives of her four suitors. And yet, clearly, none of the four has a right to so much as a say in her decision.[11] Along similar lines, Nozick retells the story of conductor Arturo Toscanini's retirement. Toscanini conducted an orchestra called the Symphony of the Air. Due to Toscanini's stewardship, the symphony gainfully employs many musicians. Eventually, he decides to retire, dissolving the orchestra. His decision, we are to imagine, effectively forces its members to find another job, without any guarantee that they will succeed in finding work in the arts. However much we imagine this negatively affects their lives, it seems ludicrous to suggest that Toscanini's retirement decision should be up to the soon-to-be unemployed members of the orchestra.

Nozick expects you to share his judgments about these cases in part because he expects that you are committed to the liberal right to freedom of association. He expects you to affirm them even if the woman chooses to marry the worst of the suitors for the most vicious and superficial reasons (leaving those not chosen lonely and depressed) and even if Toscanini could carry on conducting without significant strain. Although there is disagreement about the scope of the right to free association (along with what justifies it), it is widely agreed that there is such a right and that it is robust enough to allow people to decide to enter into (and end) personal relationships and to end cooperative ventures as they see fit.

The right to free association analytically entails the right to free disassociation. The thought is this: If I can enter into a relationship, then I can end it or alter its terms. Arguably, when employers choose to fire their employees for their speech, they do no more than this. But why think that employers, rather than just individuals, enjoy associative freedoms?[12]

---

[11] (Nozick 1974, 269).

[12] It is important to say at the outset that I do not hold that rights to freedom of association are absolute or invariant across contexts. It might be, for instance, that the state may not force White Supremacist Joe into an interracial marriage at the same time that it can enforce anti-discrimination law to ensure that persons are not fired on the basis of their sex, race, or religious beliefs. Indeed, I will

To motivate the idea, consider a stylized but familiar story. Janet begins her career as a bartender. She works diligently and spends sparingly so that one day she'll be able to open her own bar—a dream that she's had since her father died and she had to sell his bar to cover some outstanding debt. As her goal comes more closely into view, she begins talking to her co-workers and trying to convince them to jump ship. She secures the relevant permits from the relevant city, exhausts her savings putting down security deposits on the lease for the space and inventory, and hires a small number of people who seem to share her vision and that she predicts will perform well in their roles.

After some time, Janet learns that one of her hires, Nick, has been attending political rallies aimed at furthering white dominance in the United States. Upon learning of this, she sits down with Nick and generously tries to understand where he is coming from. She expresses to him why his involvement with this cause compromises values that she presumes they share. She explains, let's imagine, her own experiences with racism. In the course of conversation, however, she realizes that the two of them are terribly far apart, and that they are unlikely to see eye to eye on important issues. While Nick has performed admirably in his role, bringing in customers who have become regulars at the bar (with no indication that this sound performance is likely to change in the future),[13] Janet finds it difficult to bear to see her hard-earned resources spent employing Nick. Accordingly, she tells him to seek employment elsewhere.

Nick, of course, has a right to attend these rallies. The question is whether his associates ought to be legally obligated to continue to spend their days with him given that he does. The answer is clearly no for his friends: they may decide to distance themselves from him. Similarly with his lovers and family. Similarly, too, for any social groups to which he might belong (e.g., his church can ban him from its premises). Should Jane's business enterprise really be treated differently, just because of the kind of thing that it is?[14]

argue specifically that the right to associate varies in strength with several features of firms that serve as proxies for their intimacy and therefore the strength of their interest in free association.

[13] These are important assumptions. It is easy to simply assume that Nick's political activities will be predictive of mistreatment of others or some other on-the-job failing. Importantly, employers' rights to fire or discipline employees for their job performance is not the relevant question. Most assume that they do have such rights. Rather the question is whether employers ought to be legally authorized to discipline or fire employees when their performance is *not* at issue, merely for their off-job speech.

[14] One available rationale for arguing that commercial enterprises do not have rights to dissociate is that such rights obtain only to the degree that the ability to dissociate is necessary to the governing purpose of the association (White 1997; Fine 2017). In the case of commercial institutions, this purpose is arguably to turn a profit. In the case of non-profits, the founding purpose might be otherwise,

The idea that businesses should be treated differently than individuals (that they ought to be denied rights to associative freedom) seems to face strong headwinds when we realize that it would be perfectly above board for Jane to decide to close up shop and use her resources to do something else entirely. After all Jane's right to bring her enterprise to an end is surely no less strong than Toscanini's right to dissolve his orchestra. And it's hard to see why, if she can liquidate her business, depriving each of her employees of their livelihoods for *any* reason she wishes, she cannot fire one of them because she dislikes his speech or patterns of association.

But this is too quick. We accept that business owners can close their doors for any reason they want but deny that they can condition continued employment on sexual favors (for example). Businesses can close, but their owners cannot legally fire people on grounds of race, sex, or other protected categories. Even if employers do enjoy the freedom of association, then, that freedom appears to have limits in both law and commonsense. Why not think that those limits also bar employers dissociating from employees on grounds of their speech?

While it is possible to deny that the right to association has these limits (and hold instead that laws of these kinds violate employer freedoms), this sort of flat-footed appeal to controversial rights is unlikely to convince anyone not already sympathetic. Instead, the thing to notice is the particular nature of the burden the state would impose upon Janet if it forced her to continue to keep Nick on her payroll. Not only must she continue to advance the interests of someone she has good reason to loathe, but she also must spend precious hours of her life alongside him, allowing him to share in her success and being vulnerable to him in moments of failure. Importantly, denying Janet associative freedom significantly curtails her own ability to live in accordance with the values she most deeply holds and to build a corner of the world where those values reign supreme. Moreover, it seems to do so in a way not required to uphold Nick's own rights. Finally, while the state might have an interest in securing people in their ability to hold unpopular and in

---

but it is no less constraining. But then, unless there is a business reason for dissociations, commercial organizations, whatever their form, may not dissociate from employees. Although a coherent view, this seems to me too restrictive. People start businesses to make a living, turn a profit, true. But as others have noted, they also do so for all sorts of other reasons (to realize their values, or to live well). We should recognize organizations' rights to dissociate from others not just when *the* governing purpose of the association demands it, but when *a* central purpose of the association demands it.

some cases even unsavory views, making this duty fall so squarely on business owners like Janet can make it difficult for them to live well.[15]

These are not claims about how Janet or other business owners happen to feel. Rather they are claims about the kinds of freedoms we have reason to make space for in liberal societies. Even if we lived in a world where people were so tolerant of ideological difference that no one was motivated to act as Janet acts in our circumstances, still curtailing their freedom to buck the trend would restrict a freedom that genuinely matters. By contrast, the freedom to condition employment on sexual favors or race or sexual orientation is not, in any objective sense, very important.[16]

3.2 Intimate and Expressive Associations

Of course, Janet's is a small business. If she is prevented from firing Nick, she is effectively forced to spend her time alongside someone that she has good reason to avoid. Her ability to express her own views through her patterns of association is compromised. But, one might argue, things are otherwise with respect to larger firms (e.g., Target, Walmart, Amazon, Google, and the other major players in our economy). In these cases, the companies are owned by shareholders many of whom have little interaction with the firm's employees. Moreover, the sense in which they have views and values, the expression of which is compromised by forced association, is attenuated at best.

There is a pair of distinctions in the US case law concerning freedom of association according to which the latter right is enjoyed only by certain kinds of associations: those that are *intimate* and those that are *expressive*. If so, perhaps the problem isn't with legal restrictions to freedom of association

---

[15] The question is especially salient given that the state has additional means to pursue this goal, including improving access to unemployment insurance (Taylor 2017).

[16] One might object that these judgments are unacceptably subjective. For some people, it is genuinely burdensome to associate with different races, religions, sexual orientations and to refrain from lording power over subordinates. Yet these interests run up against the counterveiling moral rights of others, e.g., not to be discriminated against on the basis of factors beyond one's control, or not to be assaulted. Sometimes, especially when the objection to anti-discrimination law is grounded in some substantive moral view, it is sensible to carve out exceptions. For instance, a Muslim owned nonprofit might have an interest in excluding Christians or atheists or vice versa. Such exceptions are thought to allow us to respect the freedom of conscience and religion *alongside* the right against arbitrary discrimination. Though those who enjoy such exceptions violate others' moral rights against discrimination, as long as the broader institutional context recognizes such rights, the situation is tolerable. By contrast, it seems to me implausible to suggest that there is even a counterveiling moral right against dissociation grounded in objections to things that reflect upon one's character, as tend to ground firings for employee speech.

as such, but only with those that do not mark relevant differences among firm types.

As far as the court is concerned, an association is intimate in the right sense if it is highly selective in terms of its membership requirements, relatively small in size, has relatively low turnover in membership, limits participation in its central activities to members, and generally excludes strangers.[17]

Notice that commercial enterprises of varying kinds, while they vary in size, often clearly meet many of these criteria.[18] Job searches are often highly selective; employees and employers interact with a high degree of regularity; given the high costs of turnover,[19] employers have reason to keep it low; and tasks regarding the firm's mission can be done only by the persons the firm in fact hires. While a business is almost always going to be a good deal less intimate than a family or a friendship, so too will social clubs and other kinds of entities that clearly have moral rights to freedom of association.[20]

Whereas the court has tended to acknowledge that intimate associations have robust rights to dissociate, it has tended to deny such rights with respect to associations that do not qualify. One exception is for those non-intimate associations that are constituted for an expressive purpose. A firm has an expressive purpose just in case among its reasons for existence is organizing around and supporting a point of view. As with intimate associations, the court affords to expressive associations greater leeway in determining with whom to associate.

These two distinctions (between intimate and non-intimate associations on the one hand and expressive and non-expressive associations on the other) suggest the existence of four kinds of firms. We might arrange these types of firms in order of the strength of their rights to associate.

[17] *Roberts v. United States Jaycees* 468 U.S. 620.

[18] The court's list of properties possessed by intimate associations is not likely meant to be a list of necessary and sufficient conditions. It isn't the case that to count as an intimate association, a group must possess all and only these properties. Rather, it is consistent with court doctrine that an organization might be rather large, for example, but meet enough of the other criteria to count as nevertheless intimate.

[19] Losing an employee costs a firm on average 1.5–2 times that employee's annual salary (Altman 2017).

[20] Closely held corporations—those in which 50% of the company is owned by five or fewer individuals—are granted special protections in many areas. In *Burwell v. Hobby Lobby*, the court held that such corporations can enjoy religious exemptions from being bound by laws, compliance with which causes owners to violate their deeply held beliefs. It is common to think that Hobby Lobby, along with Citizens United, represents a break in constitutional law orthodoxy, treating corporations as if they were persons. As Garrett (2014) points out, this is a mistake.

On the far end of the spectrum would be firms that are both intimate and expressive (e.g., small think tanks and mission-driven for- and non-profit enterprises). These firms have the most robust associative interests not only because they are intimate but also because associating with certain persons will predictably compromise their capacity to express a message central to their founding purpose.

On the far other end of the spectrum will be those firms that are not intimately held and are not constituted to serve any expressive purpose (firms like Target, Amazon, and Walmart). Such firms have much weaker moral rights to association, and much weaker interests in excluding persons for their ideas.[21]

Squarely in the middle of the spectrum are those firms that are either intimate (e.g., family businesses, closely held corporations) or constituted for an expressive purpose (large think tanks and media corporations where there is a complex bureaucracy aimed at preserving the firm's message or orientation, or other firms which aim for a certain corporate culture).

One might grant, then, that firms that meet either or both of these conditions (being intimate or being expressive) ought to enjoy freedom from legal sanction for hiring and firing persons for their on or off the job speech. But, one might say, when it comes to those many firms that are neither intimate nor expressive, the case against state regulation of their associative liberty is far weaker.

But even if you think that non-intimate, non-expressive firms can be permissibly prohibited by law from firing employees for their speech, it is important to note that doing so may well make our speech environment worse, rather than better.

Consider: an employer's desire to discriminate in the *hiring phase* will vary with the costs it faces in terminating the employment relation. If I know that I'm liable to a lawsuit for firing you for the things you say, I'll expend more resources attempting to avoid hiring risky or undesirable personnel in the first place. (Academic readers are encouraged to reflect on how much time and how many resources go into making academic hires, especially those that are eligible for tenure.) This kind of risk aversion amplifies, rather

---

[21] It would, of course, be a mistake to suppose that this means that they will not have an interest in dismissing employees as long as they are performing well in their roles. For public outcry and social pressure can result in boycotts and other consumer activities that might impact their bottom line and give them an interest in dismissing employees for speech, even when they're otherwise performing well. By denying such employers the right to dismiss employees for this reason, we would then undercut the reason for these boycotts, which is presumably to induce a change in behavior.

than mollifies, concerns that the dependence on private employment chills speech throughout civil society. Paradoxically, if recent data that firms are *already* investing more in ensuring safe hires strikes you as bad news for our free speech environment, you should probably not want to further restrict employers' freedom to dissociate from employees on grounds of their speech.[22]

Although one could in theory address this risk by barring employers from taking political speech into account in hiring decisions, it is very difficult to enforce such a requirement. Given even just a few applicants, employers will be able to find reasons to rule out candidates out that do not touch in any way on their speech.

Even setting this problem aside, however, it isn't so easy to legislate away employer control over employee speech. Indeed, even in jurisdictions with formal legal protections for employee speech, employers often enjoy considerable powers to fire employees for their speech. Consider two contexts in which this is known to be true: The just cause dismissal regime in the United Kingdom and the case law governing public employee dismissal in the United States.

In the United Kingdom, employees enjoy considerable protection against unjust dismissal. These protections extend—at least in principle—to dismissals grounded in employees' off-the-job speech. Still, though these cases are adjudicated in courts and through arbitration more frequently than they are in the United States, they rarely dole out victories for employees. Indeed, despite the legal protections, a British report indicates a considerable increase in employers who discipline employees for their speech on social media, and scholars have noted that the disciplinary actions are often upheld in arbitration.[23] But social media is not the lone culprit. For example, in *Northwest London Hospitals NHS Trust v Bowater*, the Employment Appeal Tribunal found in favor of a hospital's dismissing a nurse for joking with colleagues (out of earshot of the relevant patient) that it had been a long time since she had been in the position of having a man under her.[24]

The same tribunal has also upheld firings for employees' off-the-job speech. For instance, in *Rustamova v. The Governing Body of Calder High*

---

[22] For the same reason, there is cause to be cautious about normalizing the practice of calling on firms to fire their employees for their speech. The costs of turnover and damage to firm reputation that these kinds of public campaigns entail can incentivize managers, owners, and CEOs to invest considerable resources in investigating a candidate's background, politics, and risk factors.

[23] (Broughton et al. 2010).

[24] (Wragg 2015, 6).

School, "a teacher was dismissed for publishing a book online . . . which was described as 'racy' and featured characters said to be recognizable as current staff and students."[25] One scholar goes so far as to complain that the European courts find it crucial to protect employee speech *only* when such speech—on or off the job—is exercised responsibly. This, he notes, offers surprisingly little protection for employees. In sum, simply having a law that protects employees against arbitrary dismissal is no guarantee against their being dismissed for arbitrary reasons.[26]

For further evidence, consider the way that US courts handle the speech of public employees. Notice that the state is—in this case—the employer. For that reason, it is widely recognized that its employees have First Amendment rights on and off the job. The state doesn't get to play censor simply by hiring someone to work for it. At least that's the theory. But in practice, the state reserves for itself considerable rights to censor employee speech—often in alarming ways. Law professor Helen Norton points out that this owes largely to two facts regarding the evolution of court doctrine.

First, courts have upheld firings in cases where employees' off-the-job speech is asserted to undermine the state's "credibility in communicating its own contrary views."[27] Thus, for example, a police officer was fired when the department discovered that he maintained a pornographic website featuring him and his wife. The courts upheld the dismissal insofar as the website was incompatible with the police force's ability to express its own message regarding the appropriateness of such content.

Second, and more troublingly, the courts held in *Garcetti v. Ceballos* that the state could regulate any employee speech as long as employees were acting pursuant to their official duties when speaking. The effect has been to prevent employee whistleblowing on matters of public concern. More concretely, courts have found no First Amendment issue with agencies that fire employees for, among other things: "their on-the-job reports of safety hazards, ethical improprieties, and other misconduct. Examples include . . . criticizing police work . . . reporting public officials' financial or ethical improprieties, and . . . criticizing administration proprieties."[28] The state, in short, has been allowed to censor employee speech where it most matters.

[25] (Wragg 2015, 6).
[26] See also (Messina 2022b).
[27] (Norton 2009, 5).
[28] (Norton 2009, 4).

Individual states that adopt explicit statutes to guarantee employee speech do not fare much better.

By themselves (i.e., without the right political culture) legal protections do not suffice to effectively protect for employee speech. Employers sufficiently interested in sanctioning employees for their speech will often be allowed to do so, even where laws recognize employees' rights to speak on and off the job.

I do not mean to suggest anything so crude as the impossibility of upholding worker speech rights through law. We could after all realize the kind of culture in which courts would scoff at these kinds of arguments. Rather, the point is that whatever your stance on the legal question, employers will continue to enjoy considerable discretion over their employees' off the job speech, at least in the short term. For that reason it is worth thinking clearly about how should use this discretion. This is a question of business ethics. We want to know: When should employers restrict or sanction speech and when should they refrain from doing so, and why?

3.3 Free Speech and the Ethics of Hiring and Firing

So far, I've argued that many employers have sufficiently robust associative rights that they should be able to sever ties with their employees as they see fit—even when they do so in response to something the employee has said. Even when the employers do not enjoy these associative freedoms as a moral matter, there are good pragmatic reasons to legally tolerate their powers to dissociate from employees when they speak in ways the firm dislikes. Paradoxically, doing so might be the best thing for our atmosphere for discussion, given the ways in which legislation can change employer incentives. For all that, though, allowing employers to fire employees for the things they say appears far from ideal for our speech environment, and it has been no part of my argument to deny that employers' exercise of discretion can compromise the latter. Given that we want people to be able to speak freely, it is reasonable to worry that the threat of reprisal from employers will impede this freedom, and that employers will coerce their employees in ways that are insufficiently sensitive to their independence as autonomous agents.

Of course, incentives matter. It is easy to make the mistake of thinking that the only person that suffers from the decision to terminate an employee is the employee herself. And there can be little doubt that employees fired face significant costs: they must forego earnings, seek unemployment benefits, seek new employment, and face the prospect of diminished wages even if they do succeed in finding new work.[29] But it is also costly for employers to fire employees. It's not just that they must rearrange schedules, take time out of their lives to conduct interviews (or pay someone to do so), and sink money and time into recruitment and training. Rather, if the employee was functioning well in her role, the employer loses out also on those services and risks hiring someone new who will be incompetent or worse. For this reason, we should be skeptical both that employers will be overly capricious in dissociating from good employees and that outsiders are better able to assess the matter than the person(s) with the most to lose.[30] Without coordination on the part of the state, it is unlikely that employers will conspire to exclude in a way analogous to what occurred during the Hollywood blacklists.[31] The temptation to defect and hire unpopular talent would be too high.

Additionally, it will often be the case that employers cannot neatly predict what will enrage the public—pressures coming from all angles will tend to balance one another out. If our circumstances are such that employers face public pressure in one direction to hire persons either of a certain political persuasion (or those who appear without politics), the chief problem is that the public is, through its informal sanctions, serving to reinforce an oppressive speech environment.

Still, none of this fully eliminates the worry that employers—acting in an uncoordinated way in pursuit of their own understanding of their interests—will create a restrictive atmosphere for speech through their patterns of hiring and firing. Whatever legal protections or other incentives against unjust dismissals there are in place, it is likely that those at the helm of business enterprises will sometimes discipline and fire in ways that amount to small-scale acts of censorship. And even if they are found innocent of legal wrongdoing by the courts, they might have acted poorly for all that.

Some are indifferent to whether they exercise their rights well or badly. But most employers are not like this: they have begun their enterprises not

---

[29] (Daymont 2001–2002).

[30] Indeed (Rudy 2002) suggests that, despite their legal freedom to dissociate without cause, a combination of social norms and costs to arbitrary dismissal combine to reinforce among employers a just cause course of conduct (importantly distinguished from a just cause legal regime).

[31] Of course, this is an empirical claim. If it is belied by the facts and employers regularly collude to exclude certain employees, this is deeply concerning. As Nizer notes in his accounting of events surrounding the trial of John Henry Faulk, the systematic coordination between employers, trade unions, and watchdog organizations is what made the blacklisting period so frightful: "the benign right of individual choice turns cancerous if exercise conspiratorially with others" (Nizer 1968, 472).

simply to exercise despotic control over others, but also to provide them with opportunities and even to make the world they live in a better, more interesting place. This is, naturally, easier said than done and there are respects in which employers acting by the lights of what they perceive to be their best interests can make our social world less hospitable to individuality, diversity of perspective, and eccentricity. How ought well-meaning employers think about the exercise of their associational rights, in view of such concerns?

In this section, I pursue two strategies in an effort to arrive at an answer. First, I argue that employers often have compelling reason to embrace ideological diversity within their workforce grounded in the narrow pursuit of their bottom lines. Since refraining from censorship is often a necessary (though insufficient) means of accommodating diversity, employers will often have narrow organizational interests in tolerating undesired employee speech. Second, I argue that even where such toleration is not within employers' narrow self-interest, they sometimes ought to extend such toleration regardless. This is because, as impactful institutions, employers play a substantial role in realizing or compromising an environment and ethos in which this kind of diversity—which has large scale benefits—can flourish.

3.3.1 Why Respecting Employee Speech Is (Often) Good for the Firm

There is a wide and growing body of literature that shows that diverse groups of people working together toward a common goal of sufficient complexity will perform better than more homogeneous groups, even if the more homogeneous groups are more talented. To the degree that they wish to aim merely at their own organizational effectiveness, therefore, employers have good reason to foster diversity within their ranks. Moreover, they have reason to do so even when this diversity causes some discomfort. That's because even though diverse groups perform better than homogeneous groups, they rarely enjoy themselves as much.

Consider an experiment conducted by psychologist Katherine Phillips and her colleagues. The experiment tasked participants with identifying the guilty party in a murder mystery. Some groups consisted of only familiar persons, whereas others incorporated strangers. The teams with out-group members reported less certainty about their effectiveness and enjoyed the task less, but did far better than the less diverse groups. Whereas the less diverse groups selected the guilty party roughly half the time, the more diverse groups had a 75% success rate—a 50% improvement.[32]

One hypothesis for explaining results like these is that the very things that make diversity so difficult also make it effective. Thus the fact that we are more skeptical of outsiders, that we criticize them more, that we are forced to defend ourselves from their criticism, helps to explain why diverse groups do better than homogeneous groups.[33] Having diverse perspectives in complex decision-making is useful because people with different approaches to problem solving can correct one another's blind spots and encourage the group to be more self-critical, digging deeper into the merits and demerits of various proposals.

By contrast, members of homogeneous groups tend to approach the problems they face in similar ways, duplicating one another's talents and insights. In coordinating on a solution, we are less likely to experience friction, we are less likely to have to disagree and convince hold-outs, and we are less likely to be confronted with powerful reasons against our approach.

To be clear, it isn't simply that more diverse teams comprised of employees outperform more homogeneous teams, holding fixed and equal the "ability" level of each team. Rather, as Scott Page has shown, people with diverse cognitive repertoires (those who use different mental models and have different background experiences, information, knowledge, and frameworks for understanding) will often outperform groups with less diversity in these areas, even if members of the less diverse group are generally of higher ability.[34] This is not just because less diverse groups of high-ability individuals can often duplicate one another's toolsets and approaches to problems, while more diverse groups will benefit from additional approaches and tools. It is also because social pressure within homogeneous groups tends to be higher, and social pressure can induce coordination on poor solutions.[35] Diversity is particularly likely to pay dividends for firms whose teams must complete complex cognitive tasks, whereas its payoffs are lessened in domains where teams perform less complex tasks.

On the basis of this research, we should predict both that employees and employers will exhibit preferences for homogeneity that will, in turn, cut against the true interests of the firm. If this research is on the right track,

[32] (Phillips, Liljenquist, and Neale 2009).
[33] (Muldoon 2018b).
[34] (Page and Phillips 2017).
[35] (Asch 1955).

employers will often have reason to insist on diversity even when their employees complain that they'd prefer to work with more like-minded co-workers or even when they think a more homogeneous team runs more smoothly.[36] This will mean refraining from dismissing employees when they begin to exhibit outward signs that they might hold certain minority positions on important questions. It offers employers reason to resist calls on social media for firing employees. And it provides at least some reason for employers to develop ways of promoting cooperation in the face of diversity rather than pursuing the easier path to harmony in homogeneity. The argument can be put this way:

(1) Among other things, firms have instrumental reason to increase their effectiveness and profitability.
(2) Workplace diversity of the right kind often helps firms increase their effectiveness and profitability.
(3) Workplace censorship often threatens workplace diversity.
(4) So, firms often have instrumental reason to refrain from workplace censorship.

On the basis of this argument, one might question the organizational rationality of firms that attempt to promote an ideologically unified workplace. Google, for instance, has been accused by a number of employees of suppressing conservative views, with some allegations going so far as to accuse the company of dismissing employees for their dissenting views.[37] There is a question of fact here, with Google denying the allegations. But if the allegations are true, Google is plausibly acting contrary to its own organizational interests.

---

[36] Naturally, this will only be true when the diversity the employees prefer to weed out is or correlates with diversity in cognitive sets and where the job descriptions involve complex problem-solving. In my view, these conditions are satisfied for many prominent speech-related firings, including Shor's. After all, the speech-related issues often arise due to differences in moral and political orientations. In turn, people with different political orientations often deploy different mental models of the world, i.e., have distinct cognitive sets (Haidt 2013, ch. 12). Still, there may be tradeoffs between accommodating ideological diversity, on the one hand, and demographic diversity on the other. Making those tradeoffs wisely depends on an assessment of which proxies for cognitive diversity are more robust in a given context and a clear understanding of the values, performance aside, the firm cares about. But the fact that there are often natural tradeoffs here also provides reasons for employers to try to ease the tensions between these kinds of diversity. Thanks to Madeleine Ransom and Ryan Muldoon for pressing me on these points independently.
[37] (Ghaffary 2019).

Even if it is not instrumentally rational to stand with an employee in a given case (because the diversity benefits are swamped by the short-term costs of keeping her around, say), there are reasons to think that the long-run dynamics favor absorbing the short-run costs. Failing to keep diverse employees around can, after all, reinforce polarization, making it difficult to sustain diversity down the road. For research shows that discussion in like-minded groups increases polarization.[38] This can make the firm structure more conducive to maintaining homogeneity even when the firm itself would be better off with more diversity. This makes it likely that the firm will face internal pressure to forego diversity benefits in the future as well. These costs can add up quickly.

Still, whatever benefits diversity might have (and whatever the costs of homogeneity), it would be naïve to suggest that a careful weighting of benefits and costs always comes down on the side of accommodation. Even staunch advocates of diversity (like Page) are careful to note that diversity initiatives can be poorly implemented and that the tensions arising from diversity can sometimes outweigh its benefits. Moreover, homogeneous workforces might be beneficial in certain respects, even if they are not beneficial in all respects. To have a diversity of bigots and a high degree of racial diversity is a recipe for an unproductive mess, not a healthy balance sheet.

3.3.2 Why Employers Should Often Recognize the Expressive Rights of Their Workers, Even at Cost

Employers will often face pressure (internal and external) to dismiss employees for the things that they say. Sometimes, it will be difficult (or impossible) to infer from the offending speech that the employee brings valuable ideological diversity to the table (and so will not point to possible benefits of resisting the pressure). Other times, this pressure will reach a sufficiently high point that the firm is unable to function harmoniously without taking action (and so maintaining more diversity is not rational). Other times still, firms will suffer negative reputational effects of continued association with persons who express certain views and might do best to part ways with those persons. Finally, it can happen that different dimensions of diversity are mutually incompatible. It would be foolish to deny any of this.

---

[38] (Talisse 2019, 105, 110–12).

What I want to suggest now is that that, even when there are organizational pressures to dissociate with people for things that they express, there are moral reasons to resist these pressures.[39] These reasons, of course, have limits. It is not plausible to suggest that every ideologically or speech-based firing is to be repudiated on ethical grounds. The problem is not simply that firms often have prerogatives to act according to their own incentives. The problem is also that sometimes there is no good ethical reason to refrain from firing an employee for her speech. Still, I argue, we ought to recognize a presumption against firings of this sort.

Consider the circumstances surrounding the 2021 forced resignation of *Teen Vogue* editor Alexi McCammond.[40] McCammond, recently named the emerging journalist of the year by the National Association of Black Journalists, was poised to be the magazine's third Black editor. Her employment situation became precarious when screenshots of some of her 2011 tweets resurfaced. In the tweets, McCammond expressed negative comments about "Asian features, derogatory stereotypes about Asians and slurs for gay people."[41] This was not the first time such tweets had surfaced. McCammond had already apologized for and deleted them in 2019.

Still, after her hire was announced, more than 20 staff members at *Teen Vogue* signed a social media letter objecting to her appointment. McCammond replied: "I've apologized for my past racist and homophobic tweets and will reiterate that there's no excuse for perpetuating those awful stereotypes in any way." As Ulta Beauty and Burt's Bee's pulled their advertisements from the magazine, pressure mounted. Days later, a meeting with other important staffers was canceled, not to be rescheduled. Seeing the writing on the wall, McCammond resigned.

Let's assume that decision-makers at Condé Nast—those who canceled McCammond's meeting with important staffers—were predominantly interested in appeasing advertisers and disgruntled employees. Let's also agree that McCammond's speech, originally uttered when she was much younger,

---

[39] (Bhargava 2020, 396).

[40] (Flynn 2021). A similar case could be made using the example of former *New York Times* columnist Donald McNeil Jr. For his side of the story, see: (McNeil Jr. 2021). The McNeil Jr. case nicely illustrates another reason legal protections are unlikely to do all the work we might want them to. After all, the *New York Times* didn't fire McNeil. They merely made it clear that he would no longer be staffed on the best stories. The lesson: firms can avoid legal restrictions by simply refusing to formally discipline unwanted employees and making their work lives miserable for them in other difficult to detect and easy to justify ways. Sometimes what they're doing will be sufficiently transparent to hold them accountable, but often not.

[41] (Flynn 2021).

was not a good proxy for meaningful cognitive diversity. In short, let's assume that the firm was acting rationally by the lights of its understanding of its own interests in distancing itself from McCammond.

I want to suggest that in cases with features like these, when persons make mistakes and other persons call for them to be punished, firms (especially those that are public facing) should often refuse to side with those who are angry. They should do so even if operations might have been smoother without the relevant employee and even if the firm might have had to expend valuable resources to ensure a productive work environment. There are several reasons for this.

First, we all have an interest in ensuring that we do not cultivate norms according to which productive relationships can be terminated for past mistakes for which persons have already atoned. The social world is perilous enough without its being the case that human enough missteps can cause irrevocable reputational damage. By siding with employees in cases like this, companies do their part in helping to reinforce norms that suggest that mistakes made in youth or prior to moral transformation need not have permanent repercussions.

Second, by capitulating to the demands of those employees that would refuse to work with such a person, companies contribute to creating a situation in which mobs get what they want. But as John Stuart Mill reminds us, when mobs can too easily enforce their conception of what counts as acceptable speech, the result can be worse than state censorship. This is an important point: To the degree that it becomes easy to pressure powerful institutions to part ways with people who say things that press the boundaries of what is acceptable, the result can be an atmosphere in which no one feels very free to question social orthodoxies. It isn't hard to see why such a state of affairs is worrisome.[42] By standing with targeted employees in these kinds of disputes, companies can help to avoid creating such a silencing climate. By failing to do so, at least so far as social trends are reproduced across firms, the overall atmosphere for speech can become stifling.

And yet not all firms are equally obliged to contribute to this atmosphere. After all, some (especially expressive) firms and organizations serve as enclaves ("safe spaces," if you prefer) precisely for cultivating and articulating certain points of view. Such enclaves can be useful for developing

---

[42] See (Joshi 2021) for a detailed account of why we want to cultivate norms according to which it is okay to speak our minds.

views among the like-minded before subjecting them to outside scrutiny, ultimately serving as a kind of incubator for them and giving them a better chance at surviving open contest in the public sphere. Insofar as they do this, then their general reasons for accommodating diversity of opinion are clearly lessened. Organizations with these kinds of missions, serving these kinds of roles, are naturally relieved of any strong obligations to accommodate perspectival diversity. Indeed, they might have strong reasons to incur costs to *avoid* significant amounts of intra-firm diversity.

One might wonder why we should have organizations like this, why we should acknowledge institutions that have the authority to "shape and censure their individual members" in terms of what they believe, especially when such firms operate for a profit rather than for an altruistic end.[43] Part of what makes it important to make space for associations of various kinds to define rules on what kind of expression they're willing to tolerate is that we have in liberal societies specifically barred states from doing so. Despite this, individuals do not believe and refine and practice beliefs alone. They take their lead from institutions and their organizing values. In turn these same values can add richness and meaning to their lives. A liberalism that subjects private associations, organized for whatever purpose, to the same norms as those of liberal states is guilty as charged of a failure to recognize community values as an organizing principle for life under institutions. But that sort of liberalism is also likely to fail to help like-minded others make the most of their cooperative partnerships.

Consider the case of academic departments. Within an economics department, you are not likely to have people in faculty meetings who are skeptical of the positive foundations of economics. To constantly deal with those kinds of objections would make it impossible to make progress, given those foundations. Similarly, in a philosophy department, you're unlikely to have to deal in ordinary contexts with mundane objections to the entire enterprise of normative science. This can help the latter gain traction in ways that would not be possible in the face of having to deal with such objections, even if such objections must ultimately be met. Some degree of compartmentalization facilitates progress, even if getting to the bottom of things requires coming together as a whole eventually.

Naturally, problems occur when these groups never come into contact with one another. It is here that we—collectively—lose out on the benefits

---

[43] (Sheahan 2020, 14).

of cross-disciplinary exchange. Truths we believe become dead dogmas. We lose out on the truths or half-truths associated with other approaches. Polarization increases, and our understanding of the world suffers. The good thing is that groups of the sort that we're envisioning here will often want to achieve social change. In order for them to do so, they will need to engage with those in the broader social and political world.[44] In attempting to vie for their views in the broader marketplace, they will necessarily meet with criticism and be exposed to other ways of thinking. Thus we should not expect groups to remain wholly segregated. Naturally, the ensuing conversation across ideological lines can be uncomfortable. This isn't necessarily a problem and indeed can be a sign of progress. But sometimes it will be uncomfortable because conversation has turned unproductive. In those cases, it is worth remembering the respects in which these conversations are best when speakers are exercising the kind of self-restraint described in the previous chapter.

3.4 Conclusion

I have defended a strong presumption in favor of (some) for-profit firms' rights to freedom of association. I then noted that whether we recognize such rights or not (but especially when we do), firms (even those that are neither intimate nor expressive) will have powers to censor in ways that are reasonably thought at odds with Millian concerns about social tyranny.

I have offered reasons for thinking that eliminating this kind of discretion might be legally difficult. But I have also offered reasons for thinking that firms generally ought to exercise their discretion in a way that leads them to refrain from firing employees for the things that they say—especially when the pressures to do so are external pressures.

One set of reasons refers organizations to their own interests, narrowly construed. Another suggests that as components of a broader institutional structure, employers often have moral responsibilities to do their part in cultivating an atmosphere of freedom in speech and to avoid rewarding those who would use their social power and clout to compromise the same. Cases like those with which we began strike us as so egregious because they

---

[44] (Muldoon 2022).

so obviously flout these responsibilities, even where we are willing to grant that the firings help their firms' operational efficiency.

Finally, I've shown that these duties are limited and that, in a range of cases, it can make good sense to think that the duty runs in the opposite direction. When it is overridingly important to a firm to cultivate solidarity around minority positions, it can make sense for those firms to police more what their employees say and think. After all, too much heterodoxy will make it difficult for them to realize their missions well, and there is good reason to facilitate conditions in which associations can realize their missions well. Refusing to do so will leave those minority positions handicapped in the broader marketplace of ideas, in addition to leaving their members importantly unfree.

If I were to end here, I suspect I'd leave you unsatisfied. What, in the end, should we think of the case with which we began, that involving David Shor and his firm, Civis Analytics? Civis Analytics markets itself as a firm that offers strategic consulting grounded in data analysis. Although it has 198 employees, its website touts its humble origins in helping the Obama campaign with its messaging. It describes the company's original staff as congregating in founder Dan Wagner's 400 square foot Chicago apartment. It thus has elements of both expressive and intimate associations. In my view this entails that the law would overreach if it were to subject it to liability for dismissing Shor.

But this is only the beginning of the analysis. After all, Shor's firing was shortsighted and harmful for the kind of speech environment that we have reason to want. There is reason to believe that it might have increased social pressure within the firm and decreased the firm's diversity in ways that intellectually matter.

Accordingly, decision-makers at Civis Analytics should be meet frank criticism for their behavior. They have abused the discretion that we have good reason to afford them given the kind of enterprise they run. Their misconduct redounded not only to Shor's detriment but to the detriment of us all. For in caving to a social pressure campaign, and in making casual speech the grounds for dismissal, the firm's leadership has helped sustain an environment in which many more will refrain from expressing themselves to avoid meeting with similar fates.

It is no mistake, I think, that Civis Analytics cited pressure from clients in justifying their decision. While I have argued that firms have duties to refrain from firing their employees under a range of circumstances, it is important for each of us to understand that our behavior can make it easier or more costly for them to act in the ways that they ought to act. Given what we know about human motivation, then, we should be cautious about our own role in making heavier the air we collectively breathe. We should, in short, remember well the lessons of the last chapter: Although there is pro-tanto reason to restrict harmful speech, and although we will try to identify such speech in practice, our competence in these respects should lead us to be cautious. When we fail to exercise caution, we too will be guilty of wrongdoing, just like Civis Analytics.

4

The "Old" Media: Censorship and Press Freedom

The freedom of speech and the freedom of the press are often treated in the same breath. It is as if the latter were merely an implication of the former. In part, this is because this is how things go in the First Amendment, which reads:

> Congress shall make no law respecting an establishment of religion, or prohibiting the free exercise thereof; or abridging the freedom of speech, or of the press; or the right of the people peaceably to assemble, and to petition the Government for a redress of grievances.[1]

Despite their close association, press freedom and the freedom of speech are not identical. The one is bound up with a particular technology—historically, the printing press, but in recent interpretation, broadcast, print media, radio, and (certain corners of) the internet. The other does not presuppose any technology in particular. I can exercise my freedom to speak simply by heading out to Jackson Square, climbing upon a soapbox, and expounding my views to anyone that will listen. Freedom of the press is institutional, arguably industrial, in a way that freedom of speech need not be.

In Chapter 1, I made the case for a kind of institutional pluralism. It might make sense, I argued, to demand that public powers refrain from censorship altogether and also to afford powers to intermediate institutions that effectively allow them to censor.[2] The best way of preventing the state from using its superior power, reach, and influence to stamp out dissent is to adopt a kind of laissez-faire or "hands off" approach to expression. And yet to prohibit the state from censoring just is to make it the case that people may say

---

[1] ("The Bill of Rights: A Transcription" 2015).
[2] See also (Horwitz 2013).

Private Censorship. J.P. Messina, Oxford University Press. © Oxford University Press 2024.
DOI: 10.1093/oso/9780197581902.003.0004

whatever they please, free from state interference (general categories of defamation, incitement, and fraud excepted).

Chapter 2 demonstrated the various ways in which such a policy might be costly in terms of the values that underlie the right to free speech itself. Recall that free speech is typically held to be worth enshrining as a right because it promotes goods like the discovery of truth, democratic deliberation, autonomy, self-expression, toleration, diversity, and freedom from tyranny. Yet when all are allowed to say whatever they want, many will act irresponsibly to the detriment of such values.

Through speech, persons can ruin reputations; powerful organizations can deceive citizens by deploying their resources to spread falsehood; those with mean views about certain groups can make them publicly known, resulting in indignity; majority views can be disproportionately represented in the public square, which (together with mundane pressures to conform) can make it more difficult for dissenters to live after their own vision, and so on. Realizing this, many commentators argue that we were wrong to think (if we ever thought) that state censorship ought to be wholly prohibited. Some regulations on speech might well help us do better by the lights of the values that justify protecting speech than laissez-faire.

Yet there is good reason to reject these calls to depart from the laissez-faire approach reflected in US jurisprudence. We simply have too much to fear from a state that is empowered to regulate speech to risk creating one. A careful study of history reinforces rather than ameliorates these fears. Still, we have reason to care about the culture that results from our largely uncoordinated activities and whether it is likely to realize or compromise free speech values.

In this chapter, I'll argue that diverse and independent press institutions are crucial institutional preconditions of maintaining a decent culture for free speech.[3] For the purposes of the discussion that follows, I will understand press institutions as those that employ journalists and produce journalism. I'll argue that, for press institutions to function as we need them to, they must be granted a strong form of editorial authority. This is so even though giving editors appropriate control over their publications and programming also hands over to them a power to censor. We ought to accept the risk of wrongful censorship as the fair price for securing a constituent element of a healthy environment of discourse.

---

[3] I do so without harboring any illusions of novelty. See e.g. (Meyers 2010, vii–viii).

Yet we should not be satisfied to leave things here. We should want to know whether traditional media institutions may be regulated in their work to ensure that it remains within the public interest. The right approach to regulating press institutions, I will argue, is to double down on and refine existing professional norms, ensuring that they are properly tailored to our changing information environment, rather than to empower states or agencies to oversee their practices.[4] But this is unlikely to be fully effective if we do not also help the public better understand these norms and how to hold the press accountable when its members fall short.[5]

I begin in Section 4.1 with an account of editorial authority and how respecting it implies a power to censor. I then offer a quick history of the old media forms in their exercise of this authority (Section 4.2). Understanding the history of newspapers, television, and radio—long sources of worries about corporate censorship—contextualizes relatively newer complaints about search and social media, the subjects of chapters still to come. But although these concerns about old media were widespread, they were largely resolved (if not to everyone's satisfaction) through a process of professionalization by which journalism became regarded as a kind of fourth branch of government.[6] Unfortunately, this progress was disrupted by the rise of "sensationalist" television and radio broadcast, resulting in regulatory efforts to

---

[4] There are opposing views in the literature. For Lichtenberg, the press is often controlled by private parties who are powerful and can exercise a kind of censorial power threatening to values of free speech (Lichtenberg 1987). Accordingly, the freedom of the press is an instrumental value—one that should be respected just insofar as it promotes freedom of speech and the values associated with the latter. By contrast, for Horwitz, the press is governed by a sufficiently robust set of norms that we need not be overly concerned that it will do anything other than promote the quality of democratic discourse (Horwitz 2013). I will suggest here that Horwitz's view lies closer to the truth. We do better to realize a healthy epistemic environment to allow the press to self-regulate, to determine what is newsworthy, and to censor, than to attempt from the top down to decide what these practices should be. This approach is compatible with concerns about the kinds of incentives that editors and journalists face and an openness to proposals for improving them.

[5] On this point, I could not agree more with Wendy Wyatt, who argues that consumers of media are bound by stringent obligations. See: (Wyatt 2010, 286–91).

[6] There are, of course, questions about how widely the press discharges these responsibilities. For a skeptical account, see (Herman and Chomsky 2002) and Chomsky (1989). According to Herman and Chomsky's "Propaganda Model," the media serve the interests of government, rather than working to keep it in check. This, they claim, is amply shown by the media's relatively favorable coverage of the United States in its foreign policy interventions compared with its relatively negative coverage of the United States' political enemies. It is difficult to know what to make of the evidence they marshal for these conclusions. Still, toward the end of *Necessary Illusions* (first published in 1989), Chomsky himself appeared to be optimistic about the direction of the trend. He wrote, for example, that "the media . . . have allowed some opening to dissident opinion and critical reporting in recent years, considerably beyond what was imaginable even at the peak of the foment of the sixties, let alone before" (Chomsky 1989, 135). For a contemporary defense of the model, see (Mullen and Klaehn 2010). At the end of the day, questions about the role the media plays in public life are crucial empirical questions. Suffice to say, if the propaganda model is correct, then there's work to be done.

correct a perceived lack of balance. Understanding the failure of this regulatory response, I argue, allows us to envision a better path forward (Section 4.3) and to articulate some principles that govern the exercise of editorial authority (Section 4.4). Section 4.5 concludes.

4.1 Editorial Authority and the Power to Censor

That the world is complex is a truism. That this complexity puts us at the mercy of numerous strangers as we try to find our way around is easy to overlook. Those things about which we have direct knowledge (the local weather, the characters of friends, family, and co-workers, the state of the local infrastructure, the working conditions in our various workplaces, our various likes and dislikes, local prices, and the variety of things that we meet with in our manifold perceptual experiences) are indispensable for governing our personal lives. But if we were to rely exclusively on these objects of direct knowledge, we would do without (even rudimentary) technology (not knowing how to create ourselves what is possible through vast economic networks and systems of innovation), medicine (most of us having no knowledge of the biological and chemical sciences so important for lengthening our lives), legal defense (the law in general being too multifaceted and difficult to understand even for practitioners in various specialized subfields to master), and knowledge of the world outside our small corner of it. In short, a world without reliance on expertise is a world in which most of us would have difficulty meeting most of our basic needs.

It's not just that this kind of reliance on what we know ourselves directly would be horribly inconvenient: it would also make us unfit to exercise the kind of self-government that republican institutions require of us. To discharge our political duties requires that we rely on strangers for testimony concerning the facts and for context to help us understand their importance. We rely on university professors to conduct basic research, on medical doctors to advise us, and on enterprise to provide us products to make our lives easier. And though many of us appear not to like it very much, we rely on journalists to bring us the news of the world and to help us to understand how current events affect our actions at the polling booth and beyond.[7]

---

[7] On the moral and political necessity of good journalism and its epistemic function, see (Borden 2010, 59–61); (Davis 2010, 101); (Singer 2010, 118–19).

It is common in our polarized political environment to lament our reliance on others in at least this last respect. As social trust wanes, so too does trust in the media. But this distrust can only go so far. Though we might complain about media bias, still, when we need to know something, rely we do. When you want to know something, you Google it. When you decide which link to follow, you prefer sources, minimally, that have not misled you in the past. Many of these are traditional journalistic outlets: CNN, *The New York Times*, *The Wall Street Journal*, the BBC, and so on. If we profess to distrust the media, our stated preferences and our revealed preferences come apart, and it is obvious which carry more weight.

Our revealed trust in media is intelligible in light of the fact that there are people and institutions that have established a reputation for reliability where it matters most. True, we might be skeptical of the more politically charged information that we find on these outlets and they are often trying to piece together a narrative on our behalf. But still, their reporting of the facts carries substantial evidential weight, and it does so because they have established reputations. These reputations in turn are possible only because they have considerable authority to protect their name by publishing and refusing to publish as they see fit. This power to publish and refrain from publishing at will is what I mean by editorial authority.

It should be clear that the exercise of editorial authority directly implies powers of censorship. If I have broad authority to publish as I see fit, I might use this authority to keep inconvenient facts from the public view. Sometimes, these powers of censorship are foregrounded and their exercise is transparent. This was the case when CBS told writers of *The Good Fight* that a scene in their show would be pulled by the network if the producers insisted on its inclusion. But it also enables the less transparent behavior that George Seldes describes in *Freedom of the Press*.[8] For instance, Proctor and Gamble is a major advertiser and purveyor of cleaning products. In 1932, it pulled its advertising support from outlets that printed a syndicated piece on how to make your own soap, which threat led some of those organizations to pull the piece. It is the abuse of editorial authority that explains why, fearing reduced revenues from health insurers, proponents of single payer health insurance have had a hard time buying advertising space in journalistic outlets in Boston and Washington, DC.[9] Even when media do decide to go ahead

---

[8] (Seldes 1935).
[9] (Soley 2002, 214).

and print a story that they predict will offend their advertisers, they will often "bury" it, placing it less prominently than it might otherwise deserve.[10]

Granting uncoordinated private interests the power of editorial authority means tolerating some bad behavior, including some censorship. But refusing to grant these powers risks something far worse: either an over-reliance on the state's determination of what information is most important or else a cacophony of information without editorial sorting. The former is bad for familiar First Amendment reasons. The latter is bad because, complex as the world is, we cannot do all the work ourselves. Not only are we often not qualified to do it, but there is simply too much activity for us to sort through in the course of our already busy lives.

In sum, today's public is heavily reliant on newspapers, radio, and television for learning about the happenings of the world. This is so not just in the realms of domestic and international politics, but also in the domains of science, medicine, business, and economy. Although the rise of social media has allowed everyone to practice journalism to some degree, still, most of what gets shared in the way of news is verified and often originally reported by major news organizations. Contemporary concerns about the trustworthiness of the media aside, our behavior reveals substantial trust in these outlets.

4.2 A (Brief) History of the Press and Attempts to Regulate It

It is easy to take this state of affairs for granted—to take it that there were always institutions responsible for finding facts, organizing information, and identifying the most important trends an informed citizenry ought to know. In fact, however, until the late 19th century, newspapers did very little reporting of this kind. When they did report on important issues of moment, they did so from a highly partisan point of view or one that heavily favored their commercial interests. The very ideas of journalistic integrity that make possible contemporary complaints about the press were anathema to journalistic practice until quite recently.[11]

---

[10] (Soley 2002, 196).
[11] (Schudson 1978; Meyers 2019).

Here's how the historian Eric Burns characterizes the (colorful) state of journalism in the United States' infancy:

> The Declaration of Independence was literature, but the *New England Courant* talked trash. The Constitution of the United States was philosophy; the *Boston Gazette* slung mud. The *Gazette of the United States* and the *National Gazette* were conceived as weapons, not chronicles of daily events; the two of them stood masthead to masthead, firing at each other, without ceasing, without blinking, without acknowledging the limitations of veracity. Philadelphia's Aurora was less a celestial radiance than a ground-level reek, guilty of "taking a line that would have been regarded as treasonable in any later international conflict." And *Porcupine's Gazette*, the Aurora's sworn foe, was barbed as its namesake.[12]

Burns continues: "there was no tradition at the time of an impartial press, either in the colonies or in Europe. In fact, insofar as there was a tradition in journalism at all, it favored bias."[13]

Before the United States broke from colonial rule, there were a few publications, but colonial leaders required that their publishers acquire a license in order to distribute their wares.[14] The degree to which this arrangement could be used by government officials to spike critical stories is difficult to overstate. It was in part against this backdrop—in which the state's sanction was required to distribute the fruits of the press—that the First Amendment's provision that the press remain free of state control was seen to be crucial.

Having to rely on the government's permission to publish would have seemed a frightful thing for those with views at odds with the state's or interests in documenting its misconduct. But the immediate result of press freedom was not to make way for a responsible, balanced, unbiased press. Instead, early press freedom made room for rowdy journalists to publish what they pleased. While it was certainly possible in this time to find commitments to impartiality and fairness, these marked merely so many exceptions to the rule.

It wasn't until the early 20th century that calls for the professionalization of journalism became widespread. In 1912, Joseph Pulitzer endowed

---

[12] (Burns 2006, 5); compare (Starr 2005).
[13] (Burns 2006, 12).
[14] (Burns 2006, 32).

Columbia's school of journalism (the first such school in the country). Before he did so, he had his work cut out for him in convincing skeptics that it was a good idea. In response to such critics—many of them journalists!—Pulitzer spoke of the trouble of restraining the "news instinct from running rampant over the restraints of accuracy and conscience."[15]

In order to better uphold restraints of accuracy and conscience, it was necessary, in Pulitzer's view, to begin taking journalism at least as seriously as medicine and law. This meant professionalization. For the field of journalism to professionalize meant for there to be "a class feeling among journalists not based upon money but upon morals, education, and character."[16] What was needed, according to Pulitzer, was to encourage a new self-conception for journalists, one which set them apart from their editors and their commercial interests. Here's how he described the way journalists ought to see themselves:

> What is a journalist? Not any business manager or publisher, or even proprietor. A journalist is the lookout on the bridge of the ship of state. He notes the passing sail, the little things of interest that dot the horizon in fine weather. He reports the drifting castaway whom the ship can save. He peers through fog and storm to give warning of dangers ahead. He is not thinking of his wages or of the profits of his owners. He is there to watch over the safety and the welfare of the people who trust him.[17]

Pulitzer hoped that journalists seeing their vocation in this way would bind them together not with reference to their monetary interests but by the bonds of "honorable association."[18] Fortunately, there was an extant model for encouraging such bonds and that model was found in professional schools. Pulitzer came to believe that the formation of journalism schools was necessary to form these bonds, encourage these self-conceptions, and provide

---

[15] (Pulitzer 1904).

[16] (Pulitzer 1904, 649).

[17] (Pulitzer 1904, 656). Importantly, this characterization has seemed to some practitioners naïve. One newspaperman put it this way: "The business of a New York journalist is to distort the truth, to lie outright, to pervert, to vilify, to fawn at the foot of mammon, and to sell his country and his race for his daily bread. We are the vassals of the rich men behind the scenes. Our time, our talents, our lives, our possibilities, are all the property of other men. We are intellectual prostitutes" (cited in Lebovic 2016, 91).

[18] It is easy to dismiss the notion of professionalism in journalism as high-minded nonsense. For reasons this would be a mistake, see (Davis 2010).

journalists an education that would prepare them for the challenges of their careers.

At the same time that journalism was professionalizing, the American Society of Newspaper Editors was re-thinking its commitment to interpretation-free reporting. In 1933, the society appeared to recognize that the world was becoming too complex for merely factful reporting. Accordingly, "editors should devote a larger amount of attention and space to explanatory and interpretative news and to presenting a background of information which will enable the average reader more adequately to understand the movement and the significance of the events."[19]

The increasing reliance on journalists' powers of interpretation would raise worries about the inevitable subjectivity of the news. It was out of these concerns—in concert with a confluence of other factors—that the ideal of objectivity in journalism became polarizing.[20] Worried that the news would be subjective, that journalists would be tempted to perform what was in fact a vocation in ways unbefitting to it, critics were vexed at least in part about the incentives produced by journalism in a world where the press is a commercial, for-profit enterprise. Echoing some of Pulitzer's original concerns in an essay published some years later, syndicated journalist Walter Lippmann wondered whether democratic institutions could maintain their integrity in a world where journalism remained "an unregulated private enterprise."[21]

And yet a largely unregulated enterprise it would remain, despite strenuous efforts of the New Deal presidency to subject it to regulations in the interest of securing a diverse and vibrant marketplace in news. Few of these measures succeeded, largely owing to a widespread fear of totalitarianism. Many—including press special interest groups—argued that any state regulation of the press threatened a slippery slope to the end of freedom in the United States. Such arguments rang true in the ears of those that mattered.[22] Even the apparent victories—e.g., a successful anti-trust suit against the Associated Press—which forced it to allow any outlet to use its wire service— were Pyrrhic, leading to more consolidation and concentration of market power, not less.[23]

---

[19] Cited in (Schudson 1978, 148)
[20] On the publicity apparatus of early- to mid-19th century government, see (Lebovic 2016, 56–62).
[21] (Lippmann 2008).
[22] (Lebovic 2016).
[23] (Lebovic 2016, 83–84).

Worries about the public costs of a media industry driven by increasingly consolidated private interests would only become more severe as news was read less and heard and watched more. While it was always the concern of the newspaper editor to assure a wide circulation to better sell commercial advertisements, the public had an appetite for television entertainment that many reasonably worried would lead news in a sensationalistic direction—one further at odds with the public weal.[24]

To mitigate some of these concerns about corporate censorship and biased media, the federal government enacted a series of regulations. First, in 1927, the Federal Radio Commission mandated that any broadcaster that allocated time to a political candidate must also allocate an equal amount of time to the candidate's opposition. This would be superseded by Communications Act of 1934, signed into law by Franklin D. Roosevelt, which not only created the Federal Communications Commission (FCC), but also expanded the equal time provision of the 1927 regulation to cover television broadcast as well.

Acting under its new mandate, the FCC enacted the Fairness Doctrine in 1949. The regulation required that all publicly licensed broadcasters cover some issues of public importance and dedicate space for contrasting views. These new requirements were geared specifically at limiting the editorial authority of broadcasters. Those who occupied airwaves were still granted broad discretion in how they filled the space. But they were forced to approach some degree of balance, on pain of penalty.

After decades with varied results, the Fairness Doctrine was repealed in 1987. This was in part because experts testified that there was no longer a scarcity of broadcast capacity, part of the doctrine's justification in the first place. This made it credible that a diversity of views could emerge from a policy of deregulation.[25]

But the repeal also marked the triumph of arguments that the doctrine itself was not particularly effective. Although aimed at laudatory ends, the Fairness Doctrine was easy to avoid, difficult to enforce, and vulnerable to being captured by political opportunists. Worse, the broad discretion the doctrine left to broadcasters allowed them to present diverse views with slant, to fail to seek out the best versions of those views, and thus to comply

---

[24] Some of these worries have been well-realized. See (Benkler, Faris, and Roberts 2018), which points to the darker side of trust in media. When trusted media sources validate misinformation, they necessarily increase its uptake and its spread. As the historian Thomas Rid points out, traditional media forms have often (and increasingly) helped misinformation (even that produced by foreign intelligence) reach a wider audience than it otherwise might (Rid 2020, 381–82, 399, 424).

[25] (Smith 1999, 484).

with the regulation formally without in any significant measure realizing its spirit.

What's more is that the doctrine was used to deny licenses to smaller more ideologically driven organizations and distribute them instead to more neutral corporate bodies.[26] And unscrupulous politicians, including Richard Nixon, encouraged aids and other associates to use the doctrine to quell any overly negative coverage of their actions. These were all unwelcome results for those who saw the doctrine as a tool for realizing healthier, more diverse, discourse. These abuses would have amplified, rather than alleviated, concerns about press incentives and their inadequacy for encouraging outlets to deliver the kind of reporting an informed citizenry needs. They would have done this while dangerously concealing the degree to which bias remained at the heart of broadcasting under a false veneer of balance. The old way may have left something to be desired in terms of bias, but at least it was easy for people to follow the money.

The effects of the Fairness Doctrine's repeal have been mixed. On the one hand, there has been a proliferation of explicitly partisan radio and television programs, with no claim whatsoever to balance.[27] As broadcast news has grown in prominence, this has, by some accounts, led to an *asymmetric* news environment. Using network analysis, for example, Benkler, Faris, and Roberts have found that extreme right-wing media sources across television, radio, and online have freed themselves from professional norms, securing an audience on the basis of providing consistently confirming evidence and narratives and generating widespread skepticism of mainstream, professional outlets.[28] These organizations are far less subject to self-correction than their counterparts on the center-right, center, and left-wing of the media ecosystem, generating an epistemic crisis for consumers of those media. On the other hand, there have been clear gains from the perspective of press freedom in expanding access to broadcast outlets. Freed from the need to apply for a broadcasting license, smaller, less well-funded organizations were better empowered to reach audiences.

Because of the costs deregulation has brought, some favor a return to a kind of (technologically updated) Fairness Doctrine. Such advocates lament the degree to which fairmindedness and diversity of perspectives have faded

---

[26] (Ammori 2008, 890).
[27] (Zelizer 2017, 189).
[28] (Benkler, Faris, and Roberts 2018).

from the public view. Others, while convinced by the case for the repeal of the Fairness Doctrine in the case of television and radio broadcast, nevertheless seek similar regulatory tools for regulating internet platforms and other new technologies that have more recently disrupted the way that Americans get their news. Others still embrace a laissez-faire approach in both contexts.

Given such disagreement about these sorts of regulations, it is reasonable to wonder who is right. Defenders of repeal have made a compelling case that there are major constitutional issues involved with allowing a federal agency of five to determine who gets a license to transmit their views through the airwaves on grounds of perceived balance. Similar concerns apply to technologically updated versions of the policy. Moreover, the doctrine's repeal represented a commitment to treating broadcast outlets and print media the same way. For decades earlier, in *Miami Herald Publishing Co v. Tornillo* (1974), the Supreme Court found that newspapers and print publications could not be forced (without offense to the press clause of the First Amendment) to comply with structurally similar regulations.[29] Such defenders of repeal note that the founders advocated press freedom at a time when the news was about as partisan as can be imagined, and when the entire nation had a total of just eight newspapers.

Ultimately, I believe it was right to abandon the Fairness Doctrine and that it would be a mistake to revive it in new technologically updated form.[30] Such a doctrine presents too few real benefits and poses too many real risks, inviting a mechanism for the covert political censorship of views critical of the powerful and influential. While the erosion of professional norms that followed coincided with the doctrine's repeal, it seems likely that repeal was incidental to the erosion of norms and that reinstating the doctrine would not bring the norms back. (Consider: would Breitbart's hosting contrasting views solve anything? Wouldn't it likely find ways of complying with the letter of the law without addressing its spirit?) What's more, there is reason to hope that we can restore sound norms without regulation, in part by teaching the public the importance of professional norms and the risks of relying on sources of information that are not liable to external corrective mechanisms. Because press institutions respond to the desires of their audiences, there is reason to believe that the worst of these issues must be addressed on the demand side.

[29] Editors and commercial presses were often powerful advocates of these arguments. For a fascinating accounting of such issues, see (Lebovic 2016, 70–79).

[30] But see (Leiter 2022) for a contrary view.

In what follows, I'll argue that the right course forward combines formal institutional elements with a less formal emphasis on recovering professional norms and educating the public about their raison d'être. I'll argue that media outlets must recognize their important public role as a kind of fourth branch of government and that, as consumers of media, we must demand and consume diverse sources of information that (though they might be partisan) adhere to professional standards. This is demanding, and fails to offer a quick fix, but, in addressing the problem at its roots, it promises real, lasting change.

4.3 Competition, Diversity, and Independent Journalism

In the previous section, we saw that the idea of journalism as a profession is relatively new. This new understanding of the social role of journalists has enabled expensive fact-finding, even when the same threatens the corporate interests of the owners of the media conglomerates. It has enabled journalists to identify with something more significant than their paychecks, and it has promised (although never fully delivered) an ability to reinforce a fragile sense among citizens that they can turn to journalists for important information when the stakes are high. It is difficult to overstate the importance of all of this for our epistemic environment and its role in enabling a healthier public conversation.

And yet it would be a mistake to pretend, as some have, that there are simply no reasons to worry about censorship in journalism, given extant professional norms. (Norms are helpful. They do not fix everything.) For example, it is common in journalism schools and (even more) in marketing schools to claim that fears of corporate censorship are overstated, that publications and broadcasters typically wall off their editorial offices from their advertising and marketing departments, and to argue that there's thus little reason to worry about censorship of important information by journalism outlets.

But for many, the mere threat that the information the public may access is determined by the corporate interests of advertisers and news organizations desperate for revenues suffices to make the case for reform.[31] The mere conferring of editorial authority implies that editors can behave in these ways

---

[31] Not only that, but there are clear cases in which editors have buried newsworthy information in pursuit of financial gain. Consider what happened when the *San Francisco Examiner* tried to publish a report on the *San Francisco Chronical*, which the parent company of the *Examiner* wished to buy. The parent company ordered the editor, Timothy White, to spike the piece, fearing that it might compromise the deal. Supposing that the piece was in the public interest, this looks less like a legitimate

detrimental to sound decision-making. If information is at the mercy of editors and journalists with private interests, we lack what we need to make wise collective decisions. As James Madison puts it, "A popular government, without proper information or the means of acquiring it, is but a prologue to a Farce or a Tragedy; or, perhaps both."[32] Less dramatically, collective self-governance is not likely to yield improvements without good information.

In this section, I argue that the best way to mitigate the risk of censorious exercises of editorial authority is to ensure a robust and diverse media environment through a variety of funding mechanisms. The intuition is as follows: Corporate censorship is concerning because it is not hard to imagine corporate incentives aligning in a way that keeps important information from public view. But if there are a number of different funding structures, which offer a number of different incentives (including exposing the errors of other outlets), this threat is significantly mitigated. If one outlet buries information that is in the public interest, others can attract readers and attention by publishing it. This is all the more likely when press institutions are responding to different funding incentives.

Of course, to some degree, we already have a diverse environment, consisting of for-profit outlets, non-profit outlets, state sources of information, universities, newsletters, and so on. But although the majority of states have at least one non-profit outlet, the majority of the news that Americans receive is from for-profit institutions like CNN, MSNBC, and Fox News. To reduce dependence on for-profit sources, we might pursue a number of strategies.

One approach is to have the state fund major institutions directly. This is the approach taken by several European and Scandinavian countries, and the BBC is among its greatest success stories. State-funded media companies secure editorial independence from market incentives. Naturally, political funding allocations can always be altered, and so choosing the state as the sole funder for journalism presents considerable risks of its own.[33] But pursued as a part of a broader strategy to ensure a variety of dependencies, this is an indispensable part of a healthy press.

---

exercise of editorial authority and more like a wrongful case of censorship. The parent company, no doubt, has a right to pursue its economic interests, but it ought to do so in a way that avoids depriving people of relevant information. See (Soley 2002, 224) for discussion.

[32] (Madison 1822).

[33] For a good articulation of at least some of these problems in Germany, see (Schwaiger 2020).

A second solution relies on philanthropy and partnership with institutions of higher learning (colleges and universities) in order to escape perverse commercial incentives. And there is indeed a significant number of non-profit outlets producing journalism in the United States. As Anderson, Downie, and Schudson point out, there are at least 200 such organizations operating in the United States, backed by over $150 million in annual funding.[34] But if non-profit journalists need not worry as much about attracting a sufficiently loyal readership to remain attractive to advertisers, the pressures they face are no less significant. It is crucial for such outlets to impress their donors, who might have interests that run counter to the public interest. Collaborations with universities do not run into these problems, per se. But as those of us in higher education know well, the funding situation is not nearly so certain as it is easy to imagine from the outside, and the pressures from within can push us away from the truth, not toward it.[35]

A third option is to endow some selection of outlets so that they can function independently without the need to have their funding renewed regularly.[36] Particularly urgent would be to fund the creation of newspapers in towns and cities where they do not exist and to provide funding for minority publications in homogeneous places.[37] This would require some up-front investment—either from government or from philanthropy—but it creates probably the most independence. Since endowments are self-perpetuating (provided relatively stable market conditions and costs), the pressures to appease outsiders (except at the moment of endowment) are much less intense. Yet true independence, after all, suffers its own problems. As the journalist John Marshall reminds us, too much independence can allow media "to be cut off from" what interests (and concerns) the readership.[38]

[34] (Anderson, Downie, and Schudson 2016, 104).

[35] See Joshi 2022.

[36] E.g., the *Guardian* is funded through a mission-oriented trust (Singer 2010, 125). Recent events suggest that some new papers could receive sizable endowments soon, as the *Tribune* changes hands: https://www.wsj.com/articles/alden-clashes-with-billionaire-over-future-of-tribuneand-of-local-news-11618027398. See also https://www.niemanlab.org/2009/01/endowing-every-american-newspaper-114-billion-innovation-priceless/ and https://www.nytimes.com/2009/01/28/opinion/28swensen.html.

[37] The first (preferring to endow local outlets where they don't exist) is urgent because the first newspaper to enter a market brings with it attractive increases in political engagement; the effect of journalism outlets beyond the first is significantly diminished (Gentzkow, Shapiro, and Sinkinson 2011). The second is important insofar as one of the things the market fails to adequately deliver is diversity in reporting (Gentzkow, Shapiro, and Sinkinson 2014).

[38] https://www.huffpost.com/entry/josh-marshall-on-the-grow_b_131571.

A final proposal is to encourage journalists to unionize, to protect them against capricious and arbitrary dismissal by the publishers that employ them. If journalists are hard to fire, the argument goes, then they can speak truth to power without fearing loss of livelihood. This approach has been variously tried in the United States and never quite delivered on its promise.[39] Part of the reason is that curtailing publishers' rights to hire and fire as they see fit by a state-backed union has been (correctly, in my view) seen as risking violation of the First Amendment. After all, press institutions are paradigm instances of expressive institutions. This means that they enjoy robust freedom of association. Moreover, successful unionization risks that the unions will *themselves* begin to police the kinds of things journalists can say. This is no idle threat and was in fact commonplace in the mid-20th century.[40] Still, other measures (like generous unemployment insurance triggered by certain kinds of dismissal) might well facilitate public-interest journalism and should be considered part of an attractive reform program.

Each model of assuring independent journalism has its own pathologies. The best shot at true independence is to pursue a pluralistic system where various different institutions operate and are subject to a variety of pressures. This means increasing public funding for media sources, continuing to interest philanthropists in the cause of good journalism, facilitating properly constrained collective bargaining, endowing a subset of press institutions, and leaving a great number of others to continue to compete in the for-profit space.

The forces of competition and professionalism under these circumstances would be much more congenial to producing a healthy epistemic environment than they are at present.[41] Journalists would have a number of options in terms of the kinds of outlets they could work at and those outlets would have to find ways to attract the kind of talent that helped them secure a good reputation. The risks of such competition (that it ultimately favors ruthless cost-cutting and maximization of ad revenue) would be substantially mitigated by the existence of organizations less subject to these pressures—institutions that could then focus exclusively on producing excellent work

---

[39] (Lebovic 2016, 88–109).

[40] (Lebovic 2016, 97–105).

[41] I think this is true at the same time that I think that concerns about our present circumstances are easy to exaggerate. As of 2007 (and I'm aware of no more recent data on this point), citizens' knowledge of the world is no worse than it was in the heyday of journalism. This, of course, is cold comfort in view of the fact this knowledge remains poor. See: https://assets.pewresearch.org/wp-content/uploads/sites/5/legacy-pdf/319.pdf.

in the public interest. Because the failings of one outlet—once discovered—would be widely reported, a diverse and healthy press of this kind can self-regulate in desirable ways, largely without distressingly involving the state in the regulation of the press. Media literacy education remains crucial to address demand-side problems that encourage people to demand information from sources that are not subject to the self-correction of a healthy media ecosystem.[42]

Nevertheless, even if these problems of diversity and perverse demand were addressed, there would remain significant latitude for editors to pursue agendas through their exercise of authority. In the next section, I argue for three claims. First, we should expect and indeed welcome some degree of partisanship in our media due to differences in editorial practices and audience needs, conditional on the media space's being sufficiently diverse[43] as to mitigate worries about one-sidedness. Media slant must not be conflated with censorial abuse of power. Still, there are a number of ways in which the exercise of editorial authority might go wrong. I outline the most important of these in the next section, presenting results from more detailed studies in media ethics.

4.4 Media Slant, Media Censorship, and Media Ethics

Some of what gets called media censorship involves editors declining to publish stories that are inconvenient for the publisher's or editor's political point of view. A news outlet with leftward tilt and an arm for scientific journalism, for example, might decline to cover a recent study that shows a significant reduction in levels of employment attends higher minimum wages. The same outlet might elect to cover instead a piece that finds that workers who enjoy

[42] For an account of why people might seek information sources that are not governed by these norms, see (Williams 2022).

[43] I've said that diversity matters here. In that direction, there is some reason to worry regarding the regulatory changes ushered in by the Telecommunications Act of 1996. This act eliminated regulations on how many AM or FM stations a person or corporate body could own, along with regulations prohibiting cross-ownership of radio stations, TV stations and newspapers in the same market (for discussion, see (Soley 2002, 219–22)). The importance of diversity in this space gives us especially strong reason to be willing to enforce antitrust law against media conglomerates. As Lebovic shows, however, this is easier said than done (Lebovic 2016, esp. 143–46, 193–96). In the absence of an ability to force change through competition law, those funding non-profit media (or who might take up the charge and endow some media outlet) would be well served to treat perspectival diversity as a desideratum for deciding who to fund (though, naturally, only one desideratum among many).

higher minimum wages have higher job satisfaction. As our brief foray into the history of the US press demonstrated, media slant is nothing new. There are organizations that purport to track it,[44] and everyone knows that the perspective you are likely to find in any given outlet depends at least in small measure upon the interests of the editorial staff and the guiding mission of the institution.

Yet this sort of partisanship strikes some people as unacceptable. They wish that reporters would be objective and balanced, giving equal time to various available viewpoints. This wish must remain unsatisfied. While it is fair to expect editors to refrain from acting capriciously, what a healthy epistemic environment requires is not several different news sources covering everything from the same neutral point of view; it's rather a variety of sources covering events from a variety of distinct points of view, which puts readers in a good position (whether they avail themselves of this or not) to piece the truth together.

In *On Liberty*, Mill notes that, for beings like us, the truth must come from conflict between parties flying opposing flags:

> Truth, in the great practical concerns of life, is so much a question of the reconciling and combining of opposites that very few have minds sufficiently capacious and impartial to make the adjustment with an approach to correctness, and it has to be made by the rough process of a struggle between combatants fighting under hostile banners.[45]

Because human beings are imperfect, because we have only at any given time a partial and inadequate sense of the lay of the land, we collectively benefit from diversity.[46] But diversity of the relevant kind requires allowing people to form associations with other like-minded individuals, associations which press their perspectives as far as they can. When they then come to the marketplace of ideas, we can better assess them in comparison with the others.[47] If this is correct, then we should not see politically motivated exercises of editorial authority as wrongful. We should instead recognize that, in curating a point of view, editors are playing an important role in our knowledge

---

[44] https://www.allsides.com/media-bias/media-bias-ratings   and   https://www.adfontesmedia.com/ but see https://www.poynter.org/fact-checking/media-literacy/2021/should-you-trust-media-bias-charts/.

[45] (Mill 2003, 114).

[46] (Sunstein 2018).

[47] (Muldoon 2022).

communities. Awareness of what they're doing and why it matters can help promote the legitimacy of these important venues, while importantly cautioning against blind trust.

Living in a world where there is a diversity of publications with different interests as editors and journalists pursue their visions in different ways is a lot of work. If every publication curated news and opinion in an identically neutral way, we could pick up any paper to find an objective accounting of the events in the world and the full range of opinion within its pages. Our work would be done. By contrast, living in a world comprised of a variety of different news gathering institutions makes for demanding duties. We cannot merely pick up one publication (or watch one channel or one radio station) in order to become informed. We must instead read a diversity of publications to know what's going on and to settle on a plausible interpretation.[48] Despite the demands of such an environment, when the things in need of reporting exceed any individual's capacity and we need to rely on others to organize information for us, things truly cannot be otherwise.

Defending the rights of publications to have slants and demanding of citizens that they put in the hard work required of them denies neither that media outlets can wrongfully censor, nor that the exercise of editorial authority cannot result in deeply unjust and distorted coverage of what matters. Coverage by the *New York Times* in World War II largely buried reporting about the Holocaust arguably to appease an anti-Semitic readership.[49] This was a massive failure—especially for a paper with a reputation as the paper of record. Outlets that fail similarly to present the most newsworthy events of the day in the proper light should meet harsh judgment.[50] Their readership should demand better.

As readers, we should demand of our press institutions that they live up to the ideal of a public watchdog, checking the excesses of state and market actors alike. But living up to this ideal requires certain patterns of behavior on the part of journalists and editors.

First, conceptualizing the mission of the media as interested (rather than neutral) watchdogs means rethinking old ideals of balance and objectivity.[51] While we should not expect that "all sides" be represented fairly in every

---

[48] (Worsnip 2018).

[49] (Harrold 2013).

[50] https://www.realclearpolitics.com/articles/2015/06/23/spike_it_when_the_media_kill_a_story_for_political_reasons_127088.html

[51] For some contemporary reflections on the rise and promise of these ideals, see (Pressman 2017) and (Hemmer 2017).

outlet, neither should the press defer to public officials in determining the "sphere of legitimate controversy."[52] Instead, the press should look to identify matters of public concern, with some sense of priority for covering the things most important to an informed citizenry. While it is perfectly in order that there should be significant variation in setting these priorities, it remains important that editors and journalists maintain a clear view of what it matters to know and use this sense as the primary determinant of what they publish and how they set their agendas. Ideological slant can be used to determine which of several newsworthy stories to print and which stories of borderline importance to drop or deprioritize. Reasonable people can disagree about what deserves pride of place on the front page. But beyond that, ideological slant should lead editors and journalists into different decisions about what they choose to criticize rather than whether they'll adopt a critical stance in the first place. When partisans complain that journalists on "their" side are playing into the hands of the opposition by criticizing politicians on the right side, we should respond with a clear accounting of why they are in fact doing something crucial.

Second, abandoning the idea of perfect balance in reporting requires outlets to more consistently and transparently inform readers of their angle. News organizations have not conducted purely fact-based reporting in decades, and it was a short-lived period when they accepted a constraint on their reporting in the neighborhood. This is as it should be, given the complexity of public life today. But when news organizations use their own sense of what matters to guide their reporting, they should not then turn around and pretend to neutrality and balance. They should instead be clear and consistent in articulating their values for the public.[53] This can help them earn the trust of their readership: even if we disagree, if you can point to your sources and your motivations as the grounds of your judgment, I am less likely to feel as though I am being taken for a ride.

Third, understanding press institutions as crucial to the health of conversations in advanced civilizations means that editors should be careful about producing misleading headlines, even when doing so will generate more clicks, eyeballs, and advertisement revenue.[54] They should repudiate

[52] The idea that there is a range of legitimate issues that the press will cover is due to (Hallin 1986). As Pressman notes, many early complaints about objectivity consisted in the fealty it seemed to require to government sources. See: (Pressman 2017, 100).

[53] (Meyers 2019, 220).

[54] Both the *New York Times* and the *Washington Post* recently failed in this respect: see (Johnson, Abutaleb, and Achenbach 2021) and (Mandavilli 2021). The *Times* suggested that those inoculated

practices of headline writing that severely misrepresent reality. For example, MSN recently ran the headline: "Teacher jailed for contempt of court in dispute over misgendering student."[55] This creates the misleading impression that a teacher was jailed for misgendering a student, when in fact he was jailed for trespassing after a suspension. Such a misleading impression is likely to generate hits, but it is also likely to fuel culture war–related panic in ways that will make it more difficult to discuss some genuinely hard issues. If the point and purpose of news organizations is to guide sound decision-making, and if we know (as we do) that most people never read past an article's headline, failure to responsibly write headlines is one of the very best ways for news organizations to subvert, rather than realize, their missions. While it might be easy for such organizations to tell themselves stories about the beneficial fact-finding that more revenue would allow, they ought to be guided by a principle to first do no harm.

Fourth, so far as we conceive a free and independent press as crucial for the health of our institutions, it is important for the member organizations that make it up to keep in mind a sense of the total picture. It is built into the notion of the press as a watchdog that much of its coverage will be negative. For the press to function well as a watchdog means taking a gently antagonistic role toward the government and major business interests. But exclusively negative reporting can give persons a distorted sense of the social world and how it has progressed.[56] Thus those responsible for choosing what to cover should bear in mind the overall media environment when making their choices. If the overall picture is one of despair and there are in fact reasons for optimism, this can influence what to prioritize and how to present information. This negativity bias of the watchdog press generates special reason for philanthropists to fund organizations that present positive news, and those that present data without spin.[57]

Fifth, journalists as a class should not shy away from new sources of competition and new models of journalism (such as the recent proliferation of

---

against COVID-19 can spread the virus just as easily as those who are not vaccinated. While there may be a sense in which this is technically correct, that is not the sense that is most immediately conveyed. The *Post* reported in its headline that three-quarters of those hospitalized in a recent outbreak were vaccinated, but did not mention that the vaccination rate in the relevant community might be as high as 114%. Both headlines generated a lot of attention. Both likely fueled vaccine hesitancy for no reason. These are not isolated cases.

[55] (Ott 2022).
[56] Perhaps no one knows this better than Hans Rosling. See (Rosling, Rosling, and Rönnlund 2018).
[57] See e.g., humanprogress.org and ourworldindata.org. Thanks to Danny Shahar for this point.

newsletters penned by journalists claiming new independence from the old institutional forms). While these models indeed reflect a changing world (and not always for better), experimentation with ways of interesting the public in quality commentary ought to be celebrated. These independent journalists may have a different set of incentives, but this can help them tell stories that more traditional outlets might not find profitable to cover.

Sixth, journalism's public role means that the common advice that journalists avoid reading and engaging with the comments sections attached to their pieces is largely misguided. While many comment sections are filled with vitriol and vice, researchers have learned that one possible remedy is to have journalists engage with their readers. This can improve the quality of discourse directly.[58] Since researchers are *also* learning that the quality of a news outlet's comments section impacts in a direct way the reputation of that outlet in the public eye, this kind of engagement is important for earning and maintaining trust.[59] Moreover, when journalists make decisions in order to maintain their integrity as professionals, sometimes these decisions are difficult for the public to understand. Journalists engaging directly with reader skepticism provides a crucial educational opportunity that can reinforce the importance of fragile norms.

Finally, though journalists should recognize the importance of interpretation and having a point of view, when reporting on matters of basic fact (as they often will), they ought to keep editorializing to a minimum. Such editorializing where it is not appropriate fosters distrust and can cause those not sympathetic with the outlet's point of view to refuse to see it as a reliable source of correction. Likewise, the necessity of having a point of view is not an excuse to suppress stories that are inconvenient for that point of view when the watchdog mission of journalism requires reporting it.

While I think that these general principles guide the exercise of editorial authority, it is easy to overestimate (and important not to overstate) the capacities of publishers and broadcasters to fix things unilaterally. In the end, commercial media outlets need a lot of help from their readership. For a substantial body of evidence suggests that, rather than publishing their own ideological message, news outlets respond to consumer preferences to deliver the news that consumers want.[60] If we do not demand diverse news, if we do

---

[58] (Stroud et al. 2015).

[59] (Weber, Prochazka, and Schweiger 2019).

[60] (Gentzkow and Shapiro 2006; Gentzkow and Shapiro 2010; Gentzkow, Shapiro, and Sinkinson 2014).

not demand accurate news (or cannot tell the difference between accuracy and inaccuracy), there is only so much that publishers and broadcasters can do. Without readers and viewers, they won't survive long.

We should be clear, though, that conceding that media outlets have substantial financial incentives to deliver news that matches the preferences of their audiences is compatible with demanding that they incur reasonable costs to ensure that people have access to quality information. Indeed, for-profit outlets ought to prefer less profit to more when foregoing profit is necessary to discharge their special responsibilities as pillars of a healthy epistemic environment.[61] But it is precisely the fact that the market will likely undersupply diversity in the marketplace of ideas that makes it important to ensure that some producers of journalism are free from these kinds of pressures (which again, can exert a disciplinary force on journalism).

4.5 Conclusion

If you're my age or older, you can remember the days before the smartphone, even the days before the internet. In those days, you could spend hours, sometimes days, without receiving meaningful outside information about the world. Now, with what would have in decades past been recognized to be supercomputers in each of our pockets and constant connection to the internet, we receive information incessantly. Some of this information is highly local: one app tells me that a potted plant has gone missing from a nearby neighbor's porch. Some of the information comes from abroad. Another app tells me that Former Alibaba CEO Jack Ma is missing. Some of it is politically important in nature: "Democrats are Drafting Impeachment Articles for the

---

[61] It might strike some readers as naïve to hang so much on the social responsibility of the media, especially when there appears to be so much pessimism about major outlets' willingness to follow through. I encourage such readers to read about the extensive voluntary censorship programs that nearly every newspaper in the country undertook to protect wartime secrets in World War II. News outlets incurred significant costs to ensure that they did not publish anything that set back the war effort. Instrumental here was the federal Office of Censorship, an Orwellian institution that guided editorial practice. (For a fascinating discussion, see Lebovic 2016, 118–34.) Arguably, without an institution like this, the censorship would have been less coordinated and less effective. But the institution securing journalistic accountability need not be a state institution and it need not be inherently pro-censorship. We might imagine boards of journalism ethics functioning analogously with medical ethics boards (see, for instance, William B. Arthur's vision sketched in (Hemmer 2017, 141)). A somewhat ham-fisted version of this measure was proposed in Georgia, but the proposal need not be implemented with fists of meat, hams or otherwise. For discussion of the Georgia proposal, see https://pen.org/press-release/georgia-bill-raises-concerns-first-amendment/. For level-headed worries about voluntary censorship schemes, see (Berkowitz 2021, 171).

President 13 Days before he is Legally Obligated to Leave Office." Some of it is mundane: "Tattoo Artists are Sharing the Worst Errors They Made on a Client."

Today, in short, there is more information at our fingertips than ever before. It comes to us largely unbidden. Sure, this has happened to some degree since the founding of the United States. People came across unfamiliar papers, confronted by what was in them. They might happen upon someone on a soapbox expounding some view or another. Education has long presented us with facts, opinions, and works of art that we'd be unlikely to encounter (or understand) on our own.

Now information comes in a more personal way. Some of this information is still subject to editorial authority. But not all of it is: you might be on Facebook or Twitter and receive information that way. Increasingly, what were once old-school newsrooms under the control of various content editors are being converted to platforms for the posting of (sometimes unverified) information.[62]

On this new model: post the story first, verify, report, and interpret next. Should this model gain additional favor, editorial control over information will continue to decline, and information will be coming to us in waves. This is a perfect environment for the spread of misinformation, and it's one that bad actors are increasingly eager to exploit.

This decline in the exercise of editorial authority to filter information is, I've suggested, cause for concern.[63] Although editorial authority formally allows media outlets to censor to promote their commercial and political interests, it does far more than this, especially when the editor must operate in a diverse, pluralistic information marketplace of the sort described in Section 4.3.[64] Giving relatively independent media the authority to choose what to publish in line with their view of what's important (to us) is one way of taking advantage of the division of labor, which has produced advances far in excess of its costs, across the many domains in which it operates.

To have the ability to rely on reputable outlets is crucial. But it does not relieve us of the responsibility to demand that these outlets are worthy of our reliance upon them, and that requires being worthy consumers of information

---

[62] (Anderson, Downie, and Schudson 2016, 75–78).

[63] Which is not to say that it is without advantages. In interviews with a number of journalists, Jane Singer found that the ability for criticism of journalists to travel quickly and without filtration has made writers more careful for fear of public reprisal (Singer 2010, 126).

[64] On the key difference between information marketplaces and other marketplaces (which complicates thinking about competition law), see (Gentzkow and Shapiro 2008, 149–50).

ourselves. Findings that media outlets respond to our preferences, rather than attempting to shape what we prefer, should be empowering. By improving our own relationship with information and consciously demanding accurate and diverse sources we discharge our social responsibility to maintain an environment conducive to public discussion's real morality.

Just as it may have been strange to think of norms as relevant to the practice of private censorship, so too might it seem odd to think of the news media as a locus of censorship. I hope that the brief history of the news has made clear that worries about non-state censorship have gone hand in hand with media criticism for decades.

The public may be fixated for now on issues pertaining to new technology (and attendant threats to our information environment), but we do well to remember that these are, in fact, old concerns in a new context. Those well versed in our increasingly vibrant public debates about, say, social media censorship, will recognize strands of those debates in these somewhat older debates about whether press freedom is compatible with commercial funding models. Calls to regulate the press were often cast in similar terms as are calls to regulate social media platforms. Understanding the history of the former helps contextualize the latter. But social media platforms are, in significant ways, unlike traditional media outlets. They raise distinctive issues, and it is to those distinctive issues that we now turn.

5

The "New" (Social) Media

By August 18, 2021, nearly 18 months into the COVID-19 crisis, Facebook had removed 20 million pieces of content alleged to violate its policies against misinformation and banned some 3,000 accounts for proliferating such content.[1] Against this backdrop, it is plausible to claim that Facebook, Twitter, and other social media giants operate "the largest system[s] of censorship the world has ever known."[2]

If so, the fact that many of us get at least some of our news and information through social media platforms (hereafter SMPs) like Twitter and Facebook raises systematic concerns about platforms' power to manipulate our information environment.[3] That public figures take to these platforms to reach their constituencies and stoke the flames of public passion raises the stakes. When platforms both remove a great deal of content and play a prominent public role, it is sensible to ask whether their moderation supports or compromises a healthy intellectual atmosphere.

In Chapter 1, I made the case that private censors don't usually violate the legal rights of those that they censor. They might treat them badly or use their resources poorly or act to contribute to a toxic climate of discourse or act deceptively or dishonestly—all important grounds for being dissatisfied or angry with their behavior. But they mostly do these things in ways that are within their own rights and that do not violate the rights of others.

Yet, as I argued in Chapter 2, there are many ways in which persons abuse their rights to free speech. When they do, others have pro tanto reason to intervene. In that chapter, we saw grounds for thinking that we are often not well positioned to play the censor in an uncoordinated way. But intermediaries

---

[1] (Bell 2021).

[2] (Benesch 2020, 86).

[3] It is not uncommon to read headlines that indicate that half of US citizens rely on Facebook to get their news. This is misleading. About 18% read news on social media "often." https://slate.com/technology/2016/12/how-many-people-really-get-their-news-from-facebook.html. Additionally, more recent data suggests that reliance on social media platforms (SMPs) for information purposes is sharply declining. (The exception is TikTok, though this is likely due to its increasing prevalence.) It is striking that these trends follow SMPs' increasing efforts to weed out misinformation on their platforms. See: (Pew Research 2022).

Private Censorship. J.P. Messina, Oxford University Press. © Oxford University Press 2024.
DOI: 10.1093/oso/9780197581902.003.0005

like modern SMPs have distinct tools at their disposal which may put them in a promising position to weed out irresponsible speech. Not only can SMPs deplatform users and prevent speech before it reaches its audience, but they can also use flags to contextualize harmful speech, arguably to the boon of our epistemic situation. The fact that they also have access to information about the overall prevalence of certain kinds of speech ostensibly puts them in a position to better engineer our information environment. And though these features of SMPs indicate that they might overplay the role of censor, it's important to remember that they have strong incentives to sustain engagement. Such incentives exert some natural pressure toward inclusiveness, giving platforms reason to tolerate speech provided it is compatible with broad participation.

And yet despite these promises, many argue that SMP content moderation overreaches.[4] Some object that SMP immunity for liability for third-party content obliges them to host such content without discrimination. Others contend that because SMPs constitute the 21st century public square (or, alternatively, because they enjoy considerable market power), they ought to be subject to First Amendment standards. But there is disagreement here, too. Relying on similar facts about SMPs, critics from the left argue that platforms should be exercising a heavier hand to moderate content, perhaps subject to government oversight. And governments are more and more given to seizing corresponding oversight powers.[5]

This chapter assesses these and related claims. I offer an analysis of SMP censorship, with special attention to how it might support or compromise the kind of intellectual atmosphere that, I argued in Chapter 2, we have reason to value.

5.1 Social Media Censorship: A Field Guide

SMPs are content hosts. They provide virtual spaces for persons, communities, and businesses to deliver their own content to other persons, communities, businesses, and so on. Some platforms enable receivers of this

---

[4] Thirty-four states have proposed to curb social media censorship through legislation. See (DeGuerin 2022).

[5] (The Associated Press 2022).

original content to rapidly reproduce and retransmit it in their own networks, giving communicators an unprecedented ability to reach a vast audience.

It is worth beginning by distinguishing between four extant SMP models. There are:

1. Web Forums: These platforms are usually organized around a topic (a particular band, genre of music, sports team, social issue, etc.) and allow users to form a community specifically around the relevant topics (e.g., EconSpark,[6] Survivors' Forums,[7] and ViaChicago[8]).

2. Meta-Web Forums: These platforms allow users to form communities around topics of their choice and make it easy for users to participate in a variety of communities without having multiple accounts (e.g., Reddit, 4chan).

3. Open Platforms: Users post content directly to the platform, which can be seen by anyone (unless the user takes steps to make the account private), but which comes unbidden only to those who "follow" the person responsible for the content, or to those who follow those who have somehow engaged with the content, or to those who have expressed interest in similar content in the past. Following is asymmetrical, and users have little control over who engages with them (e.g., YouTube, TikTok, and Twitter).

4. Semi-Open Platforms: Users post content that is immediately seen by a curated group of people and that defaults to being seen only by such people. Users can also comment on public threads, in which case their content will be seen by anyone exposed to the relevant thread, and in open or closed groups, in which case the content will be seen only by members of those groups (and is subject to moderation by those groups). Users have a wide range of control over the content they see— they control the people in their network and also the ways that others interact with their content (e.g., Facebook, SnapChat).

Any such division is bound to be artificial, abstracting from various ways in which SMPs can be customized to fit a user's preferences. But, given the diversity of social media options, it is important to be clear on the ways in which they might or might not contribute to create a (dys)functional environment

---

[6] https://www.aeaweb.org/economics-discussion-forum.
[7] https://survivorsforum.womensaid.org.uk.
[8] https://viachicago.org.

for speech. And to do this, it is important to distinguish between the structural features that make these platform-types unique, at least in terms of their typical use-case.

Web Forums are relatively small-scale experiments in online-community building. An individual or a small group wishes to cultivate conversation with like-minded persons on niche topics. Typically, a group of moderators is assigned special administrative privileges, including blocking user accounts, enforcing shared rules of conduct, and deleting posts that are irrelevant or otherwise violate those rules. Users see content on web forums only if they seek it out, making this content less dangerous and less likely to reach a wide audience that would prefer to avoid it. Communities will have strong interests in keeping discussion on topic and preventing certain kinds of abuse. They may therefore regularly delete accounts and posts and otherwise sanction users for the things that they say. Some of these interventions will amount to exercises of something like editorial authority, while others will look more like censorship. But even when forum moderation involves censorship, it is unlikely to be wrongful. Censorship in small web communities is less about preventing the ultimate spread of ideas and more about governing the relevant communities in line with a shared vision. Because these sorts of forums are often moderated by one or a small number of known users, those who think that the moderation is too tight or too loose have a direct path to making their concerns heard. When voicing their concerns does not yield satisfying change, they might break off and start a competing network.

Web Forums are effectively the internet versions of clubs and freedoms to association and speech exist in part to facilitate people building communities around shared interests.[9] We want people to be able to form groups around their ideas and ideals and this requires letting them self-govern and work out their disputes between themselves. Some level of insulation against outside influence and interference is a good way of ensuring that they are able to do so.

Meta Web Forums share many of these features, but they have an added layer of moderation on top of what the group coordinator(s) choose themselves. For instance, although the moderators in charge of the subreddit "the_ Donald" tolerated a great deal of speech, the executives at Reddit decided that much of what was tolerated violated the SMP's terms of service. Accordingly,

---

[9] Note this does not mean that they should be guaranteed a host—it only means that they ought not be barred from using the open internet to associate virtually with others at their own expense.

the group was removed from the platform (despite the objections of the moderators and community members).[10] Another feature that differentiates Meta Web Forums from the ordinary kind is that the former might expose ordinary users to communities that they do not explicitly seek out (e.g., Reddit's homepage exposes visitors to a list of the top posts from various communities).

As with ordinary Web Forums, censorship is part of having a moderated community, and so user-moderation is crucial for the smooth operation of Reddit communities. Yet it is only in a looser sense that Reddit on the whole is itself a community. While it is certainly entitled to develop terms of service, it has greater reason to tolerate a greater range of users than any particular group that uses it to organize. Moreover, since its business model depends in large part on attracting users, it has to pay a cost when it adopts terms of service that require it to ban wide swaths of communities and users. These considerations all give the platform a significant interest in tolerating a lot of speech that its founders and executives might personally see as objectionable. In line with this interest, Reddit certainly tolerates much speech that its executives and employees find loathsome, even if some think it should tolerate more than it does.

Open Platforms (like Twitter) enable asymmetric following and engagement. Here, one joins the platform less to seek out discussion on some particular topic or build community and more because the platform enables access to celebrities, news organizations, academics, journalists, and readers. Users can interact with others merely by finding their accounts. By default, users have little to no default control over how others engage with their content (though this can be adjusted). Platforms like Twitter have less claim to be organizing discrete communities and so lack good reasons to moderate just that far. This is not, as we shall see, to say that they have no reason whatsoever to moderate or censor content.

Semi-Open Platforms (like Facebook) combine elements of Meta Web Forums and Public Platforms. Users curate groups of friends and friends can communicate with one another. They can also form groups of their own around common interests, allow strangers to join (or petition to join) and moderate admissions and conversations in these as they see fit, subject to the platform's terms of service. On these hybrid SMPs, most engagement is between persons who choose to connect mutually. Accordingly, users have a

[10] (Allyn 2020).

great deal of control by default over who interacts with their posts and how. Since users have so much control over the content they engage with, platform executives have less reason to moderate content themselves. Again, less reason is not to say no reason, and Facebook has developed a set of community standards by which it expects users to abide. The latter are particularly important when it comes to the more open aspects of Facebook.

While all of these social media models enable people to communicate with strangers and acquaintances in ways that were largely impossible before their existence, each also affects our atmosphere for discourse differently. Some enable small communities to come together around common interests (with the pressures to groupthink that this entails), while others are geared more toward providing a platform for engaging on public issues of moment, well, publicly. Due to a host of worries about the degree to which social media exerts a pernicious influence on civil society (as well as fidelity to their mission-oriented goals), all social media companies engage in some degree of content moderation. (This is true even of Parler, an SMP explicitly branded around free speech.)

When platforms wish to moderate content, there are two mechanisms available to them. First, they can deploy "hard" sanctions, such as content blocks, content removal, and account bans. Second, they can deploy "soft" sanctions, which reduce visibility of content rather than eliminating it altogether. [11] . Because each type of sanction can be applied to suppress expressive content on the grounds that it is dangerous, inimical to orthodoxy, or inimical to the material interests of the platforms, each can serve as a mechanism of censorship.

SMPs typically deploy hard sanctions in response to user content that violates explicit rules that specify what will be tolerated on the platform (e.g., terms of service and community guidelines).[12] Offending content is caught

---

[11] See (Gorwa, Binns, and Katzenbach 2020, 4) for a helpful taxonomy on which my discussion draws. An additional "soft" tactic the authors point out is labeling dangerous, newsworthy, false, misleading, doctored, etc. Although this tactic raises important questions about free speech for some (including President Trump)—and although social media companies sometimes prefer this as an alternative to more direct forms of censorship—such labeling leaves consumers of the information free to access it and so is not well thought of censorship (which crucially involves *suppression*). I discuss some dangers of this approach as an alternative to censorship in Section 3.3. An additional "hard" moderation technique is to reject bids for advertisements. This is more likely to function in an ad hoc manner than censorship of content by ordinary users, but it is also less concerning insofar as advertisements are usually commercial speech, restriction of which is generally less concerning than restriction of political or artistic expression. Moreover, advertisers have always needed to find willing hosts for their content. Social media is no different.

[12] For examples, see https://help.twitter.com/en/rules-and-policies/hateful-conduct-policy?lang= browser and https://www.youtube.com/about/policies/#community-guidelines.

either by other users (who can flag it), by algorithms, or by teams of people whose job it is to catch violations. (The biggest platforms employ all three tactics, often in sequence.)

So, for instance, when Instagram briefly banned Samm Newton from the platform for posting an "inappropriate" picture of herself in her underwear, it deployed this hard sanction because moderators believed she had violated the platform's terms. Banning her suppressed her expression by removing it from view, and she was discouraged from further expression by being denied future access to Instagram—a restriction on her ability to use the platform that persisted until moderators were convinced they had made a mistake. Hard sanctions were also involved with Facebook's censorship of Fox Radio host Todd Starnes's proclamation that he was proud to be politically incorrect. Facebook's responding by banning him from the platform was a paradigm case of censorship.

Platforms that wish to avoid such hard sanctions can opt to leave the content and accounts up and active, but reduce its reach. Those in charge of less technologically sophisticated SMPs can "pin" posts that they deem desirable, such that they appear first and allow others to languish lower in the list of posts. Sophisticated and resource-rich platforms design algorithms that "deboost" or downrank undesirable content. Such downranking affects how large an audience a given piece of content reaches. Since soft sanctions, as well as hard, aim to suppress speech and can be attractive tools for those who worry that certain expressive acts are dangerous, threatening to orthodoxy, or against their material interests, they too can qualify as censorship.

Indeed, although soft sanctions leave people free to find the targeted speech, they are often less transparent, leaving users unsure when they've been targeted. It is thus untrue that soft sanctions are necessarily friendlier to free speech than hard sanctions.[13] Just the reverse is likely true, unless platforms inform users when they are being subjected to them, which they typically do not.

Importantly, whereas both soft and hard moderation techniques will often involve censorship in the sense defined, moderation is not necessarily censorial. After all, content moderation only sometimes targets threatening speech and very often is aimed instead at solving an optimization problem. That is, many platforms design algorithms to drive user engagement based on the

---

[13] Elon Musk's recent claim that Twitter's new policy of "freedom of speech" but not "freedom of reach" for hate speech (maximally deboosting such speech) is an improvement along the lines of censorship is thus questionable, with its truth depending on the details. See: (Saul 2022).

company's estimation of their users' preferences. That such optimization does not involve censorship is intuitive. When SMPs choose to amplify content attractive to other users, thereby effectively downvoting other content, the suppression of the latter is incidental to the decision. When optimizing their platforms to drive engagement, firms are relevantly like an editor who chooses the cover story based on an understanding of her readership to the inevitable detriment of those stories deprioritized. If, by contrast, SMPs should downvote or remove content primarily because they see it as a *threat*, their behavior looks more censorship.[14]

5.2 Are SMPs Obligated to Refrain from Censorship?

We have seen that SMPs content moderation sometimes involves them in censorship. Of course, since private parties often have good pro tanto reasons to act as censors, this need not raise any special issue. Still, some argue that there are reasons for thinking that social media censorship is specifically wrong (and perhaps ought to be legally prohibited).

The source of these special reasons is twofold: First, SMPs (like all online platforms and unlike publishers) are not liable for the content that they merely host. Some claim that limiting liability in this way when SMPs undertake extensive moderation is a recipe for abuse. It allows internet platforms to act as publishers without being held responsible in the same way. Sometimes this consideration is framed as a dilemma: social media companies must assume liability for the content that they host, or else they ought to refrain from (or be prohibited from) censoring and moderating content. Publisher or platform: you choose, but it can't be both.[15] Second, these platforms are alleged to constitute a new public square—a special domain in which speech restrictions must either be content-neutral or else pass a high bar of justification. The following subsections take on these arguments.

---

[14] Of course, even non-censorial filtration can create echo chambers, drive outrage and unproductive engagement among users, and make our intellectual atmosphere worse. See e.g. (*Wall Street Journal* 2021). My point is only that these byproducts of seeking engagement are separate from censorship and deserve their own treatment.

[15] This dilemma is as popular as it is because Section 230 of the Communications Decency Act essentially provides that internet platforms should be regulated as distributors of information while empowered with a certain degree of editorial authority. In the previous regulatory environment, it was either or, as the dilemma suggests, but Section 230 changed that. For details, see (Kosseff 2019, 9–56).

5.2.1 Limited Liability and the Communications Decency Act

In the early days of the internet, websites operated in a legal gray area. According to the common law at the time, certain things were clear and settled. Speakers could be sued in court for defamatory, obscene, or other dangerous speech. Traditional publishers, too, could be held responsible for amplifying these kinds of illegal speech, in view of their capacity to impact its reach. By contrast, when bookstores were brought to court for selling obscene material, they were held to a different standard. Whereas courts ruled that speakers and publishers had sufficient control over the speech associated with them to justify imposing costs on them when such speech violated another's rights, they doubted that booksellers did. To expect shop owners to read every piece of material they sold or else face lawsuits would discourage store owners from stocking any works that were even potentially unlawful— a bad result for the freedom of speech.

How did internet platforms fit into this framework? For some years, there was no clear answer. And then, in the mid-1990s, the court issued two landmark decisions that would bring things more clearly into view. In *Cubby v. CompuServe, INC* the court held that CompuServe was more like a bookstore than a speaker or publisher. After all, it exercised very little editorial control over its online bulletin boards and couldn't reasonably be expected to read everything. This laid the ground, however, for holding in *Stratton Oakmont v. Prodigy* that a platform (hosted by Prodigy) that did more moderation of content in order to keep it in line with family values could be held liable for damaging speech users posted to its forum. In effect, platforms trying in good faith to keep their spaces free of harassment and obscenity were held to higher standards than those that tolerated a free for all.

Concerned that the emerging status quo would discourage sensible moderation, abandoning the entire internet to a cesspool of defamatory speech and pornography, Congress passed Section 230 of the Communications Decency Act. According to Section 230, "[n]o provider or user of an interactive computer service shall be treated as the publisher or speaker of any information provided by another information content provider" (47 U.S.C. § 230).[16] By legislative fiat, then, internet platforms were freed from liability for any content produced by a third party.

---

[16] https://www.law.cornell.edu/uscode/text/47/230. This exception finds itself in the crosshairs of President Trump's recent executive order: https://www.businessinsider.com/full-text-donald-trump-executive-order-on-social-media-2020-5.

But what did it mean for content to be produced by another provider? Would a heavy hand in moderation involve platforms in content production? Congress ruled this out explicitly. Section 230(c)(2) expressly protects companies from liability for good faith attempts to restrict access to material that the "provider or user considers to be obscene, lewd, lascivious, filthy, excessively violent, harassing, or otherwise objectionable, whether or not such material is constitutionally protected."

And yet, according to some, legislators never intended to shield from liability platforms that engaged in politically motivated moderation. They only meant to protect moderation undertaken to make their spaces "family friendly."[17] Whatever congress's intent, they claim that platforms have grown due to Section 230 and ought now to be subject to duties to "refrain from discrimination" in exchange for their liability protection.[18]

This call for a non-discrimination norm raises a number of questions, most significantly: what does it mean to refrain from discrimination in moderating content? Isn't content moderation inherently discriminatory? Given that advocates admit that discrimination can be justified given "any valid business or technical reason," we might worry that any such requirement will either be far too restrictive (amounting to a ban on moderation) or toothless (creating regulatory bodies that must simply defer to companies' interpretations of their business interests).[19]

Consider how Facebook describes its mission: "[w]e are a service for more than two billion people to freely express themselves across countries and cultures." Before introducing its infamous community standards, the website says: "We recognize how important it is for Facebook to be a place where people feel empowered to communicate and we take seriously our role in keeping abuse off our service. That's why we've developed a set of community standards that outline what is and is not allowed on Facebook."[20] On the one hand, Facebook wishes to offer a platform for free expression; on the other, it appears to take seriously the idea that sometimes expression must be limited to allow everyone to feel empowered to speak.[21]

---

[17] (Candeub 2020, 421).

[18] (Candeub 2020, 430).

[19] As Lynn Stout notes, a corporation's business purpose is only minimally constrained by law. Boards of directors and executives can define their business purposes however they like, provided their aims are not "tainted by personal conflicts of interest" and they make a reasonable effort to stay informed about the strategies they take up in pursuit of those aims (Stout 2012a; Stout 2012b).

[20] https://www.facebook.com/communitystandards/.

[21] This is not the First Amendment interpretation of expressive freedom, which says that I get to say whatever I want without restraint. But it too has venerable roots in an ancient intellectual

Does restricting speech because Facebook sees it as inconsistent with this vision constitute a valid business reason for discrimination against certain kinds of content? If so, then barring discrimination appears not to bar very much at all. If not, however, proponents of new legal requirements owe us an account of what counts as a valid business reason showing in a principled way that this sort of discrimination is unacceptable while other kinds are fine. Such an account of what constitutes a valid business reason should be sensitive to the fact that SMPs often have a legitimate interest in shaping their terms of service in pursuit of a creative vision and their financial interests (and responsibility to shareholders) and that in many cases, their product is *precisely* a curated experience.[22]

Such an account must recognize that the most active and discriminatory moderation—that which takes the least neutral view toward content—is often undertaken by Web Forum moderators. Consider some examples.

1. The changemyview subreddit has a restrictive set of rules designed to facilitate constructive argumentation. While not politically motivated, these rules nevertheless are not about blocking obscenity and lewdness.[23]

2. Various Web Forums for victims of abuse have restrictive sets of community norms to restrict content that is harmful to such victims and might include advocacy for certain laws or skepticism about the same.[24]

3. Sports forums and message boards sometimes restrict user contributions that are hostile to the team the community is supposed to be celebrating and might wholly bar political speech.[25]

4. Message boards for discussion of art, music, literature, and film often remove content for the sake of ensuring that discussion stays on task.[26]

The list might go on. The point is that many of these platforms discriminate far more than large-scale Open and Semi-Open Platforms. If not carefully crafted to apply only to more open platforms, the new regulatory

---

tradition, one which emphasizes the equality of speakers and the degree to which speech by some can impede speech by others. See: (Bejan 2019a; Berkowitz 2021, 21; Klonick 2018, 1627).

[22] (Gillespie 2018).
[23] https://www.reddit.com/r/changemyview/wiki/rules#wiki_rule_a.
[24] http://www.aftersilence.org/.
[25] https://samcelt.forumotion.net/t15063-our-community-guidelines.
[26] https://www.jazzfestforum.com/.

requirements would effectively shutter these platforms by leaving them liable to costly lawsuits.[27]

But then the question arises: Why subject only the more open platforms to these new rules? The motivating idea is that larger companies labor under more stringent duties because they constitute a new public square.[28] Let's turn to these issues now.

5.2.2 A New Public Square?

If more open SMPs are to be subject to requirements to respect free speech (or more minimally not to discriminate against speech, unless . . .) but less significant platforms are to be exempt, we need some explanation of why. The most compelling such explanation—and the one best supported by existing legal precedent—is that major platforms have transformed the public square. Here's *Current Affairs'* Nathan Robinson, expressing the point succinctly:

> The public square is now quite literally privatized. It is not a commons. It is owned by shareholders and controlled by billionaires. And decisions about who gets to speak and whether they will be heard are no longer governed by the rule of law. They are governed by the opaque "community standards" of a private corporation whose mandate is to maximize shareholder value.[29]

To get clearer on the nature of this argument, it is worth making explicit the crucial idea of the public square.

The idea is first (albeit tacitly) introduced to US legal thinking in *Hague Mayor* et al. *v. Committee For Industrial Organization* (307 U.S. 496 (1939)). In his majority opinion, Justice Owen J. Roberts wrote:

---

[27] This is not to say that no reforms to Section 230 reflect wisdom. In particular, when your business model involves promoting defamatory, harassing, or otherwise illegal content, there is a good legal case to be made for the idea that immunizing you from legal liability is incompatible with legislative intent involved in crafting Section 230. See: (Citron and Wittes 2017, 419).

[28] Meta Web Forums like Reddit sit uneasily here. I am inclined to think that they should allow their communities to self-police. When those communities fail to do so in a way that is satisfactory to the platform executives, they should remain free to remove those communities. But ethics would, I think, recommend merely (transparently) depriving them of the extra reach that they enjoy from the community's homepage.

[29] (Robinson 2020).

The privilege of a citizen of the United States to use the streets and parks for communication of views on national questions may be regulated in the interest of all; it is not absolute, but relative, and must be exercised in subordination to the general comfort and convenience, and in consonance with peace and good order; but it must not, in the guise of regulation, be abridged or denied.[30]

Roberts expresses two crucial ideas. First, US citizens enjoy the privilege to use the "streets and parks" for expression. Second, any state regulation of this privilege must concern "general comfort and convenience" along with maintaining "peace and good order." Such regulation must specifically avoid bad-faith denials of the right. As First Amendment jurisprudence developed, these words would come to imply that in parks, sidewalks, streets, and the literal square of the city, public servants were not to interfere with persons' rights to assemble and speak as they like, except for reasons of time, manner, and place.[31] Time, manner, and place restrictions allow for laws that ban using your helicopter to drop pamphlets onto public thoroughfares and standing outside a residence at three in the morning with a megaphone. But such laws and restrictions are "content neutral": they don't bar speech because of its content, only for the sake of ensuring against public nuisance. Put differently, time, manner, and place restrictions are quintessentially *nondiscriminatory* with respect to the content of speech and the viewpoint of the speaker.

Nearly a decade later, the advent of the corporate town would force the court to confront the question of regulation of de facto public squares by private parties. On the one hand, it was well established that the First Amendment applied only to *state* restriction of speech. On the other hand, private parties were assuming some of the traditional roles of government, albeit on their own land.

This question would be (in)famously resolved in a landmark case, *Marsh v. Alabama* (326 U.S. 501 (1946)). The case concerned the town of Chickasaw, Alabama, then owned by the Gulf Shipbuilding Corporation. In Chickasaw, residents needed permission to speak publicly on town property. Marsh, a Jehovah's witness, failed to obtain such permission before taking to the streets

---

[30] 307 U.S. 516.
[31] See e.g., *Lovell v. Griffin* 303 U.S. 444.

to distribute religious pamphlets. As a result, she was convicted of criminal trespass.

The *Marsh* court held that, although the town streets in this case were privately held, nevertheless, the town did not function "differently from any other town."[32] Chickasaw, the court majority noted, consisted "of residential buildings, streets, a system of sewers, a sewage disposal plant, and a 'business block' on which business places are situated."[33] In short, the company had assumed the powers and functions of government.[34] Like other governments, then, its powers labored under constitutional limitations, including the First Amendment. Marsh's conviction was overturned.

The *Marsh* ruling was later invoked to determine that owners of shopping malls were similarly bound to respect the constitution. The argument was that the public square had shifted: people weren't congregating in (public or private) town centers anymore. Their social activity was occurring on private property, in particular, in malls. But since this was so, and since the court had previously held that private property owners might be required to provide space for the exercise of First Amendment Rights, shopping malls—newly de facto public squares—might be required to do so as well. This, anyway, was the ruling in *Food Employees Union vs. Logan Valley Plaza*.[35]

Similarly now, say some, with social media: we are no longer congregating in shopping malls but rather in virtual space provided by social media giants (compare *Packingham v. North Carolina* 582 U.S. 2017).[36] As President Donald Trump put it in the draft of his 2020 executive order, "many Americans follow the news, stay in touch with friends and family, and share their views on current events through social media and other online

---

[32] 326 U.S. 508.

[33] 326 U.S. 502.

[34] 326 U.S. 501.

[35] Hugo Black is sometimes cited to defend rulings like this. In the original case, he wrote: "the more an owner, for his advantage, opens up his property for use by the public in general, the more do his rights become circumscribed by the statutory and constitutional rights of those who use it" (326 U.S. 506). Yet, in *Logan*, Black notes that the decision (which he authored) in *Marsh* was "was never intended to apply to this kind of situation. Marsh dealt with the very special situation of a company-owned town, complete with streets, alleys, sewers, stores, residences, and everything else that goes to make a town . . . I can find very little resemblance between the shopping center involved in this case and Chickasaw, Alabama" (391 U.S. 330–331).

[36] One note about *Packingham*: Although the court here recognizes the importance of the internet for a real right to speak, they are still considering a clear case in which it is the state (in this case North Carolina) restricting access to these platforms, wholesale, for anyone listed on the registry of sex offenders. It may well be the right of a particular platform to refuse to host your content without its being the case that the state is permitted to intervene when the platform would otherwise host the relevant users and content.

platforms. As a result, these platforms function in many ways as a 21st century equivalent of the public square."[37] If Trump is right, the major platforms are on the hook for respecting the First Amendment norms constitutive of a public square—just like shopping malls and company towns. They too must refrain from content-specific speech restrictions. Or so the argument goes.

It is helpful to note that *Food Employees Union vs. Logan Valley Plaza* was overturned in 1976. A 6-2 majority in *Hudgens v. National Labor Relations Board* held that shopping malls and company towns were not functional equivalents and that the law should distinguish clearly between them (424 U.S. 507 1976). The court reasoned that because shopping malls do not perform all of the functions of a government (e.g., they do not provide sewerage), whereas the corporate town does provide all of these functions, there was no sense in which the duties of the latter to protect the First Amendment rights of its residents extend to the former.

I believe the court's decision to overturn the *Logan* ruling achieved the right outcome for the wrong reason. It remains unclear to me why the court thought an entity had to perform *all* the same functions of a government to be so constrained to respect First Amendment rights to speech and assembly. (What does *sewerage* have to do with *speech*?) It is more plausible to simply observe that, when the company town leverages state laws against trespass to bar speech, the state reasonably sees itself implicated in a kind of censorship that the 14th amendment disallows.

Let me explain. Initially, the constitution was read to apply only to laws made by congress. Later, the court held that the equal protection clause of the 14th amendment required extending the protections of core rights against infringements by state and local governments, in addition to the federal government. The idea was that citizens could reasonably complain if state and local authorities in some places protected residents' fundamental rights and liberties in ways that those in other places did not. As Black wrote in *Marsh*:

> Many people in the United States live in company-owned towns. These people, *just as* residents of municipalities, are free citizens of their State and country. *Just as* all other citizens, they must make decisions which affect the welfare of community and nation. To act as good citizens, they must be informed. In order to enable them to be properly informed, their information

---

[37] https://www.cnn.com/2020/05/28/politics/read-social-media-executive-order/index.html; compare (Benesch 2020, 93).

must be uncensored. There is *no more* reason for depriving these people of the liberties guaranteed by the First and Fourteenth Amendments than there is for curtailing these freedoms with respect to any other citizen.[38]

Just as the claim of equal protection under the law exerts pressure on the courts to ensure that state and local governments respect the constitution, it exerts the same pressure to ensure that company towns do the same. Citizens living in company towns must enjoy the same rights as those living in more traditional municipalities.

The real problem with the original holding that shopping malls are equivalent to company towns is that there just isn't any case to be made that users of shopping malls have different rights than shoppers who avoid them. Both can exercise their rights in the public square of the town they live in and none lives in a shopping mall. By contrast, Chickasaw acted in a governing capacity. As a result, residents living within its limits might plausibly have claimed that its ability to skirt the First Amendment was incompatible with their claim to equal protection. Compared to residents of municipalities, residents of company towns had genuinely different rights in the places they lived. Those in ordinary municipalities had the right to campaign on town property, subject only to content-neutral restrictions. Those in company towns did not.[39] The fact that the Gulf Corporation provided for sewage disposal is neither here nor there.

Importantly, just as no one lives in malls, no one lives on SMPs. Those who use SMPs and those who do not enjoy equal protection for their rights. Indeed, when you are banned from Facebook, or have your content removed from its pages, you may still speak out in your town's center or in local parks (not to mention a host of other online platforms). You might not receive as wide an audience, but the constitutional right to speak has never guaranteed a sizable audience. (If it did, there would be a violation of the equal protection clause that some live in Manhattan and others in very small towns.) Users of these platforms do not, then, have a compelling claim of unequal protection. They have just the same legal rights as non-users. In these ways, SMPs remain

---

[38] 326 U.S. 508, emphasis added.

[39] It is fair, of course, to wonder whether one can consent to terms like the ones company towns asked of their residents and thus whether *Marsh* was correctly decided. My only point is that accepting that *Marsh* was correctly decided does not entail thinking that its logic extends to malls and SMPs.

more like malls than a private town. Accordingly, they are not legally bound to refrain from restricting speech.

To this point, our focus has been on arguments that there are extant legal duties according to which SMPs are subject to enforceable duties to refrain from censoring content (or to censor content only in a non-discriminatory manner). But it is possible to argue that, independently of existing law, we ought to constrain them in these ways by legislative means.

5.2.3 SMPs and Public Goods

Sometimes people claim the major social media players need to be regulated in their censorship activity because they share features with other industries that are regulable under common carriage or antitrust law.[40] Such industries are so regulable for two reasons.

According to the first, monopoly justification, they simply have too much market power, which they can exploit to users' detriment.[41] The typical response to monopoly power—breaking it up—is often held not to work for these industries, because it is estimated that they operate in an industry that contains pressure toward natural monopoly. The thought is that market incentives make it the case that a single firm will be dominant and that therefore must be regulated in the public interest. This line invites the question: is the social media space characterized by pressure toward natural monopoly?

Even Meta, which controls the majority of the market for social media companies through Facebook and Instagram controls only about 56% of that same social media market.[42] Strictly, there is no monopoly and the market for social media remains eminently contestable: the most downloaded social media app as of 2021 was a relatively new entrant, TikTok. Still, there is considerable *market concentration*. But such market concentration is not unheard of. For instance, Anheuser Busch Inbev controls about 46% of the

---

[40] For instance, one regularly hears that at least some SMPs are de facto "common carriers." Strictly, a common carrier is a body that transports persons, goods, or communications, is absolutely liable for damages, and has been granted the authority to operate by a regulator that then imposes conditions on the quality, price, and conditions of its service. Paradigm instances of common carriers in the United States are telecommunications and rail companies. See e.g. (Wu 2011a).

[41] Of course, since consumers do not pay to use their services, their dominant market power does not result in high prices except for advertisers. This is one (limited) respect in which a monopoly in the social media space is less worrying than monopolies in other important areas.

[42] https://www.statista.com/statistics/265773/market-share-of-the-most-popular-social-media-websites-in-the-us/.

global beer market, and that market is extremely competitive, in the sense that players in the beer market are under constant threat of new entry and under constant pressure to innovate and keep prices low.[43]

If no social media player enjoys monopoly power, any claim that we need to regulate SMPs on the monopoly power reading would be prospective: we anticipate the development of monopoly and think that the threat of new entry is not sufficient to discipline firm behavior. But why should we think this?

The typical analysis concerns network externalities. Because an SMP's value to a consumer depends upon how many others use it, and because the costs to the SMP of accommodating additional users is zero (perhaps negative, given the value of additional users to advertisers), we might expect smaller firms and new entrants to have a difficult time competing with entrenched and established networks. As Jonathan Tepper puts it, if "you want to be on a network with all of your friends, there is really only one network to be on, and it is on Facebook."[44]

And yet it's important to notice that when SMPs behave badly, people respond. In 2019 (following concerns about free speech and privacy), for instance, Facebook was among the major corporations with the fastest falling reputations.[45] Moreover, Facebook is especially unpopular these days among the younger generations, which suggests that if it is to continue to dominate, it will have to innovate.[46] And, if Tepper's claim does not feel dated yet, I suspect that it will soon. In this connection, notice that, although MySpace had at one point cornered the social media market (in a way that makes Facebook's current market share look quaint), it has since been completely displaced. While not dispositive, these considerations suggest that users can and do seek alternatives and that the threat of exit disciplines existing players.

In the case of other natural monopoly industries (e.g., electric and telecommunications industries), there is a worry that barriers to entry are sufficiently high (and competition sufficiently wasteful) that competition is neither to be expected nor sought after.[47] It is true that already developed

---

[43] The fact that the beer market is competitive in this sense is consistent with the antitrust challenges that have been brought against it.

[44] (Tepper 2019).

[45] https://theharrispoll.com/axios-harrispoll-100/.

[46] https://theharrispoll.com/axios-harrispoll-100/.

[47] Moreover, it is worth noting that those industries regulated as public utilities are not often very consumer friendly. https://www.utilitydive.com/news/do-utilities-have-a-terrible-reputation/140702/.

SMPs have networks and existing technologies that make entering the social media market difficult and that a want of competition can make the social media market suboptimal in the sense that users might prefer a different network that cannot get a foothold. But there appears to me at this time little reason to worry that a single network is so vast and important that new entrants offering better products cannot be competitive.

For these reasons, I suspect that if social media companies ought to be regulated due to their social role, it is less because fears about the development of monopoly power are credible and more that cultivating certain means of open communication is publicly beneficial. The thought is that regulation should enable communication across networks to make everyone reachable.

For example, the Trump administration lawyer Adam Candeub has recently argued that SMPs provide a *public good*. To the degree that this is true, they can be subject to regulatory carrots and sticks for keeping their activities in the public interest.[48] On Candeub's reading, Section 230 is a step in this direction, but fails to contain sufficient (any) sticks to discipline SMPs. For this reason, statutory reform is necessary, minimally, to ensure that SMPs do not discriminate against users by, e.g., censoring them.

Yet social media companies appear not to be public goods any more than they appear to enjoy monopoly power. For a good to qualify as a public good in the strict sense, it must be both non-rivalrous and non-excludable. Non-rivalrous goods are those that can be enjoyed by any number of people without diminishing the quality of service. SMPs—at least those structured as Meta-Web Forums, Open Platforms, or Semi-Open Platforms—plausibly satisfy this condition. Not only can an additional user enjoy the service without diminishing it, arguably each additional user improves the value of the network. Non-excludable goods are those that (like the national defense) cannot be provided to *anyone* without also being provided to *everyone*. SMPs clearly do not satisfy this constraint. SMPs readily exclude all of those who are unwilling to part with their data or sign onto the terms of service.

Failing to qualify as a public good in the strict sense does not mean that SMPs cannot be regulated for other reasons. But making the case for such interventions requires distinguishing SMPs from a variety of other services that are not regulated in this way. This case has not, to my knowledge, been made well.

---

[48] (Candeub 2020, 399–400).

In sum, the arguments so far offered for subjecting SMPs to regulatory oversight seem to me inadequate. In fact, regulation in this direction carries with it substantial risks.

For regulation that applies to the entire industry will limit the ways in which future SMPs can experiment with regimes of content moderation. In turn, this will limit consumers' abilities to choose the communities they wish to join. Additionally, the costs of complying with these sorts of regulations will not impact new entrants and existing players equally. Those that already enjoy networks of users and massive budgets can more readily absorb them than new entrants. Even if the regulatory solutions are initially narrowly tailored to exempt new entrants, entrenched interests can capture the regulatory bodies to the detriment of new entrants. But if SMPs differentiate their products in part by providing different content curation and moderation services, we should not want to discourage new market entrants.

But nor is it easy to justify constraints that apply only to "big" platforms. After all, if exemption from the policies allows new entrants to attract those users who prefer more heavy-handed content moderation, then the burdens on existing players look unfair.[49] This is why many of these regulatory tools often carry with them protections for the market power of affected firms. But protecting existing firms' market power is sure to stifle innovation and entrench existing players in an environment where such entrenchment is perilous.[50]

I have made much of the fact that it is difficult in practice to define a category of discriminatory moderation that would be barred through regulation. But it might be objected that I'm missing an obvious answer: platforms respect the non-discrimination principle when they do not censor content that is legal under the First Amendment.

Yet there is reason to worry about forcing SMPs—even just the largest Open and Semi-Open platforms among them—to respect First Amendment norms. This is for two reasons. First, the kinds of content that they would have to host under such a regime might well make them highly undesirable

---

[49] It is possible to grant smaller SMPs access to the networks of larger SMPs by reviving the essential facilities doctrine. This would involve allowing users of, say, Twitter and Snapchat to transmit their content to users of Facebook without needing an account with Facebook. But it is not clear how cogent this proposal is, given the different use-cases of the different platforms. For fuller discussion, see (Guggenberger 2020). In my view, this remedy makes much more sense in the e-commerce, app-store, and search engine spaces than in the social media space.

[50] For additional reasons for skepticism, see (Thierer 2013).

to visit.[51] Second (but relatedly) if SMPs *were* bound to respect the First Amendment, this would create intense public pressure to narrow protections for speech to avoid the first eventuality. The likelihood that we would see the erosion of constitutional protections against state interference with bad speech if internet platforms were required to host all constitutionally protected expression is, in my estimation, non-negligible. For that reason, if you care about free speech, it's better to tolerate a status quo in which platforms moderate content in admittedly flawed ways, but we continue to enjoy strong protections for our basic liberties against state interference.

And yet the case for extending the First Amendment to protect against infringement by SMPs does not exhaust the case in favor of regulation. Some think that content moderation on SMPs is so urgent a matter that the law must step in and ensure that it happens in accordance with democratic principles.[52] Others don't go that far, but argue that SMPs themselves ought to be a doing a lot more than they are to structure our speech environment. Let's turn to these issues now.

5.3 Are SMPs Obligated to Censor?

Since the speech they host reaches such a wide audience, many argue that SMPs have a duty to protect users (and our broader democracy) from misleading or harmful speech. Worried about the capacity of privately run companies to do this on their own, some go so far as to argue for a congressional role in ensuring that SMPs' pursuit of their financial interests does not come at the expense of the public interest.

In Chapter 2, I argued that there were defeasible reasons to suppress speech that is objectively irresponsible (e.g., defamatory speech, harassment, dangerous speech, discriminatory speech, uncivil speech, and falsehood).[53] I also argued that there were powerful defeaters for these reasons. Not only should we be cautious about our capacity to identify speech worthy of suppression

---

[51] Indeed, if Gillespie is correct, then what SMPs offer is a schedule of content moderation—this is the product they're selling (Gillespie 2018, 13). Change the product, and you may well change the users' interest in using it. On the other hand, if it were possible to do this, why not think a "public option" is the way to realize it? For some concerns about such an option, see (Balkin 2020, 15–16).

[52] See: (Simons and Ghosh 2020).

[53] Previously, this list may have included certain illegal activities, like sex trafficking and copyright infringement. But the law has caught up with these issues. On the first, see (Kosseff 2019, 66); on the second, see (Kosseff 2019, ch. 13).

in practice, but we should also worry that our attempts to suppress speech through social sanctions will be ineffective or worse. Here, I argue that there is good reason to think that SMPs can do better than uncoordinated individuals in some of these areas. In others, however, the risks of wrongful and ineffective censorship loom large and should caution executives against yielding to public pressures to moderate. Moreover, although SMPs have fiduciary duties to moderate content of certain kinds, we should be skeptical of legal and regulatory requirements in this direction.

5.3.1 Defamation and Harassment

In Chapter 2, I argued that defamation and harassment can compromise our environment for free speech by diminishing their targets' standing in the community or else by leading them to exit conversational space.

Just as you have a duty to throw away a newsletter falsely impugning the character of a member of the community rather than passing it along, social media companies have duties to refuse to allow their spaces to serve as convenient tools for ruining innocent persons' lives and reputations.[54] Likewise, if you own a coffee shop and one of your customers is constantly bothering the others, it is not merely good business but also the decent thing to do to tell him to leave.

When SMPs set and enforce guidelines to keep their own (virtual) spaces free of these kinds of speech, they are acting in a recognizably similar way. All else equal, then, they should be praised for their refusal to merely provide space for bad actors to bother those who come to the platform for its intended purposes. By striving to keeping their spaces free of harassment and defamation SMPs not only prevent direct harm and complicity in the same. They also take a small step toward ensuring that a diverse group of users will continue to come to the table. In doing so, they take small steps toward realizing a better atmosphere for discussion.

Are there reasons to worry that platforms will fail to satisfy the effectiveness constraint when they censor harassing and defamatory speech? One thing to notice is that there is pressure for more false positives (content that gets flagged for removal despite being non-harassing or non-defamatory) than

---

[54] Such possibilities are not abstract and are treated at length and with great care by Jeff Kosseff: (Kosseff 2019).

false negatives (content that does not come to the attention of moderators but is in fact defamatory or harassing). After all, harassing and defamatory speech make clear victims of those targeted by them. Due to the distressing nature of this kind of speech, victims will be motivated to bring it to the attention of moderators.

Yet there will be difficult decisions to make. A business owner or politician drawing harsh and persistent criticism from a customer or constituent might complain that she is being defamed or harassed. She might flag the content, which risks it being taken down. And yet often, speech of this kind will be vital to our information environment. Sensitive to such dynamics, platforms might overcorrect in favor of tolerating more content, even when it is flagged. In turn, this can result in platforms being overly hospitable to bad speech. Moreover, platforms' immunity from liability for third party content means they often lack strong incentive for removing speech that is disastrous for ordinary persons' reputations and psychological well-being. When so, victims can find it difficult to obtain relief. Although they can pursue tort remedies against those guilty of libelous speech, the responsible parties often lack resources adequate to compensate for the harm done.[55] This suggests that platforms will tend to do well to distinguish in their policies between celebrities, business-owners, politicians, and public figures on the one hand and ordinary users on the other. In cases of libel and harassment against ordinary users, the *least* platforms can do is stop the spread of the problematic information once it is brought to their attention. When they fail to do even this much, they are liable to boycotts and other social sanctions.

The fact that high-value speech can find itself in the crosshairs of moderators aiming to clear platforms from defamation and harassment raises again the risk of uneven enforcement. If moderators tend to identify harassing speech more when it targets people or firms with which they are sympathetic, the result can introduce a kind of perverse arbitrariness to the marketplace of ideas and the real marketplace alike. Yet there are ways to avoid this. Platforms can find ways of ensuring that the teams making the decisions to keep up or remove harassing or defamatory speech are ideologically diverse. They can carve out exceptions for speech that is in the public interest. And they can introduce (as many have) a clear, reliable, and unbiased process for appeals focused on treating like cases alike.

---

[55] See again (Volokh 2021).

Given the typical low value of harassing and defamatory speech, platforms should prefer (admittedly imperfect) safeguards against biased enforcement to a hands-off approach. Often doing this will align neatly with their organizational interests, narrowly construed: users often have reason to avoid spending time in (virtual) spaces rife with harassment and defamation. But even when it is not, platforms should protect ordinary users from the harms that result.

5.3.2 Incitement and Failures of Due Care

In a move that would give rise to his executive order against online censorship,[56] Twitter flagged the following Donald Trump tweet for violating its rules against glorifying violence.

> These THUGS are dishonoring the memory of George Floyd, and I won't let that happen. Just spoke to Governor Tim Walz and told him that the Military is with him all the way. Any difficulty and we will assume control but, when the looting starts, the shooting starts. Thank you![57]

Despite labeling the tweet in this way, Twitter left it up, in case it was of public interest. Facebook was harshly criticized for not doing at least as much. Trump's tweet, it was argued, satisfied a common-sense notion of incitement to violence, encouraging property owners and law enforcement to shoot looters.[58] Not only that: the SMPs that hosted the speech had policies against that sort of thing, and so were in-effect exempting the already powerful from their rules.[59]

Issues surrounding SMP duties to moderate incitement came to a head in January 2021, when a mob of Trump supporters in the grips of a groundless theory regarding election fraud stormed the Capitol Building soon after a rally.[60] He told listeners that they had to show strength in the face of a grave

[56] (CNN/AP 2020).
[57] (Johnson et al. 2021).
[58] Recall from Chapter 2 that the legal standard of incitement requires that violators aim to direct a party to imminent lawless action by means of speech that is in fact likely to result in such action. SMP standards for incitement are considerably broader than that.
[59] To exempt certain accounts from moderation has been Facebook's official policy for some time: (J. Horwitz 2021).
[60] At the time of writing, no systematic evidence of fraud has been, to my knowledge, unsurfaced. See e.g. (Eggers, Garro, and Grimmer 2021).

procedural injustice. "I know that everyone here will soon be marching over to the Capitol building to peacefully and patriotically make your voices heard," the president said, while encouraging supporters to "stop the steal."[61] What ensued was not peaceful, not even close.

The video of the speech was posted to Trump's Twitter account. Twitter accompanied the video with a disclaimer—"claims about election fraud are disputed"—along with a link to resources investigating such claims. Shortly thereafter, Trump took to Twitter again. He told the rioters to go home, that he loved them, that they should remember that the republicans are the party of law and order. Then, Twitter suspended his account. When he got access back again, Trump tweeted the following.

> The 75,000,000 great American Patriots who voted for me, AMERICA FIRST, and MAKE AMERICA GREAT AGAIN, will have a GIANT VOICE long into the future. They will not be disrespected or treated unfairly in any way, shape or form!!!
>
> To all of those who have asked, I will not be going to the Inauguration on January 20th.[62]

Those would be his final tweet before being indefinitely[63] banned from the platform owing to concerns about the potential of further tweets to incite further violence. When Twitter did this, Facebook and Instagram followed suit. Parler refused to take a similar stand and had its access to Amazon's Web Services suspended.[64] In this way, terms of acceptable use and community

---

[61] (Naylor 2021).

[62] (Twitter 2021).

[63] At time of writing, Trump's account has been reinstated by Facebook and Twitter.

[64] Parler sued Amazon for breach of contract for failing to give 30 days' notice for the suspension of its services. Amazon alleges that the 30-day notice period does not apply for persistent breaches on a client's part of its own Acceptable Use Policy and says that it gave Parler notice to increase moderation to remove violations. Whatever the merits of Parler's case against Amazon, the incident has raised serious worries about private censorship. But Amazon is not the only provider of cloud services and it was Parler's choice to use Amazon as their sole source of cloud services. They accepted the terms of acceptable use when they signed on. The situation is as if the owner of a building hosted a community's meetings, subject to the condition that their space not to be used for plotting a revolt. Aware now that the building is being used for that purpose, the owner forces the community out, but it cannot find another space for its meetings in time (suppose the only unbooked space is hours away). Just as the building owner need not suffer for this lack of foresight, nor need Amazon host content it explicitly said it would not host because Parler now wishes to host it or cannot bring its behavior into compliance with the terms of service in a timely manner. Indeed, forcing Amazon to grant access to Parler even when the latter breaches contract reduces incentives for platforms to invest in server infrastructure of their own. In turn, this can tend toward further market concentration. For discussion, see and (Balasubramani 2021); (Fung 2021).

guidelines resulted in a coordinated effort to remove a great deal of political speech, much of it doubtless protected under the First Amendment.

It was unprecedented. Some celebrated the moves as evidence that SMPs and service providers were finally stepping up to the plate and seriously addressing the damage their platforms can do. Others lamented the move as one more piece of evidence that popular discourse was being controlled by wealthy Silicon Valley ideologues. Whatever your own reaction to these events, it is worth noting a few things about recent calls for more stringent censorship of incitement by SMPs.

First, in thinking through the stance we wish for these companies to take, we must once again beware the Streisand effect: sometimes our zeal to suppress bad speech results in its reaching a much wider audience than it might otherwise have reached. Indeed, my first time seeing Trump's tweet was in a newspaper headline. Someone's first time reading the words themselves might be in this book. Given how newsworthy it was for Twitter to flag his tweet as violating its community standards, it was more or less inevitable that Trump's words would reach a wider audience than they would have if left alone. If the words themselves are dangerous, then censorship might have been counterproductive.[65]

Second, even if these attempts to flag or remove this kind of content are successful in reframing it or stopping its spread or allowing passions to cool, it is important that we stop short of doing things that block adult citizens from powerful persons' distasteful speech. If the president is inciting violence, we need to know about it. In Western democracies we must press law enforcement to prevent people from responding to this sort of speech violently. But the speech itself is relevant to the sound exercise of our democratic duties. There is a reason why the president's words were big news.

Third, it is important that there are laws against insurrection and incitement on the books. Social media activity can alert law enforcement to the

---

[65] Compare what happened when Anderson Cooper (critically!) covered a story about the "Jailbait" subreddit (which featured sexually suggestive photos of young looking women): traffic to the community quadrupled (Marantz 2019, 211). An anonymous reader suggests another interpretation of Twitter's behavior here: the removal of Trump's tweet was not meant to suppress it, exactly, but to engage in a kind of counter-speech: speech designed to convey disapproval for the president's contrary speech. While I agree that there is an expressive element to content-moderation decisions of this kind, I have a hard time seeing removing content as counter-speech. This is simply because counter-speech is taken to be an alternative to removing something from public view. So the counter-speech interpretation requires thinking that Twitter was expecting it to reach a larger audience, and that its dissent would be that much better heard. While possible, I'm not sure this makes good sense of the company's public statements on the decision. See again (Twitter 2021).

plans of lawbreakers just as easily as it can host violations of these laws. When the laws are violated, the violators can be sanctioned. But when they aren't detected by the relevant actors, for example because they are flagged by an algorithm which suspends their dissemination, harm can result without anyone's being the wiser. There is, indeed, good reason to believe that law enforcement was well aware of the risk of violence on January 6, and that social media activity (particularly on Parler) was partially responsible for that awareness.[66] Forcing violent speech underground may succeed in limiting its reach, but it also arguably impedes our ability to respond to it in a timely way.

These are reasons to worry either that SMPs will tend to censor at least some incitement ineffectively or else that their doing so can have negative unintended consequences (making illegal activity more difficult to detect). For all that, however, if SMPs have reason to think that their removing some violent or inciting content will stop some imminent harm, they ought to do just that.[67] For similar reasons, SMPs should take care not to take affirmative steps that help extremist groups organize, as Facebook did when its algorithm automatically created groups for ISIS and right-wing militia organizations.[68] They are more likely to be effective in pursuing these goals when the content is not posted by public figures and is not for that reason newsworthy. Since such speech is quintessentially low-value speech, SMPs are less likely to err in removing it. But they should take care to ensure that they do so in a consistent manner.

5.3.3   Misinformation

In Chapter 2, I argued that environments too inundated with misinformation make deliberation about important issues much more difficult. They also make it difficult to act collectively in ways supported by the evidence. Many are worried now that new media forms are leading to the spread of harmful misinformation and that something needs to be done about it.[69]

---

[66] (Woodruff and Wu 2021).

[67] There are troubling questions about enforcing rules against incitement insofar as we recognize the possibility of legitimate or justified violence. These questions are put in sharp relief by the Arab Spring uprisings, largely thought to be facilitated by social media. For discussion, see: (Brown, Guskin, and Mitchell 2012).

[68] (Miller 2021).

[69] Importantly, despite all of the panic, researchers at Princeton and New York University have found that sharing misinformation is a relatively uncommon phenomenon. Around 90% of social media users do not share any at all. For ordinary users, those that share misinformation trend older and more conservative—both traits which plausibly negatively correlate with technological savvy

This case has been perhaps most forcefully made by Cass Sunstein.[70] On his view, current conditions might well require changes to Section 230 of the Communications Decency Act to make SMPs liable for the falsehoods they host on their platforms, at least if they fail to take them down in a timely manner when they are aware or should have been aware of them.[71] This can seem uncontroversial. What could be less objectionable than requiring social media companies to take down obvious falsehoods?

Yet there are reasons to worry about this proposal. As a purely legal matter, making platforms liable for misinformation is likely to result in their removing vast amounts of content that are, in actuality, wholly unobjectionable. Faced with the choice between liability-free unjust censorship and toleration risking legal action, companies will sensibly choose the former.

The law aside, it can seem that allowing people to live as autonomous individuals means allowing them to respond to the reasons others offer, even if their response to those reasons leads them into preventable and harmful error.[72] Indeed, before ultimately taking it back, T. M. Scanlon

and media literacy. See: (Guess, Nagler, and Tucker 2019). This suggests a bifurcated approach: moderation for organizations that regularly engage in bad-faith production of fake news and media literacy for ordinary users. SMPs make our beliefs visible.

[70] In addition to thinking that SMPs should be doing more than they currently are doing to regulate misinformation, Sunstein endeavors to move us away from First Amendment absolutism. In particular, although he takes it that speech should be generally protected, he believes recent jurisprudence has gone too far in limiting the state's ability to combat misinformation. If the government can show that the speech is both false and sufficiently harmful then it might warrant restriction (Sunstein 2021, 4, 72, 131).

[71] Importantly, some of those who wish to see more regulation (and in any case believe that SMPs have a strong social responsibility to police content) set their sights relatively narrowly: on misleading political advertisement and speech which attempts to mislead or suppress voter activity. This kind of call for regulation involves speech that is the political equivalent of commercial speech: speech proffered by groups advancing their self-interest by means of falsehood. US law already restricts what corporations can say to sell their products: I cannot claim that my new serum will make you immortal without violating restrictions imposed by the Federal Trade Commission. It is reasonable to wonder why laws don't similarly protect voters against lies that attempt to sell them a false bill of goods or prevent them from exercising their political liberties. If laws against fraudulent commercial advertising do not interfere with free speech, then neither should laws against fraudulent political advertising.

[72] There is a little noted irony of many claims that social media threatens democracy by refusing to censor misinformation. This consists in the fact that the threat is caused by nothing more than letting people engage with content on terms that they set and by their own lights. Many seem to suppose that people, left to their own devices, will be mechanistically taken in by swaths of nonsense. What seems to escape their notice is that, if this is a problem for democracy, it is a problem of democracy's own cloth. If social media threatens democracy by failing to censor misinformation, it is precisely by giving voice to more people and allowing them the responsibility to assess the content that they engage with. Now, one might argue that people simply aren't very good at assessing information and that misinformation will more or less mechanically induce them to believe badly. But this is an empirical claim, and one that appears belied by research on advertising efforts, which show that people are remarkably resilient against efforts to persuade. See: (Cooper, Blackman, and Keller 2016;

forcefully argued that respect for persons' autonomy meant rejecting coercive attempts to prevent certain kinds of harms that might result from expression. Specifically, harms "which consist in [persons] coming to have false beliefs" because of someone else's speech must be tolerated. So too must those harmful consequences that result from speech that convinces people that certain acts harmful to the actor are "worth performing."[73] In these cases, because the agents simply act on the reasons others offer, coercion to prevent their access to these reasons would compromise their autonomy, expressing a kind of disrespect for their agency. Autonomy does not involve simply acting in line with one's interests, but doing so in one's own way.

For example, suppose you are a professor and take to social media and argue that it is a good idea to take on a massive amount of debt to acquire a newly offered graduate degree from your university. Allow that your belief in this respect is genuine, though not formed with a responsible and clear-eyed view of the opportunity costs of such a degree and the poor prospects for graduates. In view of those opportunity costs and middling prospects, your advice is lousy and you should know better. While obtaining the degree would be okay as a consumption good (and might even materially benefit some rare persons), it would be a poor investment for most people. If so, you are culpable for your bad advice (and those that notice have a responsibility to hold you to account). After all, if people listen to you, it will harm them, and your privileged position as a professor makes uptake all the more likely. Nevertheless, one might think that respecting listeners as autonomous decision-makers means allowing them to hear your case alongside those less sanguine about the program's benefits. If listeners choose badly, it's ultimately on them.

If this is right, then SMPs that value autonomy should not restrict speech just because those exposed to the speech would be better off if they weren't exposed to it. What's more is that autonomy is a prized value in market contexts.[74] Because persons come to the market in search of exchanges mutually beneficial by their lights, there is something objectionable about

---

Bernstein 2021). Note that this is distinct from worries that SMP engagement efforts involve them in *amplifying* misinformation. The latter can be concerning for democratic reasons even if failure to suppress misinformation is not.

[73] (Scanlon 1972, 213).
[74] (Hasnas 2013).

corporations that substitute their own judgments about what benefits users for the judgments of consumers.[75]

SMPs' market-oriented reasons to respect autonomy, coupled with their desire to avoid being arbiters of truth, push them in the direction of soft rather than hard sanctions for misinformation. For example, many platforms have preferred labeling and contextualizing posts containing misinformation to removing it. Whatever concerns there may be about taking content down, surely these are reduced when users are able to engage with it and told that it is disputed, debunked, or otherwise problematic. Not only does flagging content appear to tread lightly on persons' autonomy, it might also *enhance* it by encouraging more critical reflection.

But there are reasons to worry, too, about labeling content thought to be false. First, even doing this much necessarily singles it out, which can draw attention to it. If the flagged content was newsworthy (or produced by a public figure), then there's a real risk that, in flagging it, one will increase, rather than decrease its influence. This matters, in part, because preliminary research suggests that flagging content as disputed does not typically reduce its pernicious effects.[76] For readers that are disposed to believe the content before the flag, corrective efforts will typically fail. Moreover, overuse of flags during polarizing crises risks further politicizing the platforms (potentially opening them up to legal repercussions like Trump's executive order and undermining their credibility where it matters most).

Regarding the latter risk, many republicans worry that social media companies are partisan in their enforcement of their community standards. Set aside the truth of this claim. The mere fact that people believe it can induce people to respond to flagged content by disbelieving the *flag*, rather than the *flagged content*. As the authors of a Stanford University report put it, "Given Facebook's alleged history of preventing conservative stories from appearing in the Trending News section of an individual's news feed, conservative groups especially seem reluctant to accept the 'disputed' label."[77] Given the political orientation of SMPs, there is reason to think that they

[75] It is true that one can have a view of autonomy according to which one can violate it at t1 in order to promote it at t2, e.g., by enabling better decision-making power and a more independent cast of mind. But I take it that most who take autonomy to be of value are reluctant to instrumentalize it in this way. I certainly am.

[76] (Garrett and Weeks 2013).

[77] (Finkel and Herman 2017, 41). Note that it doesn't necessarily improve things to have users correct one another, rather than having the platform introduce the correction: (Mosleh et al. 2021).

will flag content from conservative sources as misinformation more often.[78] But then the flags will seldom help those who moderators believe most need correction. In concert with the exposure effect, which suggests that the first exposure to misinformation yields uptake, the danger that labeling misinformation can make the problem worse will likely induce SMPs to reduce exposure in the first place, either by being more aggressive about taking content down or by deboosting questionable content. This will put pressure on SMPs to find ways of being transparent about what they're doing without simultaneously undermining their efforts to curb exposure to offending views.

What's more is that flags appear to increase the perceived accuracy of content without flags.[79] But since it is not feasible to flag everything false or misleading, this exerts a strongly distortionary effect on our information environment[80]—one that predictably favors the priors of the fact-checkers or those flagging the content.[81] The result is not just unfairness resulting from similar content receiving differential treatment. Rather, uneven standards allow some kinds of falsehoods to flourish without being counterbalanced by opposing ones.

There is, then, no easy way for SMPs to both address misinformation on their platforms and also respect user autonomy. But even leaving considerations of autonomy aside, there are several reasons to worry about SMP attempts to tackle the misinformation problem.

First, it is not so clear that SMPs are competent to identify misinformation. The SMPs that have taken on misinformation in the wake of COVID-19 and the January 6 Capitol riots have tried to sidestep this issue by relying on independent fact-checking agencies and public authorities to avoid making controversial judgments of fact themselves.[82] But even such fact-checking agencies rely on official sources, which are sometimes mistaken.

[78] Note: this is compatible with the fact that Facebook in particular has a track record of holding conservative news sources to a lower standard and also that its most popular content is often aimed at conservative audiences. See: (Horwitz and Horwitz 2021).

[79] (Pennycook et al. 2020) call this the "Implied Truth Effect."

[80] (Guess, Nagler, and Tucker 2019, 30) note that this sort of selective censorship is one of the prominent ways of ensuring the effective dissemination of misinformation.

[81] Indeed, the current state of artificial intelligence does not allow SMPs—even the richest and most technologically sophisticated among them—to identify all of the potentially troubling posts that there are (Gorwa, Binns, and Katzenbach 2020; Gillespie 2018).

[82] In the wake of these events, YouTube, Twitter, Facebook, and Reddit each adopted statements on COVID-19 moderation. Many of these statements prohibit posting demonstrably false information—especially that which can lead to serious harm—to the platforms. See: https://web.arch ive.org/web/20211221153024/https://help.twitter.com/en/rules-and-policies/medical-misinformat ion-policy; https://support.google.com/youtube/answer/9891785?hl=en; https://www.reddit.com/ r/ModSupport/comments/g21ub7/misinformation_and_covid19_what_reddit_is_doing/;   and https://about.fb.com/news/2020/03/combating-covid-19-misinformation/

For example, for months during the early stages of the pandemic, posts claiming that the coronavirus might have originated in a laboratory setting were variously labeled misinformation or removed.[83] Now, the hypothesis is credible (though far from proven) and content exploring the hypothesis is tolerated. Similarly, official sources early in the pandemic cautioned that masks did not offer protection to those wearing them. This turned out to be exactly wrong. Yet even when official sources are not demonstrably mistaken, they exhibit a kind of status quo bias, which can impede new discovery and otherwise disadvantage new perspectives.

Additionally, regulating misinformation can lead the platforms to legitimacy-compromising decisions, especially around elections. In this regard, consider moves by Facebook and Twitter to censor a *New York Post* story connecting Hunter Biden's laptop to foreign influence peddling. Although early reports indicated that the story was unverified and likely the effect of a Russian disinformation campaign, its authenticity has been verified now by several major outlets.[84] Not only does this raise questions about moderators' motives (were they trying to protect the Biden campaign?), it also reduces the platforms' credibility in other domains.

Second, the more people come to believe that platforms are addressing misinformation, the less incentive they themselves have to ensure that they're checking their information.[85] Given that one of the classic justifications for free speech principles is to cultivate critical thinking skills necessary for democratic deliberation, there is reason to worry that such measures will encourage people to think that they do not need to do their due diligence.[86]

---

[83] (Hern 2021).

[84] (Nelson 2022).

[85] Compare a Stanford University Research report finding that when SMPs address misinformation explicitly, this fosters a "trust bias"—users believe that the misinformation problem is being addressed and so that they can rely on what they read on the platforms more robustly (Finkel and Herman 2017, 12).

[86] To be clear, the idea that too-tight moderation will breed complacency rests on an empirical hypothesis advanced by others in other domains. For instance, Wilhelm von Humboldt worried that for each task the state undertakes, the community will see itself as having less reason to be concerned. He makes this point particularly strongly concerning the provision of welfare: "As each individual abandons himself to the solicitous aid of the State, so, and still more, he abandons to it the fate of his fellow-citizens. This weakens sympathy and renders mutual assistance inactive; or, at least, the reciprocal interchange of services and benefits will be most likely to flourish at its liveliest, where the feeling is most acute that such assistance is the only thing to rely upon; and experience teaches us that oppressed classes of the community which are, as it were, overlooked by the government, are always bound together by the closest ties" (Humboldt 1993, 21). Additionally, in a provocative law review article, Fagan and Meares argue that increased state involvement in norm and law enforcement weakens community enforcement mechanisms, partially explaining why tough on crime policies seemed to lead to an increase in criminal activity (Fagan and Meares 2008). Arguably something similar has occurred with the COVID-19 crisis. Whereas before lockdowns, GPS data shows that people

Third, there is a risk—already realized—that politicians will pressure SMPs to censor content, even when it's the sort of thing that would ordinarily be beyond the reach of law.[87] For example, the Biden administration has been monitoring social media activity, flagging user posts to be evaluated and taken down.[88] The Surgeon General is meeting with Twitter executives to create a plan for taking down dangerous misinformation. The Department of Justice plans to dedicate more resources to monitoring social media activity. Elon Musk's release of the "Twitter Files" reveals persistent attempts by state actors to flag content for removal that might've otherwise remained up. In some cases, such "jaw-boning" from officials succeeds.[89] Abroad, Facebook and Twitter caved to pressure from Indian politicians to remove user posts complaining of state misconduct.[90] Canada has laid out a plan to create a new political position to oversee internet speech.[91] And the European Union has just imposed sweeping requirements via the Digital Services Act that SMPs of every size comply with orders to remove content deemed misleading by officials.[92] These trends demonstrate that platforms' good-faith efforts to moderate can be seized upon by politicians keen to circumvent the First Amendment and other speech protections by using political carrots and sticks to get SMPs to censor in the ways that benefit them. If politicians could generally be relied upon not to exploit powers like this for private purposes, we wouldn't need robust protections for free speech in the first place. The best way for platforms to avoid these pressures is to refuse to have policies of moderating misinformation.

radically decreased their movements, as soon as states lifted their lockdowns, people may have taken this as a cue that it was safe to return outside, leading to big spikes in GPS movement data. An additional concern is that SMP removal of misinformation deprives users of the ability to determine the facts, e.g., on important matters of value, treating them as passive in a problematic way. See: (Forestal and Singer 2020). This favors flags generated by users (such as those built into Twitter's "Birdwatch" feature). It is an open question whether the latter suffer similar drawbacks as context provided by platforms themselves.

[87] (Benesch 2020, 99); (Klonick 2018, 1622–25).
[88] (The Editorial Board 2021). Such coordination between governments and SMPs is not always to be repudiated. Still, there is a long history in which state actors attempt to muzzle the press. For discussion, see (Gentzkow and Shapiro 2008).
[89] (Tuccille 2023).
[90] (Purnell 2021).
[91] (Leavitt 2021); for criticism, see (Macnab 2021). Noteworthy in the proposal is the mandate that SMPs remove content deemed illegal within 24 hours or face sanction. This will likely result in SMPs censoring a great deal of unproblematic content, preferring removal to the threat of sanction.
[92] ("EU Poised to Impose Sweeping Social Media Regulation with Digital Services Act" 2022).

These considerations combine to make it the case that SMPs usually do better to avoid censoring or flagging misinformation. So far as they insist on continuing to moderate this kind of content, they ought to have strong principles in place that allow them to resist pressure from legislators to censor content that really ought to be left up. Generally, they should prefer introducing *good* information to taking down or flagging *bad* information. Curating some degree of reliable content for users is likely to help the truth win out without inviting the perverse effects of censorship. Changes, especially, to the architecture of their sites such that reliable sources appear alongside trending sources are promising avenues for further experimentation and potentially lasting change.

The duty against SMP censorship of misinformation that these worries generate is weighty but defeasible. In cases where a piece of misinformation is demonstrably false (e.g., in the case of lies about polling places and other matters of public importance) and the estimation of harm extends beyond harm to the listener and extends to the public at large, SMPs may have little moral choice but to act. In these cases, the relevant content will not typically be created by a normal user, but by coordinated campaigns of such users which attempt to manipulate platform rules to gain an outsized influence.[93] SMPs have good reason to ensure that the content they host is authentic. When SMPs respond to concerns about inauthenticity or mass disinformation campaigns, they should do so in the full awareness of the manifold ways in which their action can ultimately undermine the very goals they're trying to pursue by its means. But it stretches credibility to think that worries about unintended consequences categorically prohibit taking action.

---

[93] Three examples of this kind of coordinated campaign: social media disinformation campaigns orchestrated by foreign operatives (of the sort described in (Rid 2020)); widespread campaigns of climate change denialism by special interest groups (of the sort described in (McKinnon 2016)); and anti-vaccine campaigns aimed at undermining public confidence in inoculation for profit (Ahmed 2021). In each case, the actors are not plausibly acting in good faith. Such bad-faith actors surely enjoy First Amendment protections. But SMPs need not serve as a megaphone for them. In each case, there are ordinary users who are good-faith purveyors of similar claims. (The difference between good- and bad-faith claims is sometimes thought to be the hallmark of the distinction between disinformation and misinformation.) SMPs do well to target bad-faith action and leave good-faith speech alone—even when the two kinds of speech are indistinguishable in terms of their content. Notably, even coordinated disinformation campaigns have unclear impacts. See e.g. (Allcott and Gentzkow 2017; Tucker et al. 2018; Rid 2020).

5.3.4 Discriminatory Speech

Though it wasn't always so, SMP community standards now nearly universally prohibit hate speech (Parler and Gab are notable exceptions).[94] Hate speech, a subclass of discriminatory speech, targets persons for abuse based on their "protected characteristics," things like race, ethnicity, gender identity, sexual orientation, religious affiliation, and so forth.[95] Such speech is often accompanied by stereotypes and slurs, but can occur independently of these. In Chapter 2, I argued that, in addition to having the capacity to set back its targets' dignitary interests and potentially expose the vulnerable to the risk of harm, this kind of speech can encourage minorities to refrain from participating in important public conversations.

Were you to own a bulletin board vandalized to gratuitously attack some person or group of persons for their race, you should remedy the situation. And if an unidentifiable person were to spray paint a swastika on your house, you ought to incur the expense to paint over it, even though there's some cosmic unfairness in that. I take such judgments to be relatively uncontroversial. They do not imply that the *state* should punish hate speech. Rather, the idea is that property owners have good reason to minimize the extent to which their property is used to subject persons to wrongful abuse. Reasons to rid spaces of these kinds of speech are stronger still when the presence of such speech compromises the goals of the property owners. In the case of social media, platforms have reason to worry that engagement on their platforms will suffer if they tolerate these kinds of speech. Even when engagement as a general matter would not suffer, still they appear to be interested in fostering certain kinds of engagement in line with their vision for the communities they seek to build.[96]

Still, SMPs must balance the case for keeping their communities free of these kinds of bad speech against the possibility of backlash and the risk that

[94] Much of this speech was not regulated at all until European authorities put pressure on platforms to do more regulation. See (Citron 2018, 1038–41) for discussion, including how demands for removal quickly extended to speech not covered by European law.

[95] Conservative critics complain both that political discrimination is not included on these lists and also that some of the items on the list amount to discrimination against content on political grounds. On the first front, this reflects current law. But on the second front, SMPs have good grounds for thinking that political affiliation is meaningfully different from the other protected classes. Whereas the latter are often not chosen, the former often are. And when something is a matter of choice, in your control, it becomes more reasonable to discriminate on its basis.

[96] For example, some research suggests that negative representations of groups on social media encourage further negative commentary, whereas positive representations combat it. See: (Miškolci, Kováčová, and Rigová 2020).

too-heavy moderation will drive bad actors underground, where they may be more likely to radicalize. Moreover, because hate speech standards are vague (leaving considerable discretion to moderators to distinguish between speech which genuinely violates the policy and speech which does not), it is important to develop safeguards against biased enforcement. Because of the risk of abuse (and cases in which hate speech policies result in taking down speech by the very minorities they are designed to protect), it is encouraging to see many of the largest platforms develop appeals procedures for those who believe they are unfairly subjected to such restrictions.

The upshot is that, although SMPs are and ought to be legally free to censor content on their platforms, and though there are good reasons for them to try to address bad speech by consistently enforcing community standards, we might expect them to have more success in some domains (harassment, defamation, violence, pornography, discriminatory speech) than others (misinformation). Even in domains they are most likely to be successful, there are clear and convincing reasons for platforms to exercise caution in their moderation endeavors. As SMPs set their priorities and compete along the dimension of moderation policies, they should emphasize transparency and consistency of enforcement. Because they deal with a vast amount of speech, there is good reason for them to develop a body of "case law" to guard against enforcing standards in a distortionary way. To their credit, as SMPs continue to come under attack for distortion and discriminatory enforcement, they have done just that.

These measures will plausibly increase the perceived legitimacy of their moderation activities. But there is a danger here, too: given SMPs' interests (distinct, whatever their public roles, from the public interest), challenging the legitimacy of their particular decisions is crucial for holding them accountable. The more that users know about the patterns of enforcement, the less they will be tempted to uncritically take the distribution of views on any particular platform as representative of the broader views and attitudes of their fellow citizens. Fortunately, moderation decisions deploying hard sanctions create clear victims who have ways of bringing the decisions to light (e.g., by means of blog posts, media engagement, op-eds, and so on). This allows the public to observe the orientation of platforms to certain classes of speech and to understand when this orientation is inappropriate.[97]

---

[97] As a result, to the degree that SMPs are "shadow-banning" users without notification, they are engaging in unacceptable behavior.

As Danielle Citron points out, there are numerous features (including definitional ambiguity, global enforcement, and opacity of moderation practices) that can empower platforms to censor speech in ways that go beyond their narrow mandate and we need to be on watch against them.[98]

The complexity of the problems that SMP content moderation is designed to address implies that we are to some degree shooting in the dark. It is unlikely that there is one set of standards appropriate to all platforms. Additionally, the real-world impact of any particular set of standards is uncertain. As a result, calls to subject SMP censorship to regulation appear premature.[99] At the same time, it is important that SMPs continue to appreciate their public roles as intermediaries of discourse. They ought to continue to experiment with the development of professional norms that will allow them to resist political pressure to censor where appropriate.[100]

Independent of the open questions that remain about the effects of censorship, I want to conclude this section by offering a quick argument to those who yearn for steady regulatory action to ensure proper content moderation. The argument begins from the observation that one of the many ways in which the Supreme Court has found reasons to hold private companies responsible for respecting the First Amendment concerns the degree to which the state is involved in regulating the relevant private party.[101]

If congress were to impose requirements on SMPs to moderate content according to its desired pattern, and a plaintiff were to sue a platform for violation of her First Amendment rights, precedent would put pressure on the court to find in the plaintiff's favor. This is because it would be quite easy to show "entwinement," namely that there was a "sufficiently close nexus" between the state's regulatory activity and the company's alleged violation of the party's First Amendment rights.[102] For this reason, those who long for more responsible content moderation should address themselves to the firms currently empowered to undertake it under Section 230 of the Communications Decency Act. To involve the state is likely to give up the game to those who yearn for an internet governed exclusively by First Amendment norms.

Nor should those who yearn for an internet governed by the First Amendment engage in a cynical play to regulate the platforms to secure

---

[98] (Citron 2018, 1051).
[99] See for example ("NY State Assembly Bill A7865a" 2021).
[100] Compare (Balkin 2020, 12).
[101] See e.g., *Public Utilities Comm'n v. Pollak*, 343 U.S. 451 (1952).
[102] *Jackson v. Metropolitan Edison Co.*, 419 U.S. 345 (1974).

their desired result. For, as I suggest above, the internet that would result would be difficult to live with. Accordingly, an internet regulated by First Amendment standards is, in my view, the fastest way to erode the real protections against state censorship that the past six decades have won. And we have good reason to fear what such erosion might mean for our access to information. In sum, although SMPs' experiments in censorship might leave a lot to be desired from an ideal perspective, they might be the best we can do at present.

So far as we follow my advice here and resist calls for regulation, we are essentially allowing companies to conduct various experiments in censorship. Experiments are great, but unless we have the information we need to properly evaluate them, the amount we can learn is limited. This fact generates extra reason to make the data from these experiments available to researchers who can help the public better understand their social effects.

5.4 Conclusion

Some believe that SMPs are a big threat to democracy and they may be right. There are legitimate concerns about the presence of false accounts operated potentially by foreign or domestic operatives that might substantially affect our understanding of what our fellow citizens believe. They make it easy for misinformation to spread and technology can readily make fake content appear legitimate. Social media executives are scrambling to de-activate the accounts of individuals and organizations engaging in a concerted effort to spread misinformation. These efforts are to be cautiously applauded, even if they involve recognizable censorship, and even if policing misinformation generated authentically is misguided.

Given that I think it is right to be worried about these kinds of things, it is a good thing that social media companies are not obligated to provide a First Amendment forum. And for different reasons entirely, it is a good thing that they are not required by law to censor in specific ways. Regulations in this direction are likely to be either overly broad or inefficacious. Even if they are narrowly tailored and effective in limiting speech, they might push our legal environment in undesirable directions. And even if they do not push our legal environment in undesirable directions, they can encourage a sense of complacency among us that can lead us to be less responsible citizens than we already are.

In view of the challenges we face, it is important to give citizens tools for evaluating content and understanding the complexities of expertise, to be vigilant to take our information from a diversity of sources, and to be wary of our own impulses toward tribalism and associating with only like-minded others. In these respects, the best way for SMPs to address the pathologies of our current information environment is not through censorship or fact-checking, but by experimenting with ways of increasing engagement with reliable sources and investing in media literacy and good quality educational resources.[103]

Some, including Facebook, are already making substantial investments in these areas. This, rather than the moderation they undertake to keep their platforms usable, is the real story regarding the steps they're taking to reduce the harmful effects of online speech and the only one that can treat the underlying disease rather than merely masking its symptoms. If we fail to invest as a society in good mission-driven journalism and education, even the most extensive and perfect regime of SMP content moderation will not make responsible citizenship a reality. The tech giants cannot save us from the hard work that goes hand in hand with freedom. Neither—I might add—can our elected officials. At least not without giving up the very freedoms they are entrusted to protect.

---

[103] Twitter, for instance, prompts users to read articles before sharing them. Both Twitter and Facebook indicate to users what's "trending." Each could also recommend to readers a diverse number of high-quality pieces in a more directly editorial role. These choices matter and might explain changes in fake news diffusion across platforms. See: (Allcott, Gentzkow, and Yu 2019).

6

Search and Monopoly

The year 2020 saw the century's most significant global health crisis in the coronavirus pandemic. In addition to testing the limits of the public spirit, that
year—more than any in recent memory—demonstrated the degree to which
information crucial to our health and safety is controlled by private parties.
To understand how (not) to behave, many of us turned to search engines for
help in locating the best information. In doing so, we put ourselves at the
mercy of choices made by corporations hundreds, sometimes, thousands of
miles away from us. Not only do search engines have algorithms that determine the order in which results appear, but the largest among them (Google)
has also admitted to taking some manual steps to control the kinds of news
sources that are prominently displayed on its results page.[1] Between uncertainty about the degree of manual censorship and the certainty of algorithmic sorting, many worry that Google employees will use their own
sectarian understandings of the public good (not to mention their own private interests) to shape the information users can access, with potentially
grave distortionary effects.[2] It is difficult to find clear and uncontroversial
cases in which these effects have obtained. But the anxieties are real.

For instance, during the height of the pandemic, there was a brief period
of panic when Google was not returning results for the Great Barrington
Declaration—an open letter signed by a number of medical professionals
and other individuals in objection to the use of lockdowns as a mid- to late-
stage tool for addressing viral spread.[3] Signers of the petition advocated a set
of policy objectives that would have prioritized protecting the vulnerable instead of lockdowns, which, they argued, were subject to expensive trade-offs

---

[1] (Bloom 2019).

[2] Some internal company documents have amplified the sense of concern. See, for example the
document "The Good Censor," which can be found here: https://s3.documentcloud.org/documents/
5002023/The-Good-Censor.pdf.

[3] (Myers 2020). At the time, I was able to test this myself. My early searches for the declaration
didn't return anything pandemic related at all. The second, some hours later, buried the declaration
itself under a series of highly critical articles. Subsequent searches displayed the declaration among
their first results.

Private Censorship. J.P. Messina, Oxford University Press. © Oxford University Press 2024.
DOI: 10.1093/oso/9780197581902.003.0006

no longer justifiable by the best understanding of the facts. Whether the policies the declaration laid out were right or wrong, it would be clearly be troubling if we were denied access to them by tech executives who know little about epidemiology and public policy. Fortunately, as complaints mounted, the problem resolved itself, and eventually the declaration was prominently displayed in Google's results.

It remains unclear exactly what explains the incident described above. But there are plenty of innocent explanations. For instance, due to imperfections in search engine optimization, websites do not always appear prominently in search results, even when their search terms indicate that they should be. This is especially so when they are new. (New websites do not often have the kind of broader web presence that signals to the Google algorithm their importance.)

Whatever was the case, the story drives home just how big a deal the possibility of search engine censorship is. To Google something, after all, has become a synonym for looking it up. In light of Google's role in directing much of the world's eyes to the content they search for, it's reasonable to wonder about its considerable power to censor—especially in times of emergency when pressures from public officials can quickly escalate. If company operatives—not themselves experts in either science or social science—can determine the information that even experts can disseminate, our information environment is at risk.[4]

In Chapter 1, we noticed that, under certain conditions, the morally salient differences between private and state censors begin to fade away. Massive publicly traded companies can enjoy monopoly power that makes exiting our relationship with them difficult. In the domain of information services, this means that private powers can come to control such a wide array of the architecture that citizens use to make important political decisions that one

---

[4] This problem, so far as it exists, may prove legally difficult to remedy. After all, courts have found that search engines' rankings of results constitute protected speech under the First Amendment. This means that regulations in how these results are returned must pass the bar of strict scrutiny. That is, they must be shown to be in the service of a compelling state interest and narrowly tailored to pursue that interest (as the least speech-burdensome way of achieving it). Additionally, courts will not accept First Amendment interests of search users as satisfying the state's need for a compelling interest in the regulation. See *Search King, Inc. v. Google Technology Inc.*, Case No. CIV-02-1457-M (W.D. Okla. May. 27, 2003). What's more is that courts have held that the right to free speech includes the right not to speak. Since ranking results constitutes speech, courts will hold that there is a constitutional issue with requiring Google or other search engines to rank results in any particular way. See *Langdon v. Google, Inc.*, 474 F. Supp. 2D 622, 626 (D. Del. 2007). Finally, Section 230 of the Communications Decency Act appears to protect Google and search engines for any attempts they make to moderate content they find objectionable. Compare (Woan 2013).

might wonder how far their control differs from the state control of information. In circumstances like these, the thought that these institutions might be best regulated in line with First Amendment values (rejected as a general response to private censorship earlier in this book) appears more plausible.

To many, Google fits this description—at least with respect to its search engine arm. The Silicon Valley company controls somewhere around 90% of the search engine market share, and search engines have become the dominant mechanism for accessing information. But it would be wrong to say that everyone is equally vexed about Google's powers for censorship. For many, Google and similarly positioned companies have a duty to exercise a steady censorial hand to ensure that public health is not compromised by a slew of misinformation (especially during emergencies). Google—as the internet's largest gatekeeper—has an especially strong duty, some argue, to ensure that reliable results are prioritized. Its imperfect judgment in this matter is not an objection to the need to rely on it. Instead, it's an argument for holding Google legally accountable for doing the right thing. These opposing calls for regulation reflect a bipartisan dissatisfaction with the status quo.

In this chapter, I argue that things are better than they seem and that we should be cautious to avoid taking action that may well make things worse. I begin in Section 6.1 by sketching a theory of search censorship. In Section 6.2, I argue that antitrust remedies that are and have been sought against Google might have one of three effects on the market for search. Section 6.3 treats two of these potential outcomes—those which involve the re-emergence of a dominant firm—and examines the potential remedies for this situation (including their risks). Section 6.4 considers the third outcome, according to which competition is restored and argues that ethical, rather than political, remedies are advisable. On the whole, the chapter thus delivers less a knock-down argument for pursuing one or another course of action and more an exploration of various proposals that lays out their potential benefits and limits.

6.1 Search Censorship

Before turning to structural issues, it is worth making more determinate whether and how search engines can engage in censorship. To begin, it will be helpful to start with a few words about search engines and how they work. This might seem unnecessary in light of their ubiquity—don't we already have a sense of this? To some degree, yes. And yet the failure to be explicit about how search engines return results—and a profit—will leave our account vague at crucial points.

The major piece of intellectual property that makes search engines function is a sorting algorithm. Sorting algorithms are essentially complex rules for organizing information. In the case of internet search, a successful algorithm evaluates a vast number of websites that might or might not be useful for the person conducting the search. In addition to search terms, sophisticated algorithms account for things like recency, search location, past browsing history, and prominence of results (usually captured in a metric that reflects the number of other weblinks that reference each result). The point of the algorithm is to deliver a list of search results that gets the person who makes the query to the best result(s) as quickly as possible. Accordingly, designing an effective algorithm is crucial to attracting users back to the search platform. If a search engine too regularly returns irrelevant results, it's of limited use. To train their algorithms, search companies collect user data and employ software engineers to evaluate how such data might allow the algorithm to be fine-tuned.

To pay for all this, search engines usually sell space to advertisers (though subscription models have existed). In exchange for a prominent place in the search results (usually to the side of or on top of the unpaid results), advertisers pay search companies a sum of money. In Google's case specifically, advertisers pay a certain rate (determined at auction) per keyword per click. In addition to returning search results by machine learning–trained algorithms, search companies can employ persons to fine-tune them when things appear to be going haywire.

Naturally, one need not pay Google for advertising space in order to appear in its list of search results. Instead, those interested in attracting users to their websites through search can work with search engine optimization experts and web-design tools to ensure that their site ranks highly in the *organic* search results for associated keywords. These organic results are not flagged in the way advertisements are (and are often more attractive to users for that). They are the ones that usually appear below or to the left of the paid results. (In this way, it is worth noting, Google's organic results compete with its paid advertising results. Advertisers will only pay to list on Google to the degree that doing so results in more traffic to them than search engine optimization at lower cost.[5])

---

[5] This has interesting implications for the degree to which Google is able to extract monopoly rents from advertisers. See: (Manne and Wright 2011, 199).

Anyone who has designed a website knows that the process of search engine optimization is somewhat arduous and that it can be challenging to make it the case that your page appears in the desired searches. It is in part to sidestep problems with optimization and in part to appear in results for other products that makes paid advertising attractive.

That should be enough to fix ideas. Now, search engines deploy algorithms to organize vast sums of information. In doing this, they exert considerable influence over our information environment. But this doesn't by itself prove critics (e.g., Tulsi Gabbard[6]) are right when they accuse search engines of censoring web content in a politically motivated or problematically profit-driven way. What would it mean to deliver on such claims? What, specifically, would count as censorship by search engines?

I take it that, if search engine executives were to act manually and intentionally to bury inconvenient political news (e.g., to the disadvantage of one over another political party or candidate), it would be perfectly natural to speak of censorship.[7] In this sort of case, corporate actors suppress expressive content for the sake of shoring up their material interests. Likewise if they manually buried such content because they judged it harmful or threatening to orthodoxy.

But nothing hangs on the manipulation being manual, carried out directly by human actors. Something similar would be true were this to this happen algorithmically. Algorithms, after all, are created and set in motion by people. When those people design an algorithm to suppress content, the algorithm is an instrument of censorship. Even if not *intended* to suppress content in this patterned way, if engineers are aware of the possibility, could stop it from actualizing, and decline to on censorious grounds, this too fits the model.[8]

Thus, we have two basic ways in which companies that own search engines can engage in censorship:

---

[6] (Birnbaum 2019).

[7] Arguably the Associated Press and associated telegraph companies behaved in roughly this way during the late 19th and early 20th centuries. See: (Blondheim 1994). It is an open question how successful they were in using their outsized market power to influence the course of history, but there is doubtless something concerning in the power itself.

[8] In the case that this censorship is executed by someone in a corporate role, acting in an official capacity, the censorship is attributable to the corporation. If the corporation does not inform users that it is engaging in this behavior, then it may be guilty of fraud or deceptive business practices (Woan 2013, 319, 328). In that case, the corporation may be liable for the actions of its employees under the legal doctrine of *respondeat superior*. Likewise, when an algorithm is designed by a company, the company has control over it, and the company benefits from the operation of the algorithm, what the algorithm does is arguably attributable to the company. Compare (Diamantis 2021).

(1) A search engine's operatives manually remove results that would be seen to be relevant by the person conducting the search on the grounds that it is dangerous, threatening to orthodoxy, or inimical to the material interests of the firm.[9]

(2) An *algorithm* set in motion by a search company is designed to automatically remove results for censoriousreasons, or does so foreseeably in a way welcomed by engineers or executives.

Naturally, there is a question of fact: how often do search engines engage in (1) or (2)? Google executives repeatedly deny that the organic search results are manipulated in these ways and at least one study supports their claims.[10] Although this is far from settling the matter, it should be relatively easy for evidence of such manipulation to surface.[11] Notice that many people use search engines *knowing* what they want to find (rather than memorizing URLs).[12] Moreover, people can check their status in the search results themselves. If search engines regularly buried sought-after results, the problem should readily surface. (Recall how quickly complaints surfaced that the Great Barrington Declaration was not appearing in searches and how quickly the problem was resolved.)

Whatever the facts (and it is not the philosopher's place to decide them), we can safely advance the following normative principle: provided a search

[9] Returning relevant results is seen by both proponents and opponents of regulating Google as the chief virtue in search. According to Mays, for instance, this is the very essence of search neutrality, which obtains "when a search engine produces the most useful results to the internet user and displays them in order of best to worst quality" (Mays 2015, 731). By contrast, search neutrality is compromised when search engines prefer their own content (Mays 2015, 733). Compare (Manne and Wright 2012, 163). Whereas for Mays, a search engine's preference for its own content necessarily entails failing to return the most relevant results, Manne and Wright argue that this need not be the case. Quality search (understood in terms of relevance) might well be facilitated by bias.

[10] (The Economist 2019). Importantly, censorship is just one way that Google impacts our information environment. Search orderings might, for instance, impact perceptions of quality, allowing non-censorious algorithmic choices to impact electoral outcomes. For a summary of research on these questions, see (Metaxa et al. 2019). For a sophisticated account of how such filtering can exhibit a form of social power ("skewing power") that can undermine users' epistemic agency, see: (Miller 2022).

[11] What Google does seem to do is create a blacklist that stops certain unreliable sources of news from appearing in its curated "news" sections or prominent "information boxes." Since these tools are curated by Google and very explicitly draw user attention to them, it strikes me that there is nothing inherently censorious about this practice. Indeed, for reasons we saw in Chapters 4 and 5, there is reason to believe that Google is exercising a kind of editorial authority over this section of its website. This authority does bring with it the power to censor, but this is a price worth paying for much needed curation of content.

[12] Additionally, research suggests that when users know what they're looking for, they can overcome algorithmic impact by attempting multiple queries, differing somewhat, until they arrive at their desired results. See: (Slechten et al. 2022).

engine does not explicitly and prominently announce that it blocks some search results (potentially with a link to deliver the results if asked), provided, indeed, that it regularly *denies* doing so, it ought not to engage in (1) or (2).

Why not? In ways encouraged by the search engines themselves,[13] users tend to justifiably see search engines as neutral gateways to the internet. They tend to reasonably believe that when they search for something and nothing relevant comes back that it simply does not exist. Without an explicit explanation of the ways in which results may be skewed due to deliberate decisions, search engines are misleading their users, even if their behavior would be otherwise justifiable.

But even if we knew with certainty that (1) and (2) did not occur without the appropriate transparency, this would not, I think, completely resolve worries about search censorship. Notice another possibility in the neighborhood.

(3) Someone conducts a search. Rather than removing the undesirable content from the list of search results, the search algorithm or a corporate employee acting in an official capacity buries the best result for a user's search under a bevy of less relevant content.

Most users (either owing to the efficacy of Google's algorithm or to search fatigue) do not venture past the first page of results. So moving a result sufficiently far down the list with the intent that fewer people are able to find it (and it receives less engagement) appears to differ little from de-indexing or removal.

As with (1) and (2), (3) invites difficult-to-assess questions of fact. Do search engine employees or their algorithms regularly bury results that the executor of the search would find relevant? Do they do this to control access to information (perhaps for ideological reasons)? Or do they do it more innocently, in failed or failing attempts to provide the best search results? Whatever the facts, we might say that *if* search engines do this covertly for reasons not related to the quality of the search results, then they are engaged in a kind of wrongful censorship. They should either desist or make abundantly clear to users what is going on.

But now consider a fourth possibility:

---

[13] https://www.google.com/search/howsearchworks/mission/.

(4) A user enters a general search term, say, "white supremacy." In a way that amounts to corporate action, the company in control of the search engine places the active white supremacy propaganda well below other highly relevant search results (e.g., histories, activism campaigns against white supremacy, and so on).

When a search is nonspecific in this way, there are myriad different possible orderings of results, each of them faithful to the search engine's goal of returning relevant results.[14] Because this goal can be met in several different ways, it is less natural here to speak of censorship and more natural to speak of curation or editorial authority. As we observed in Chapter 4, tolerating editorial authority means tolerating the existence of powers that might well be exercised in a corrupt and censorial manner. But without it, we would be left in an incomprehensible morass of content.

Now, notice that accepting that the behavior described in (4) is above board does not give search companies carte blanche. Instead, it acknowledges that search engines might use a variety of criteria to choose between several equally good results orderings.

Thus, we might say: the governing value of general search is the results' relevance to the user. When relevance does not suffice to deliver a unique ordering, employees and algorithms can appeal to other values to choose among the options. Such values might include:

- Informativeness: if one ordering prioritizes results from non-credible sources, the search engine might reasonably prefer an ordering in which these appear lower down in the results. Likewise, if one ordering prioritizes relevant results that aim at action and another prioritizes that offer information, the search engine might prefer that.
- Justice: if one ordering prioritizes results that advocate or perpetuate violence, harm, or injustice, the search engine might prefer to choose a different one.

[14] There is a wrinkle here, concerning the tailoring of results to a person's taste. Suppose that past searches indicate that the user really is interested in the pro-white-supremacy content? Is the search company permitted to refrain from delivering the results it knows its user wants? My own view is that the search engine has a right to act as it sees fit in these difficult cases, understanding well that a search engine's failure to return the relevant results will likely lead the user to go elsewhere, to perhaps a less well-curated search engine. Accordingly, there may be limited up-side of such decisions. At the same time, there is something repugnant about profiting from helping these kinds of searchers find what they want to find.

- Profit: when one ordering prioritizes a business partner or would generate additional revenue, the search engine might reasonably prefer it.
- Diversity: when one ordering presents results only from a single ideological perspective or delivers mostly mainstream results, the search engine might prefer a more diverse ordering or one that prioritizes minority views.

As above, there are questions of fact: are search engines using these kinds of values to order results? If they use are, are they meeting basic conditions of transparency? As long as they are, then it is hard to think that they're unfairly or unreasonably distorting our information environment. Different search engines, like different publications, can have different priorities, including different views about when they should make certain kinds of content harder to find. Unless, of course, there's only one game in town.[15]

This last consideration raises a separate question of fact: is the market in search sufficiently competitive to justify extending editorial authority (with its attendant de facto powers to censor) to search engines without intolerable risk of distortion? Many look at the current search environment and conclude that the market is *not* sufficiently competitive to defray significant worries about search censorship. Given the type of worry this is, it is natural to reach for solutions in antitrust and competition law. In the next section, I examine these laws, how they work, and their limitations in addressing search censorship.

6.2 Search and Antitrust

Now that we have the basic mechanics of internet search censorship on the table, it is worth saying a thing or two about the search space's major player, Google, specifically with respect to the share of the market it controls. On the one hand, it is challenging to define its market share because it is difficult to define its market. Is Google's market the *search advertisement* space, competing with, e.g., DuckDuckGo, Bing, and Yahoo!? Or is it a player in the

---

[15] Notably, this guidance applies only to search engines that do (through word or deed) claim a kind of neutrality. It isn't hard to imagine search engines optimized to appeal to those with distinctive ideological interests.

advertising space more generally, competing with sellers of advertisements everywhere?[16]

Fortunately, we need not settle the question. Recall that we are primarily interested in the degree to which Google's omnipresence in internet search raises worries that our information environment is compromised. Thus, for our purposes, we can set aside some of the complexities of market definition, though they'll certainly matter for the prospects of any actual antitrust action. What's important for our purposes is to observe how much search traffic goes through Google and to ask: are there resources in current competition law for addressing worries about Google's powers of censorship, given how much of our access to information is mediated by it? If not, are there ways that the law can be updated to deliver a better environment for search? And what are the risks of regulation and how might we think more productively about the trade-offs between these risks and the uncertain benefits regulation promises?

Thus we can begin our investigation by noting that, as of February 2021, 86.6% of global search traffic is routed through Google; 6.7% of the same traffic is routed through Bing; 2.71% through Yahoo!; and just over 0.5% through the Chinese company Baidu. The remaining 3.5% or so of traffic is shared by DuckDuckGo and other smaller search engines.[17] To contextualize these numbers, note that the Herfindahl-Hirschman Index—the measure used to guide the Department of Justice in its evaluation of prospective mergers—would assign to this market a score of roughly 7,564.[18] According to this index, a pure monopoly market earns a score of 10,000. The Department of Justice is directed to view any market with a score above 1,799 as highly concentrated. By this metric, the search services space is *extremely* concentrated, at least so long as we are interested (as we are here) primarily in the control that Google has in directing internet traffic to some, rather than other, websites.

The fact that the search marketplace is as concentrated as it is gives Google an impressive degree of control over our access to information. This has led many to reach to the antitrust provisions of the law as a source of reigning in Google's power. If the problem is Google's size, the argument goes, we have a set of policy tools for addressing it. If these tools are not up to the task and we

---

[16] (Manne and Wright 2011, 220–23).

[17] https://www.statista.com/statistics/216573/worldwide-market-share-of-search-engines/.

[18] https://www.justice.gov/atr/herfindahl-hirschman-index; compare (Sherman 2008).

agree the problem is grave, then perhaps the toolkit itself needs to be updated to deal with these new challenges.

The United States' arsenal of antitrust provisions has developed over decades of legislative effort dating back to 1890 with the Sherman Anti-Trust Act. This act—inspired by a growing dissatisfaction with the practices of the major players in the oil and rail industries—made it illegal to enjoy a monopoly or attempt to monopolize. The Federal Trade Commission Act was passed in 1914 to supplement the Sherman Act and authorized the new federal agency to pursue antitrust actions and eventually regulate mergers by means of the Clayton Act.[19] Further legislative actions have authorized individual states' attorneys general to pursue antitrust action themselves.

When a firm is found guilty of violating antitrust laws, governments can seek a variety of remedies. In some cases, the offending corporations are fined and the responsible executives jailed (up to 10 years). In others, those demanding "structural" remedies, companies are forced to separate (or "break up") their operations in order to more directly foster competition. In yet others, firms with an interest in consolidation are prevented from consolidating, or are allowed to consolidate only if they accept certain conditions ("consent decrees") or grant the remaining firms access to their essential facilities.[20] Finally, in a number of cases especially relevant for the issues under consideration in this chapter, firms that have developed monopoly power are classified and regulated as public utilities. Often in exchange for the legal title to monopolize, the government is authorized to regulate the prices firms are able to charge, the returns they're able to garner, and subject them to certain legal duties to keep their operations in the public interest.

The dominant (though not sole[21]) justification for antitrust actions of these kinds is that they are anticipated to promote consumer welfare.[22] Antitrust action can promote consumer welfare by preventing firms from

---

[19] https://www.ftc.gov/tips-advice/competition-guidance/guide-antitrust-laws/antitrust-laws.

[20] The latter remedy is especially common when one (usually larger) competitor controls a facility that is essential to providing service of a certain kind. A prominent example involved the court's determination that AT&T had to grant long-distance competitors access to its local networks. In more contemporary circumstances, scholars have argued that the vast amounts of data to which the major tech players have access should be shared with competitors under a renewed essential facilities doctrine, e.g. (Meadows 2015).

[21] For instance, especially under the Brandeis court, antitrust action has also been used to promote the interests of smaller firms and promote competition regardless of its anticipated effect on consumer welfare. These kinds of antitrust rationales remain controversial.

[22] (Bork 1993); (Posner 2019); contrast (Wu 2018).

exploiting their outsized market power to capture monopoly profits or from colluding with other players in the market to form a cartel (an organization that controls prices or works together with other firms to make production decisions that may conflict with consumers' interests). When markets are sufficiently competitive and consumers have many alternatives, firms have little leeway for bad behavior in these respects. Those that fail to set competitive prices or that offer low-quality goods and services will tend to fail, while those that satisfy consumer preferences will tend to succeed.

Returning to the case at hand, Google is currently facing numerous antitrust challenges. Most of these do not address its search algorithm per se (much less its specific capacity to compromise our free speech environment). Rather, current antitrust challenges address themselves to: (1) arrangements with hardware manufacturers to make Google the default search engine on products it does not produce;[23] (2) the firm's role in being both the gateway to a marketplace and a seller in it;[24] and (3) its potential ability to overcharge advertisers due to its market concentration.[25] The Department of Justice (along with various state attorneys general) is petitioning the court to find Google in violations of Section 2 of the Sherman Act. As a remedy, they seek not just an injunction against these anti-competitive practices but structural reform that would see Google broken up.

For our purposes, we can set aside both the merits of these antitrust charges against Google and an assessment of merits of the proposed remedies. These are complex legal and economic matters better left to experts in the law and economics of competition (and, ultimately, to the march of history) to decide. Instead, let's suppose that the antitrust charges are sustained and that the state pursues a structural remedy of the kind it has long sought.[26] There are three potential outcomes of interest.

(1) Google re-establishes dominance despite the remedy.
(2) *Another* firm comes to dominate the market for search.
(3) The structural remedy succeeds in introducing more players to the marketplace in a durable way.

---

[23] Exclusive dealing violates the prohibition on attempting to monopolize set out in Section 2 of the Sherman Act. For details about this complaint against Google, see (Department of Justice 2020, 3).

[24] For details on this complaint against Google, see (Gillett 2021).

[25] (*US Department of Justice v. Google LLC*, 2020).

[26] For a principled approach to structural reform in information industries, see (Wu 2011b). Wu argues that information markets ought to be separated into those that provide network infrastructure, those that create content, and those that distribute content.

The realization of outcomes (1) or (2) would provide further evidence that the search space is characterized by features which render it a natural monopoly (more on which below). In that case, lawmakers have at their disposal further remedies available for ensuring that dominant firms do not act in ways that harm consumers. I discuss these remedies in the next section, along with some of their problems. In the case that the antitrust intervention succeeds in introducing competition between firms, the situation is otherwise. Because we are not dependent on any one firm, the relevant questions are what kinds of moral principles govern running a search engine in a competitive environment. I address this possibility in Section 6.4.

6.3 Natural Monopoly Regulation and Its Limits

This section supposes for the sake of argument that the market for search is characterized by conditions that make it unlikely to sustain competition. Even if structural remedies were prescribed and well calibrated, we are imagining, they would fail. Many commentators already believe this to be true about the market for search engines, and if they're right, this tells us something about how to approach their regulation because it suggests that the market has a tendency to produce monopoly power.

Natural monopolies result when markets are not contestable, i.e., when markets are—by the measure of existing technologies—unlikely to incentivize new entrants and to sustain multiple competitors.[27] When markets are

---

[27] Markets are likely to fail to be contestable in circumstances where there are substantial economies of scale (or scope), where entry involves substantial sunk costs (costs that cannot be recovered upon exit from the market), and where network externalities make it the case that substantial benefits redound to consumers when all users deal with a single firm. These and other factors can result in a situation in which competition between multiple firms is likely to push the market price below each competing firm's marginal cost (resulting in running an operating loss and an incentive for all but one firm to exit the market). Some of these features characterize the market for search. For instance, search engines involve network externalities, both direct and indirect. There are direct network externalities because the more users interact with a search engine's algorithm, the more useful the algorithm is in returning relevant results. There are indirect network externalities, so far as the more users a particular search engine enjoys, the more attractive it is to advertisers. These effects can make it the case that it is difficult for multiple providers to compete. They also make it the case that new entrants to the market face an uphill battle, insofar as market incumbents already enjoy an active user base, increasing the likelihood that competitors will enjoy a fringe share of the market and little more. Additionally, the search space is characterized by economies of scale: providing additional search results to additional users is likely to be cheaper than it was to provide such results to the first. By the same token, once one has a search algorithm up and running, there are benefits to providing the service to additional users, insofar as doing so allows one to attract more advertising revenue. Finally, the industry is characterized by at least some measure of sunk costs: designing an algorithm

not contestable in this way, competitive forces to discipline firm behavior are reduced to the *threat of entry*, a threat that might not, in the end, be credible.

Markets might be non-contestable because of anti-competitive behavior by a dominant firm. But anti-competitive practice is not necessary to ensure non-contestability. When a market is characterized by the pressure toward natural monopoly, therefore, structural remedies, injunctions, and punishment are not likely to help.

Fines and jailtime are out of place because there is a sense in which the monopoly power that results from markets with this kind of structure need not be the fault of the firm that enjoys it. Again, in these kinds of markets, the firm need not be engaged in any anti-competitive behavior. In the case under consideration, any fines have already been paid post-settlement. It might simply be difficult for multiple firms to maintain profitability. In such circumstances, the firm might compete on fair terms and monopoly might result nevertheless.[28]

In markets that yield natural monopolies, structural remedies (those which "break up" the dominant firm) are unstable. For the now separate firms face the same pressure in the direction of single-firm provision. Prosecution for illegal mergers and consolidation is similarly beside the point: market consolidation in these industries does not necessarily result from unscrupulous executives vying to control ever greater market share,[29] but from the market incentives themselves.

---

requires investing in engineering outputs that are not easy to recoup upon market exit. This raises the costs of entering the market and contributes to the already substantial barriers to entry.

[28] It is worth pausing to note that, although Google is currently dominant, it is not obvious that the market for search is not contestable, even pre-structural reform. Even as things stand in advance of any antitrust action against the search giant, venture capital sees fit to fund alternatives to Google. Microsoft is investing heavily in its own search algorithm. Google itself is investing heavily in research and development. And it seems clear that if Google were to begin behaving badly in a transparent way, a competitor would emerge to better satisfy consumer preferences. (Already some say that Google search is "dying." See: ("Google Search Is Dying," 2022).) Finally, search technology is not fixed once and for all. While Google's sorting algorithm is perhaps the best of its kind, it would be naïve to rule out the possibility that new technology might emerge to make Google—for all its dominance—obsolete. (Despite the weak antitrust action, Microsoft's market share has fallen considerably since it raised the suspicions of regulators.) These facts—all of them true as far as they go—have been variously rehearsed a number of times throughout the debate over whether Google should face antitrust action. For affirmative answers, see e.g. (Wu 2018; Clemons and Madhani 2010; Bauer 2010; Mays 2015); for more skeptical takes, see (Manne and Wright 2011, 2012; Witt 2019).

[29] As a matter of fact, court documents demonstrate that Google does want to dominate the market for search and snuff out the competition in ways that offend a Brandeisian palate. But this desire explains a good part of the firm's dynamism, drive for innovation, and competitive edge, the benefits of which have redounded largely to consumers. It is thus at least questionable whether desire to dominate is anything to worry about. When not pursued by illicit means, it may even be something to celebrate.

In these circumstances, we must live with monopoly power. Since the existence of monopoly power carries with it substantial risks (especially in uncontestable markets), regulators tasked with pursuing consumer welfare are left to find ways of ensuring that the provider does not come to exploit its position. Traditionally, there are two main options for ensuring that the monopoly provider does not engage in practices that significantly reduce consumer welfare. The first, called public provision, involves bringing the market under the control of the state. The second, called public utilities regulation, often involves having the state grant the dominant provider with a legal (de jure) monopoly (at least in a certain geographical area of service), shielding it from outside market entry. In return, the state claims the right to subject the provider's service to principles to keep its exercise of monopoly power in the public interest.[30]

Given that I am not aware of any serious proposals to nationalize the market for search (and that indeed it seems overwhelmingly likely that any such measure would exacerbate rather than alleviate worries about censorship in search), I focus in this section on the case for regulating search as a public utility.

Talk of public utilities should rightly call to your mind things like electricity, water, sewage, and telecommunications. Each of these industries could be (and has been!) provided in a more or less standard, unregulated market. But because each of them requires massive infrastructural outlay (making it highly costly for competitors to enter the market) and because (in at least some cases) network effects make it the case that users of a service might prefer to belong to the same service,[31] competitive pressure in these markets is wanting. Moreover, at least for many consumers, the products in these markets are not differentiable except by means of price (and sometimes network considerations), consumers care that they be provided competently at a low price, but not that they be provided by one firm, rather than another.[32] As a result, the risks of single-firm provision are relatively low.

---

[30] Naturally, conditions of natural monopoly are not the only conditions which call for regulation in the public interest. As Simon and Ghosh put the point in a recent piece for the Brookings Institution, the "purpose of antitrust is to protect and promote competition, not to address every concern about corporate power" (Simons and Ghosh 2020, 7). We can, then, be agnostic about whether an antitrust justification is available and ask: is there a case for regulating Google in the public interest? If so, then we have a case for potentially updating the laws to include new grounds for action.

[31] See e.g. (Tirole 2017, 398–400).

[32] Importantly, algorithms are not impossible to differentiate in the way electricity and water arguably are. Whereas I may be indifferent between a gallon of drinking water provided by one firm at a certain price and a gallon of drinking water provided by another at a certain price, a list of search results can be better or worse depending upon the quality of the algorithm. Insofar as this is

It is not surprising that the most typical constraints that natural monopolies face are constraints on the prices and products they provide.[33] Monopoly provision of goods can reduce consumer welfare by allowing the monopoly provider to charge higher prices than would be possible in a perfectly competitive market. Alternatively, firms can skimp on quality in ways that more competition would predictably prevent. One might address the current antitrust issues with Google, for instance, by regulating the prices Google charges to advertisers and by regulating the "price" consumers are charged in the form of data collection.

Notably, neither measure will do much to address worries about search engine censorship. But to say that these are the standard regulations is not to say that they're the only possible regulations for search engines deemed public utilities. In exchange for a de jure monopoly, regulators might require, for example, that monopoly providers of search are held to a duty of non-discrimination when returning search results or that they interfere with search results when the public interest requires it or that search results display

so, there is diminished cause to consider search to be a utility. After all, others (Bing, or Duckduckgo, or some new entrant) might offer a product that is more appealing to customers. Indeed as various tech companies come under scrutiny for the way they do business, consumers do indeed appear to be growing dissatisfied with them. Google in particular has, in the eyes of many users, lost a great deal of its power as it has adapted to respond to public and political pressures. Insofar as there are alternatives, we should eventually predict that consumers will switch to these other options. If so, it is reasonable to think that search engines face constant pressure to deliver a product that satisfies consumers. If a search engine fails, it will lose market power. I am sympathetic with this line, but many are not. To better address myself to those who disagree with me, I take on board the assumption that search engines are like utilities in these ways.

[33] At the same time, the focus of public utilities regulation on prices makes it difficult to see readily how it is intended to apply to internet search, at least in a way that touches upon free speech concerns. For consumers do not pay (in dollars, directly) for use of the services search engines provide (see, Department of Justice 2020, Section 25). Instead, they must accept certain conditions for using it, including consenting to certain patterns of data collection. Thus appeals to consumer welfare in these circumstances require some care to suss out. It is one thing to note that in a competitive market in a certain space, a certain price below the current market price would be offered and safe enough to assume that users are better off at lower prices. It is another to make good sense of the claim that in a competitive marketplace, patterns of search results would have a certain shape, and that this shape would be to the benefit of consumers (especially so when data collection itself is not separable from algorithmic quality). But even if we might expect a different pattern of data collection practices, algorithm features, and other conditions for use in a more competitive market, there remains reason to worry about the degree to which a perfectly competitive marketplace is the relevant baseline for comparison. To wit, a more competitive marketplace may do better in realizing consumer preferences over search, but the concerns about the market power of search engines do not reduce easily to worries about consumer welfare. They are easier to state in terms of the public interest. We worry that the incentives that private parties face are inadequate to secure an optimal information environment. This means that regulators cannot in any simple way appeal to standard welfarist criteria if they are to regulate well.

some measure of balance or that they are accountable to First Amendment standards.[34]

But although the case for regulating search engines in circumstances of natural monopoly is strong in theory, public utilities regulation in the area of a service so intimately tied to the freedom of information is a risky proposition. In the case of internet search, we might note that the status quo leaves us better able to access information than ever before, in large part because firms like Google have designed technology that lowers the cost of accessing it. If so, we are better off for Google's presence despite its market power. Though aimed at making our information environment *better yet*, there is no guarantee regulatory efforts will succeed: they may make things worse, especially if they are not carefully crafted to deprive the state of an ability to manipulate search results for their own advantage.[35]

More generally, public utilities regulation can stifle innovation by barring new market entrants who might otherwise compete. Open markets—even when characterized by significant network externalities, high sunk costs, and other seemingly insurmountable barriers to entry—at least leave other competitors free to try to do better by the lights of consumers. Sometimes—especially after a technological shift—a new firm will enter the market against all odds. The threat of entry under renewed circumstances can exert a surprising disciplinary force even on natural monopolies.

For instance, George Stigler tells the story of how trucking emerged in the early 20th century as an alternative to shipping by rail. Rail executives, then heavily regulated under antitrust law, responded by lobbying governments to restrict the amount of weight that could be carried by truck. In many jurisdictions, they succeeded in getting their way. While it may not have been foreseeable to regulators that trucking would emerge as a competitor to rail in shipping cargo, it isn't hard to imagine something similar happening with search algorithm technology. For example, experts are already wondering if new advances in artificial intelligence might disrupt traditional internet search.

The twin threats of regulatory capture and stifled innovation partially explain why public utilities regulation has been a mixed bag. On the one hand,

---

[34] Public utilities regulation of a firm can, under certain court doctrines, make it the case that that firm's activity counts as state action. See: Burton v. Wilmington Parking Auth., 365 U.S. 715, 722 (1961).

[35] (Manne and Wright 2012, 200).

the case for intervention is theoretically clear. On the other, intervention in the real world is messy and frequently courts unforeseen consequences.[36]

These concerns about the real-world effects of public utilities regulation—raised most seriously and systematically by economists like F. A. Hayek,[37] George Stigler,[38] and (more recently) Donald Boudreaux[39]—do not amount to an easy knock-down argument against such regulation. It remains necessary to take a close look at the particular regulatory proposals—as yet not on offer—and examine the incentives that they create.[40]

At the same time, it is worth noting that the trucking case concerns an area in which the sought-after regulation involves relatively simple constraints of non-discrimination and fair pricing. Even such limited interventions allow firms an outsized influence over further regulations that shape the landscape in which they operate. There are further ways for things to go wrong when attempting to regulate something as complex as search engines' moderation practices. For once we move beyond simple questions of pricing and have to consider more complex questions of what it would be for a monopoly search engine to keep its operations in the public interest (e.g., by refusing to discriminate or auditing the firm for wrongful censorship), difficulties multiply. These questions—especially those concerning whether and to what degree the public search utility should regulate speech—are deeply polarizing.

To get a sense of the thorny issues regulators would have to deal with to settle on utilities regulations that would address these issues, consider the following questions:

(1) Suppose I search for the KKK's website (or the website from a similar hate group). Should the search engine prominently display it in the results (as DuckDuckGo does)? Or should it display it (as Google currently does) only after displaying several other pages which offer (largely critical) information about the hate group? Does it depend on facts about the searcher?

(2) Suppose we're dealing with a global pandemic and someone enters search terms that would, without manipulating the algorithm or manually changing the results, direct them to a controversial treatment of

---

[36] (Manne and Wright 2012, 202–3).
[37] (Hayek 1996).
[38] (Stigler 1971).
[39] (Boudreaux 2017).
[40] For a review, see (Dal Bo 2006). For an analysis of the ways in which cognitive bias can negatively impact regulators in the domain of antitrust, see: (Cooper and Kovacic 2011–2012).

the relevant health and safety issues. Should the search engine deliver this as the first result without disclaimer? Or should it first include a disclaimer? Or should it do something else entirely?

(3) Should search engines default to a safe mode to shield children and others who might not want to encounter obscene, though constitutionally protected, information? Should such a safe mode make other assumptions about what an ordinary person wants to encounter, beyond obscenity? What do free speech principles say about such matters?

(4) When someone conducts a search regarding a political issue (a defense of a higher minimum wage, say) should a search engine's algorithm be designed to deliver the results that a user most wants to see (based on her search and browsing history) or should it strive to present results that convey the balance of information on a question? If the latter, who decides what counts as balanced, and how might any oversight mechanisms be abused in ways analogous to the abuse of the Fairness Doctrine decades ago?[41]

(5) If someone searches for something, how much (if at all) should other searchers' search histories affect the results returned? For example, Safiya Noble has criticized Google's search for "baking in" existing inequities by delivering search results that reflect current preferences.[42]

We disagree deeply about these and many related questions. Such disagreement renders public regulation of search extremely difficult. And since taking a stand on them would doubtless affect the user experience, handling things democratically is likely to impose costs on the dominant firm that may well undercut its dominance, save for a grant of a de jure monopoly. But a de jure monopoly in search seems especially prone to abuse, public regulation aside.

Of course, public regulation of a dominant search firm can be more modest than this discussion suggests. Perhaps it can be so modest that it does not require granting a dominant firm a de jure monopoly. To investigate this possibility, consider proposals advanced in a recent Brookings Institution report.

---

[41] For a case in favor of a fairness doctrine for search that suffers similar defects, see (Pasquale 2008).
[42] (Noble 2018).

As authors of the report note, a dominant firm might be required to make data available to researchers who could then conduct regular reviews of the way its algorithm affects the public interest to better inform consumers.[43] Such a requirement would allow consumers to make better choices in light of the provided information without unduly burdening the firm's operations requiring the grant of a legal monopoly. Although Google and other search firms credibly claim that they cannot make their search algorithms publicly available without ruining their service (by allowing users to manipulate search results to serve their own narrow interests), more limited data sharing regulations need not have this effect. Firms might hand their algorithms over to research teams or certifying agencies that could publish reports on their features under strong non-disclosure agreements. Such a requirement could be imposed on a firm arguably without unacceptably impeding innovation or adversely affecting the quality of the existing product. The report cites four further regulatory proposals that are likewise neutral with respect to how specifically search engines should order results.

First, the report's authors argue, a dominant firm must be made to "respect certain public values and rules of the road designed to protect the public interest."[44] More specifically, Google must be made to respect equal access, non-discrimination, public safety, consumer privacy, and serve marginalized or underserved communities (though they should have "considerable discretion" about how to implement these requirements and "work closely with regulators, civil society groups, and academic experts" to determine best-practices.[45]

It's easy to say things like this. But platitudes always roll readily off the tongue. Without something more determinate, calling for legal duties at the same time that one wishes to grant to the firm regulated by means of them "considerable discretion" in implementation is a recipe for failure (a recipe followed with exactness by the FCC in crafting the Fairness Doctrine). Proposals like this allow politicians to claim victory for solving a problem and give the public a sense that something has been done without doing much more than signaling fealty to the right kinds of values. Such regulations often do little more than breed complacency.

Second, the authors continue, a dominant firm can be held to a duty of transparency, in the sense that it "should be required to explain how [its]

---

[43] (Simons and Ghosh 2020). This is one aim of the Algorithmic Accountability Act of 2019.
[44] (Simons and Ghosh 2020., 12).
[45] (Simons and Ghosh 2020, 12).

systems are designed and articulate the principles that underpin them." [46] But of course, Google already does a good deal of explaining how its system works in general terms. It is unclear what more is reasonable to require of the firm in this regard, aside from making room for independent assessments of its curation procedures (already discussed above).

Third, a dominant search firm must do what newspapers have previously done and sharply separate its advertising interests from its editorial interests.[47] Google already does this in part—paid advertisements appear clearly labeled and distinct from their organic search results, and the two do not have any obvious relationship with one another. If Google were to allow paid advertisers to manipulate the organic search results, this would be troubling. And although there is no evidence that it does so, a regulatory requirement against this need not be overly costly.

Finally, the authors argue, Google must "experiment with" systems of democratic government, especially where its operations concern matters of public importance. This might involve instituting citizen juries as a legitimacy building exercise. As the authors put it, "[c]itizen juries could be used as regular components of internet platforms' governance of public debate by involving citizens in the design of high-stakes content moderation algorithms."[48] It might also involve using mini-publics "to connect corporate decision makers with the concerns and demands of citizens and policy makers."[49] If we do not act politically to answer questions about search engines, we might think, then they get answered anyway—by executives at the dominant firm. What could be the costs of ensuring by law that the way they made these decisions was at least informed by the public's views on the matter?

And yet a major issue is that the public doesn't have a clear sense of what makes for a good search algorithm. It might think it wants a search algorithm to have certain features without its being the case that it much likes using one that actually has those features. For instance, many say that they don't want Google to track their search histories. I certainly share the unease that motivates these responses. Indeed, I feel it strongly enough to have attempted a full-on transition to DuckDuckGo, which explicitly refuses to collect user data. In doing so, I've been forced to confront just how much

---

[46] (Simons and Ghosh 2020, 12).
[47] (Simons and Ghosh 2020, 13).
[48] (Simon and Ghosh 2020, 13).
[49] (Simon and Ghosh 2020, 13).

better data collection makes Google search.[50] I still use both, because I think pluralism is important. But if Google were to become like DuckDuckGo in this regard through public oversight, my ability to locate high-quality information would be made worse, not better. Google, unlike voters or the public, has an overriding interest in ensuring that its product delivers the goods. The incentives for others—even voters or select groups of them—are not nearly so good.

Still, it is useful to remind ourselves that dominant firms are *not* necessarily acting with the public interest clearly in view. Even when they deliver a great product, they can do so in ways that subtly distort our information environment. Accordingly, it is important to conduct internet searches—especially those that concern matters of public importance—on multiple different search platforms, when available. It is also important crucial to refuse to treat search engines as exhausting our access to information. There are still the old ways, and there are new ways cropping up every day. We might do better than we currently do to diversify our sources.

The measures I've suggested in circumstances of natural monopoly can be supplemented by state efforts to provide their own search services.[51] One might think of this as the 21st century equivalent of a public library. Recall that the reason a monopoly in search is anticipated to be the natural result of market forces is that network effects, barriers to entry, and sunk costs make it the case that new entrants would either lack prominence or struggle to operate profitably at scale. Note that because the state is not accountable to market forces in this way, it can operate certain services at a running loss. Additionally, because the state is (at least in some communities) a trusted source of information, lack of prominence is less of an issue. Having a public alternative to one dominant firm might not solve all of our problems, but it would help adjudicate disputes (by allowing persons to cross-check private searches with the public option) and admits of easier regulation in line with the state exercise of power than do other options in circumstances of natural monopoly. Additionally, it would leave in place incentives for other private companies to introduce technological innovations that might improve our epistemic environment in ways we find difficult now to imagine.

---

[50] This was true at the time of drafting this book. More recently, I have noticed a decline in the quality of Google's search results that has me using alternatives much more regularly now. What explains the perceived decline in quality is an interesting and important question.

[51] Though, as Jack Balkin points out, there are significant First Amendment challenges in implementing something like this (Balkin 2020).

6.4 Competitive Search

The conclusion of Section 6.3—that we must rediscover information literacy and its demands—is one that has come up in each preceding chapter of the book. It's one for which I believe there is no replacement. Similarly, the idea that the state needs to update its approach to allowing citizens to find the information necessary to exercise soundly their epistemic duties appears sound whether or not we're dealing with natural monopolies. If these are less urgent matters once we relax the assumption that structural remedies must fail to deliver a more diverse search environment, it is only by degrees.

To see this, let's imagine that structural remedies succeed in restoring competition to the market in internet search. Then, any residual worry about search engine censorship presumably shifts from one regarding the supreme power of a particular search engine to a more generic one that we seem to face whenever private companies control access to information that is crucial for public life. In these cases, we might continue to ask how public authorities can supplement the private sector solutions to these problems, giving us a richer set of options. Beyond this, it is crucial to reflect on the kinds of principles we want to see search engines incorporate into their algorithms.

Much work has been done to criticize the ways in which search algorithms can reinforce an unjust status quo.[52] Search engines have responded, e.g., by creating an "autocomplete blacklist"[53] which is a list of words that the search engine will not autocomplete for users. The idea is to stop reinforcing stereotypes and to keep perverse preferences widespread in the population from reinforcing themselves through search. Some complain that this is itself a kind of censorship.

While it is true that it is a way in which these search companies intentionally control our information environment by refraining from suggesting things that we might well mean, claims of censorship seem to amount to considerable overreach. The blacklist does not mean that users cannot find the results they want, and it does not mean that results have been scrubbed. It means only that the search engine will not prime users to complete these kinds of searches. It makes sense that search engines would want to avoid doing so. After all, autocomplete is a feature added to search engines for its

---

[52] (Noble 2018).
[53] https://slate.com/technology/2013/08/words-banned-from-bing-and-googles-autocomplete-algorithms.html.

convenience, giving firms that use it a competitive edge and benefiting them accordingly. As a result, the company is morally liable for any deleterious effects it might have on the social world. Search engines do well to take care to reduce these to the degree that they can.

Worries about the ways in which search algorithms reinforce an unjust status quo extend well beyond the autocomplete results. Indeed, because search engine algorithms return results in part based on popularity, the ordering of results themselves reflects majority interests that may lead to the continued marginalization of the vulnerable. Fortunately, a competitive search environment encourages product differentiation. And for beings like us, who might have different interests when we sit down to search, that's usually a good thing. Consider: it might make sense to make use of different search tools for different purposes. Sometimes, it matters to see the most popular results—this helps us understand what the rest of the world is thinking and reading. Other times, we might want to see results that are more carefully curated to highlight minority views and interests. A competitive environment without de jure monopoly allows for innovations along these lines that might serve our plural interests in search.

As we saw in Section 6.3, one of the most daunting features of the idea of search regulation is the prospect of coordinating around a single set of principles for designing an algorithm to order search results. There are simply too many diverse and conflicting interests at stake for this to be feasible. The promise of restoring competition to these marketplaces (provided we agree that it is wanting) is that it would obviate any need to coordinate in this way.

Still, to say that competition might provide benefits to the search marketplace is to stop well shy of supposing that it would solve all of our problems. Incentives might still exist for search executives to conceal information for bad reasons or in harmful ways despite attempting to respond well to genuine crises. In an internal presentation at Google, the presenter wonders whether it's possible for firms like it to act as Good Censors. I'm afraid that this is easier said than done. To be a good censor requires knowing not only which truths are too dangerous to be allowed in public view, but also estimating the effects of withholding them on public trust. If backlash against search censorship is already widespread in a time when search executives exercise a relatively light hand, we might imagine widespread legitimacy crises were they to do more.

In a competitive environment, of course, companies in charge of search results should be free to experiment with different practices of returning search results. In such an environment, we might expect some firms to exercise a relatively heavier hand than others—not only by using political principles to design their algorithms but also by more actively curating results. So long as people have a plurality of good options, there is nothing wrong with this,[54] especially since users often learn quickly to find information they seek despite algorithmic ordering.[55] But so far as search engines do these things, they have duties to be transparent about what they're doing. If perfect transparency remains unachievable because it only helps users game the search results, search engines that take on a greater role in curating content should offer mechanisms by which web developers can inquire about why their content is not favored in search results generated by apparently appropriate queries.

And yet it would be too strong to demand that any search engine achieve this level of transparency. Only the biggest corporations with the deepest pockets can afford to pay people to adjudicate disputes and look into issues concerning particular search results. To adopt a requirement like this as a *regulatory matter* would increase the pressure toward monopoly and ultimately undermine prospects for competition.

In short, sufficiently competitive markets might allow lots of different search engines, encoding lots of different values, to flourish. In the absence of coordination between them to exclude the content you wish to find, it should be possible to find what you're looking for (and to be found when you want to be found). There is no more danger in private power in competitive markets for search than there is in the market for bookstores. Still, even if antitrust action restores competition to the search space we should continue to invest in information literacy. It may make sense also to invest in a public option free of advertising pressures and revenues, but market research would be crucial to determine whether consumers would make use of such an option. We should, in short, be grateful for competition without naively assuming that we can trust whatever results it produces.

---

[54] Indeed, Woan notes that, in such an environment, we might take each search engine as offering a list of *recommendations* regarding the answer to our queries (Woan 2013, 329–30). As we learn about the character of each search algorithm, we can use their differences to our advantage.

[55] See again (Slechten et al. 2022).

6.5 Conclusion

It is difficult to know how the present day's anxieties about the capacity of search engines to act as censors will resolve themselves. There are also substantial questions about how they *should* resolve themselves.

It is perfectly possible that the current market for search is characterized by sufficient pressure in the form of entry threat and cheap exit options to render any significant changes unnecessary. I have considerable sympathy with this view. Alternatively, improving competition in search might pay dividends in the form of greater innovation. It's important, however, that the latter outcome is not inevitable. Not only might structural reform fail to make things better, it also might fail to yield durable change (as in the case of natural monopoly).

In the latter case, states can consider public utilities regulations. But these are beset by sufficiently high risks that they are to be approached with great caution, especially when they grant the regulated firms *de jure* monopoly status in a domain that concerns our access to information.

Moreover, the typical mechanisms for public utility regulation (price controls and universal service requirements) are not particularly well suited to address concerns about censorship by the most powerful firms. Thus, if we decide to pursue regulation in the public interest, it may be best to abandon the typical public utilties framework and develop a new one. But we should not be blind to the challenges of coordinating around a single set of principles to govern search (to say nothing of the dangers of state censorship that a regulatory approach courts). These challenges may support more modest regulatory requirements to push firms to cooperate with independent researchers and submit to fines if they are found to manipulate organic search results in ways incompatible with our interests in information. If the companies fear that these requirements might compromise their intellectual property or the smooth functioning of their platforms, they may wish to voluntarily submit to independent reviews by agencies that they can better trust.

Even in circumstances of natural monopoly, it is important to note that public providers of services do not need to claim de jure monopolies. Just as the USPS is not the sole provider of shipping services, and the various public transit authorities are not the sole providers of transportation services, we might think it prudent to work toward updating our public information services to include a public option (alongside those privately provided).

This is likely to result in a productive conversation, whatever we think about Google.

It is natural, I think, to have a certain reaction to this chapter: I identify several issues with several popular proposals, without settling clearly on an answer. This is because I think the valuable work of this chapter has been less to tell you what to think than to help you think by clarifying the terms of the debate—a debate that frequently moves quickly from worries about censorship to proposals to break up big tech companies that do not obviously promise to alleviate the initial concerns. If you're unsatisfied by this, suffice to say that my current considered judgment is that the risks of strong regulation of search algorithms at this time outweigh the potential benefits. Our information environment is as good as I ever remember it being, and I fear worsening matters more than I desire a shot at making things better yet. Still, this judgment reflects my own risk assessment. For this reason alone, I caution you against using it to replace your own.

7

(Not So) Final Thoughts

The phenomenon of private censorship brings out a tension that has been deep within liberal thought at least since Mill's *On Liberty*. On the one hand, liberalism affirms that individuality and liberty of opinion are sacrosanct. On the other, it upholds a schedule of rights, understood as domains free from state interference, which effectively grant to persons and associations powers that can stifle individuality and promote conformity of opinion.

Being at liberty to express yourself enables you to speak truth to power or to play a part in legitimating power soundly exercised. But it also enables you to cow others into submission or to marginalize them so that their own expression falls on deaf ears. Having the freedom to associate allows you to choose your friends and co-workers and to shape your family and professional life after your own vision. But it also entails an ability to impose acute social costs on others for the choices they make in their own domains. And property rights, which entail broad rights to exclude, give you space in which you can pursue your interests without anyone's say-so. But they also enable you to exclude people for no good reason. Accordingly, liberal rights both enable eccentricity and can make it difficult for eccentrics to find their place.[1]

As new technologies have enabled new social movements to take hold and assert their influence over individuals in record time, these tensions have become salient. When the stakes are highest, the tensions threaten the liberal project at its foundations. As one commentator puts it, if leaving individuals and groups "to operate freely . . . impedes the development of individuality, then there is something self-undermining about the [liberal] project."[2]

---

[1] One must, of course, ask, *compared to what*? Will a society of conformists do better or worse to accommodate individuality with or without a system of liberal rights? Considering that curtailing, even limiting, such rights will create capacities for institutions to decide how far they extend, the advocate for an alternative to liberalism faces an uphill battle.

[2] See: (Threet 2018, 540). As Waldron puts the point, social coercion is "*nothing but* the upshot of people's actions and inclinations in a social context." He continues: "They comprise things people want to do . . . Placing limits on people's ability to act on these feelings and inclinations may itself give rise to an issue of liberty. People may have a right . . . to do the things which, at least when taken en masse, constitute the social coercion which Mill is attempting to stop" (Waldron 2003, 231).

Private Censorship. J.P. Messina, Oxford University Press. © Oxford University Press 2024.
DOI: 10.1093/oso/9780197581902.003.0007

For all that, liberals are not of one mind about the severity of the threat. Jeremy Waldron, for example, can sometimes seem skeptical that there is much of a problem at all. Here's what he says:

> The threat to liberty and individuality comes from the collective action of the public, inadvertently but lethally embodied in a concerted public opinion and a monolithic social atmosphere . . . But in our time even more than Mill's, with an increase in mobility, an increase in commerce and man- ufacture, an increase in the scope of the media, and an increase in common education, people are terribly vulnerable to mass public opinion. People "now read the same things, [. . .] go to the same places, have their hopes and fears directed to the same objects," and so on ([*On Liberty*,] p. 137). There is no need, really, for partisans of individuality to concoct an equally con- certed campaign to oppose that, because, on Mill's account, liberty will have a chance of flourishing whenever the social environment is *disconcerted*, whenever it is *not* collectively organized. This is one of those wonderful instances where the term "collective action problem" actually means what it says—it is collective action that is the problem, and there is no need for collective action in order to secure a solution. Any form of chaos, any lack of coordination, in individual views and lifestyles will help.[3]

Waldron seems to say that as long as there are domains free from "collective action"—in other words, collectively unregulated spaces—individuality will have a chance to flourish. So long as there is a bit of chaos, we need not be overly concerned with social tyranny or the exercise of private power that reflects it. Yet the mere chance that individuality will emerge is hardly an an- swer to the question at hand. Surely small pockets of chaos will not do if most people feel compelled by their peers to avoid them.

Fortunately, the quoted passage gives at best a partial flavor of Waldron's position. After all, he also emphasizes that there are "ways of exercising [our] associational and other rights better or worse, so far as individuality and progress are concerned."[4] Once we see that exercising our rights in the ways we might immediately be inclined to can keep our fellows from developing as individuals, we might refrain from exercising them in those ways. Such a reminder, I've argued throughout this book, is especially important to bear

---

[3] (Waldron 2003, 241).
[4] (Waldron 2020, 240.)

in mind when we are in charge of intermediate institutions and have a role in setting the terms of engagement.

Of course, in addition to too much collective action and too little room for liberty, there can be danger also in too little collective action. For example, one problem with sorting people into echo chambers is that it deprives us of a shared world and fragments our understanding of the problems we face.[5] This can make it difficult to address problems that require coordination. If so, intermediaries might do more to try to expose people to information that they might otherwise ignore and to frame information in ways that help address collective action problems. Or they might form alliances in which they articulate shared standards in an effort, not to suppress dissent about the standards, but to signal their strong support for them and encourage coordination that way. Whether these measures are likely to succeed is an empirical question.[6] Still, recognizing the ways we can exercise rights to our own collective detriment allows us to begin to describe the responsibilities that we have to ensure that things do not go badly awry.

Many prominent responses to the challenges of the current moment see this kind of response as inadequate. For various reasons, they suggest that we respond best so far as we limit liberal rights, or prioritize some over others. For instance, those most worried about the reach of private power and its effects on speech recommend weakening rights to speech, association, and property in response, at least for certain prominent actors. Those who believe the deleterious effects on speech are just the result of the exercise of rights to association and property, by contrast, can underestimate the importance of our real capacities to express ourselves, challenge narratives, and develop as individuals—capacities threatened by the exercise of the rights they rightly recognize. It is thus no surprise to see one and the same pattern of behavior described by some as accountability and the exercise of rights and by others as tyranny and oppression.

I have tried to take a different approach in this book—one that seeks to uphold strong rights against legal interference with expression, association, and property, while arguing in favor of moral limits to the exercise of the relevant rights. I have urged that we all have a role to play that consists in the responsible exercise of our own rights. This, Waldron might agree with.

---

[5] (Sunstein 2018).

[6] There is reason specifically to worry that simple exposure to opposing views might backfire, leading people to double down on their previously held beliefs. See: (Bail et al. 2018).

To recap: We began by discussing free speech and why it is valuable. We saw the appeal of accepting a pluralist account, according to which free speech isn't valuable for just one or a few but for many reasons. Appreciating this allowed us to see acutely the risks censorship and silencing carry with them. We also saw that there's no good reason to suppose that worrisome censorship is inherently a creature of state. Finally, we saw that nonstate censorship and state censorship merit different treatments.

From there, we went on to discuss the kinds of self-restraint that help realize a healthy epistemic environment—one where minority voices and heterodoxies can find their way into the marketplace of ideas. Where self-restraint fails, I argued that there were defeasible reasons for censoring those who fail to exercise speech rights responsibly and also powerful defeaters for those reasons. When reasons to censor are defeated, we must make do with rational engagement or strategic disengagement.

Of course, standards of responsible speech are demanding, and we often fall short. Our failures are many: We are bad at assessing information; we treat one another as enemies in the face of disagreement; we taunt others by lording our (own sense of our) superior intelligence or more seasoned experience over them; we harass out-groups and minorities sometimes with the (intended or unintended) effect that they continue to find themselves excluded from conversations that concern them.

For all this, and even holding fixed strong protections against state censorship, our information environment is not wholly at the mercy of our foibles. News editors and broadcast executives impose order on a sea of complex information so that there are credible sources against which various claims can be checked. The keepers of social media companies offer different moderation packages that try to strike a balance between various values. Search engines might transparently order or curate results in ways that are sensitive to common sense values while also delivering high-quality information, sensitive to user-preferences. Employers have reason to discipline the worst abuses of speech rights by employees in order to protect their public image (and our common values) and ensure a harmonious, respectful workplace.

Although responding to real failures, it would be implausible to hold that these intermediary regulators of speech never go too far. Throughout this book we've seen numerous real cases of bad action by persons in each of these positions of private power.

Still, the threats to which private censors are responding are real. Some appear existential in nature. We worry about dangerous speech, misinformation, partisanship, violence, harassment, and the strength of our political institutions. We witness our friends and family members taken in by nonsense, radicalized by individuals and groups on the internet and through the airwaves. We see our friends and co-citizens fired for innocent things that they've said or for truly awful things they've said recently or long ago. We see lives, careers, relationships ruined by online harassment campaigns, and we witness state secrets threatened by leaks. Private censors can mitigate some of these problems by moderating and curating content responsibly. But their exercise of their powers (which are continuous with their powers to censor) is subject to an effectiveness constraint and must at all times be guided by the importance of tolerating high-value speech (even when harmful).

Much of this book has occupied a skeptical position with respect to some popular proposed remedies for our sometimes toxic climate of discourse. I have suggested that ambitious proposals to regulate private powers are risky and misguided, even if the regulations ostensibly move platforms in a more speech-protective direction. I have also suggested that expecting large-scale intermediaries to assume the role of gatekeeper and editor is too much to ask given the limits of their competence. Of course, my own proposals— education and responsibility for individuals; professionalism, diversity, and competition in the press; transparency, public accountability, and experimentation for search and social media companies; and an ethics for private employers—can seem a naïve response to circumstances that require drastic measures.

If this is your reaction, I understand. Our current political moment appears untenable. It can seem like we need big changes, or else. I feel that, too. But although the current moment presents challenges, I believe that it is in facing these challenges and refusing to overreact to them that we will continue to show that our broader institutional framework is worth fighting for. Our current knowledge-preserving institutions are more diverse and robust than we often appreciate. Accordingly, I believe that there are lessons in the current moment that are more modest than those imagined by visionary planners and technocrats that recall hard lessons about how to be human in a rapidly changing world populated with others who think differently.

In my view, there is no panacea for the problems we face and dreams of a perfect world are better left to restful twilight than used to guide political action in waking life. Even if everything goes well, human beings will act individually and collectively in ways that are irrational. They will join movements for bad causes and they will believe theories that they shouldn't believe. The best we can hope to do is equip ourselves and each other with the tools necessary for living well. Whether (we) they use these tools for this purpose or not is ultimately up to them (us). This kind of self-governance (collective and individual) is as treacherous as it is worth protecting.

We face problems, it is true. But it is also well worth remembering that our access to good, reliable information has likely never been better than it is now. Never before has it been possible for ordinary people to not only make themselves heard in the great conversation but to listen to and access the best information that humanity has to offer. For those still without access to the internet due to want of infrastructure or authoritarian government, great advances still lie in wait. Things are alright, to some degree, and it would be a shame to address our problems in ways that undo the progress we've made. Many solutions currently on the table would create power structures that bad actors can turn against us. Others would lock us into relationships with the major tech companies of today (at the expense of those that might otherwise emerge tomorrow).

But although I do reject or at least have doubts about several popular proposals to address concerns about the pathologies of private power, and although I do think that it's worth not losing sight of just how good we have it, still, this book has not been a sanguine celebration of the status quo. Indeed, throughout the pages here I have suggested that a healthy speech environment well suited to the modern world requires certain institutional preconditions—preconditions that, if they exist at present, exist only tenuously.

We need reliable information and we need people to do some of the sorting for us (along with the determination of what is most crucial). Those who assume this work have a responsibility to behave as professionals and to resist their superiors when they are invited to abandon professionalism by the short-sighted pursuit of easy profit or political gain. To be able to genuinely deliberate, we want access to platforms for exchanging views with those unlike us and for sharing abuses publicly.[7] And to be able to find the best information quickly, we need search engines to organize the Web. There are things that firms, philanthropists, and governments can do now to shore up this environment.

---

[7] It is not surprising that many of those who will find themselves criticized on such platforms are fighting hard for the right to muzzle us by holding our platforms liable. But not everything worth resisting needs to surprise.

For example: Governments can undertake investments in state infrastructure for search and modernize the institutions designed to afford public access to information, including how to differentiate between reliable and unreliable sources. Philanthropists and governments can endow local news organizations, fund investigative, local journalism, and help practitioners build social trust. Social media platforms can improve their content moderation policies to better calibrate them to both the challenges of censorship and the harms of speech. Since many areas of content-moderation are contested, they can facilitate helpful debate about the concepts they deploy by publishing case files. They can submit to independent review of their moderation policies, as many of the largest among them already have. And they can form associations, as many professionals before have, for defining and understanding their rights and responsibilities. Search engines—especially when markets are highly concentrated—can make their data and algorithms available to researchers, under confidentiality agreements. They can commit, publicly, to refuse to manipulate organic search results, and submit to independent certification so that users can verify that they've kept to the principles they publicly avow. We can invest in information literacy for our populations at an early age, and employers can adopt policies that explicitly commit to standing by employees during times of controversy. All of this promises to move us closer to a situation in which deviant speech is less threatening and propaganda less effective than it is at present.

Even if we were to succeed in all of this, however (and certainly in the meantime) we ourselves have a lot of work to do—work that we need to help one another along in. Productive discussion on topics that concerns us all is as difficult as it is important. It is easy to misunderstand one another. We have different backgrounds and different skills. Some of us are well versed in logic and dialectics; others not. Some of us have read widely and deeply; others not. Some of us have benefited from years of education; others are beginning; still others are grown and need help understanding how things have changed.

There is a tendency in public conversations to presume that each of us is on an equal footing, and on one interpretation, that's all well and good: we should not condescend to one another and in an important normative sense, we are all equals. But in many other ways, we are not equals. This isn't a bad thing! It's crucial, I've suggested, to converse with people unlike ourselves. Doing so not only promises to help us along in learning about the world and about those we live with: it also promises to encourage creative thinking about the appropriate solutions to our collective problems. So far as education predicts a lack of worldly experience and the initiation into communities with norms that may be corrupt, those less educated have a lot to offer in our common conversations. Although a proclivity for dialectics can often be helpful in discussing matters of common concern, so too can too tight a dialectical focus induce us to forget that the sentiments matter, too. Those less inclined to abstract reasoning of the sort that might take place in the seminar room can correct pathologies in the ways of thinking best suited to that cloistered environment.

These concluding reflections, like the arguments throughout this book, reflect my own presuppositions of what we owe to other people and what will move us stably toward greater justice. Yet it is not lost on me that many of these presuppositions (e.g., the importance of institutional pluralism, the paramount importance of liberty as non-interference for ensuring an open future, and belief in the ability of individuals and groups of individuals to address areas of shared concern productively on their own) are in danger of becoming dead dogmas, empty husks of ideas that have lost their vital force.[8] As this danger intensifies, the defense of these ideas will become increasingly difficult.

If this trend is worth pushing back against, as I am confident that it is, we can no longer simply assume that the fundamental political questions are settled.[9] We must re-engage in the deepest questions about human nature and collective life. And we must do so in a way that does not merely dismiss the concerns of those who have become uncertain about once unquestionable traditional enlightenment liberal answers to these questions. To refuse to formulate good responses to the illiberal currents moving through our civilization is to give up the game, and the stakes are high. As we continue to navigate a world rife not just with private censorship but also with serious problems to which it is a response, we must ultimately accept the burden of defending positions we have become accustomed to take for granted. Ever the optimist, I trust that we will rise to the challenge.

---

[8] Compare (Mill 2003, 106–7).

[9] As the philosophers Dzenis and Nobre Faria suggest, even those who insist most strongly that all arguments deserve a hearing often refuse to question the foundations of liberalism, accepting the merits of the latter as settled and beyond dispute (Dzenis and Nobre Faria 2020). In the main text, I am suggesting that continuing in this way is no longer an option.

References

Adkins, Karen. 2019. "When Shaming Is Shameful: Double Standards in Online Shame Backlashes." *Hypatia* 34 (1): 76–97. https://doi.org/10.1111/hypa.12456.

Ahmed, Imran. 2021. "Pandemic Profiteers: The Business of Anti-Vaxx." Center for Countering Digital Hate.

Allcott, Hunt, and Matthew Gentzkow. 2017. "Social Media and Fake News in the 2016 Election." *Journal of Economic Perspectives* 31 (2): 211–36. https://doi.org/10.1257/jep.31.2.211.

Allcott, Hunt, Matthew Gentzkow, and Chuan Yu. 2019. "Trends in the Diffusion of Misinformation on Social Media." *Research & Politics* 6 (2): 205316801984855. https://doi.org/10.1177/2053168019848554.

Allyn, Bobby. 2020. "Reddit Bans the_Donald, Forum of Nearly 800,000 Trump Fans, Over Abusive Posts." NPR. June 29. https://www.npr.org/2020/06/29/884819923/reddit-bans-the_donald-forum-of-nearly-800-000-trump-fans-over-abusive-posts.

Altman, Jack. "How Much Does Employee Turnover Really Cost?" 2017. HuffPost. January 18. https://www.huffpost.com/entry/how-much-does-employee-turnover-really-cost_b_587fbaf9e4b0474ad4874fb7.

Aly, Waleed, and Robert Mark Sampson. 2019. "Political Correctness Gone Viral." In *Media Ethics, Free Speech, and the Requirements of Democracy*, 1st edition, edited by Carl Fox and Joe Saunders, 125–43. New York, NY: Routledge. https://doi.org/10.4324/9780203702444.

Ammori, Marvin. 2008. "The Fairness Doctrine: A Flawed Means to Attain a Noble Goal." *Administrative Law Review* 60 (4): 881–93.

Anderson, C. W., Leonard Downie, and Michael Schudson. 2016. *The News Media: What Everyone Needs to Know*. What Everyone Needs to Know. New York: Oxford University Press.

Anderson, Elizabeth. 2017. *Private Government*. Princeton, NJ: Princeton University Press.

Andersson, Lynne M., and Christine M. Pearson. 1999. "Tit for Tat? The Spiraling Effect of Incivility in the Workplace." *Academy of Management Review* 24 (3): 452–71. https://doi.org/10.5465/amr.1999.2202131.

Applebaum, Anne. 2021. "The New Puritans." *The Atlantic*. https://www.theatlantic.com/magazine/archive/2021/10/new-puritans-mob-justice-canceled/619818/.

Asch, Solomon E. 1955. "Opinions and Social Pressure." *Scientific American* 193 (5): 31–35. https://doi.org/10.1038/scientificamerican1155-31.

Austin, J. L. 1962. *How To Do Things with Words*. Oxford: Clarendon Press.

Bail, Christopher A. 2021. *Breaking the Social Media Prism: How to Make Our Platforms Less Polarizing*. 1st edition. Princeton, NJ: Princeton University Press.

Bail, Christopher A., Lisa P. Argyle, Taylor W. Brown, John P. Bumpus, Haohan Chen, M. B. Fallin Hunzaker, Jaemin Lee, Marcus Mann, Friedolin Merhout, and Alexander Volfovsky. 2018. "Exposure to Opposing Views on Social Media Can Increase Political Polarization." *Proceedings of the National Academy of Sciences* 115 (37): 9216–21. https://doi.org/10.1073/pnas.1804840115.

Balasubramani, Venkat. 2021. "Court Rejects Parler's Demand That Amazon Host Its Services." January 22. Technology & Marketing Law (blog). https://blog.ericgoldman.org/archives/2021/01/court-rejects-parlers-demand-that-amazon-host-its-services.htm.

Balkin, Jack. 2020. "How to Regulate (and Not Regulate) Social Media." Occasional Papers Series. Knight First Amendment Institute. https://knightcolumbia.org/content/how-to-regulate-and-not-regulate-social-media.

Barr, Alistair. 2014. "Mozilla CEO Brendan Eich Steps Down." *Wall Street Journal*, April 4, sec. Tech. https://online.wsj.com/article/SB1000142405270230353270457947974112 5367618.html.

Bauer, George. 2010. "eMonopoly: Why Internet-Based Monopolies Have an Inherent 'Get-Out-of-Jail-Free Card.'" *Brooklyn Law Review* 76: 731–73.

Behrouzian, Golnoosh, Erik C. Nisbet, Aysenur Dal, and Ali Carkoglu. 2016. "Resisting Censorship: How Citizens Navigate Closed Media Environments." *International Journal of Communication* 10: 4345–67.

Bejan, Teresa. 2019a. "Two Concepts of Freedom (of Speech)." *Proceedings of the American Philosophical Society* 163 (2): 95–107.

Bejan, Teresa. 2019b. *Mere Civility: Disagreement and the Limits of Toleration*. Reprint edition. Cambridge, MA: Harvard University Press.

Bell, Karissa. 2021. "Facebook Has Banned 3,000 Accounts for COVID-19 and Vaccine Misinformation." *Engadget*, August 18. https://www.engadget.com/facebook-removed-3000-accounts-covid-vaccine-misinformation-184254103.html.

Bell, Melina Constantine. 2021. "John Stuart Mill's Harm Principle and Free Speech: Expanding the Notion of Harm." *Utilitas* 33 (2): 162–79. https://doi.org/10.1017/S0953820820000229.

Benesch, Susan. 2020. "But Facebook's Not a Country: How to Interpret Human Rights Law for Social Media Companies." *Yale Journal of Regulation Online Bulletin* 3: 86–111.

Benkler, Yochai, Rob Faris, and Hal Roberts. 2018. *Network Propaganda: Manipulation, Disinformation, and Radicalization in American Politics*. New York: Oxford University Press.

Berkowitz, Eric. 2021. *Dangerous Ideas: A Brief History of Censorship in the West, from the Ancients to Fake News*. Boston: Beacon Press.

Bernstein, Joseph. 2021. "Bad News: Selling the Story of Disinformation." *Harper's Magazine*, August 9. https://harpers.org/archive/2021/09/bad-news-selling-the-story-of-disinformation/.

Bhargava, Vikram R. 2020. "Firm Responses to Mass Outrage: Technology, Blame, and Employment." *Journal of Business Ethics* 163 (3): 379–400. https://doi.org/10.1007/s10551-018-4043-7.

Billingham, Paul, and Tom Parr. 2020. "Enforcing Social Norms: The Morality of Public Shaming." *European Journal of Philosophy* 28 (4): 997–1016. https://doi.org/10.1111/ejop.12543.

Birnbaum, Emily. 2019. "Tulsi Gabbard Sues Google over Censorship Claims." The Hill. https://thehill.com/policy/technology/454746-tulsi-gabbard-sues-google-over-censorship-claims.

Blondheim, Menahem. 1994. *News over the Wires: The Telegraph and the Flow of Public Information in America, 1844–1897*. Harvard Studies in Business History 42. Cambridge, MA: Harvard University Press.

Bloom, J. Arthur. 2019. "EXCLUSIVE: Documents Detailing Google's 'News Blacklist' Show Manual Manipulation Of Special Search Results." https://dailycaller.com/2019/04/09/google-news-blacklist-search-manipulation/.

Bor, Alexander, and Michael Bang Petersen. 2022. "The Psychology of Online Political Hostility: A Comprehensive, Cross-National Test of the Mismatch Hypothesis." *American Political Science Review* 116 (1): 1–18. https://doi.org/10.1017/S0003055421000885.

Borden, Sandra L. 2010. "The Moral Justification of Journalism." In *Journalism Ethics: A Philosophical Approach*, edited by Christopher Meyers, 53–68. Practical and Professional Ethics Series. Oxford: Oxford University Press.

Bork, Robert H. 1993. *Antitrust Paradox*. 1st edition. New York; Toronto: Free Press.

Boudreaux, Donald. 2017. "Antitrust and Competition from a Market-Process Perspective." In *Research Handbook on Austrian Law and Economics*, edited by Todd J. Zywicki and Peter J. Boettke, 278–95. Cheltenham, UK: Edward Elgar Publishing. https://doi.org/10.4337/9781788113106.

Brady, William J., Killian McLoughlin, Tuan N. Doan, and Molly J. Crockett. 2021. "How Social Learning Amplifies Moral Outrage Expression in Online Social Networks." *Science Advances* 7 (33): 1–14. https://doi.org/10.1126/sciadv.abe5641.

Brehm, Jack. 1966. *A Theory of Psychological Reactance*. New York: Academic Press.

Broughton, Andrea, Tom Higgins, Ben Hicks, and Annette Cox. 2010. "Workplaces and Social Networking: The Implications for Employment Relations." Advisory, Conciliation and Arbitration Service (ACAS) Research Report.

Brown, Heather, Emily Guskin, and Amy Mitchell. 2012. "The Role of Social Media in the Arab Uprisings." https://www.pewresearch.org/journalism/2012/11/28/role-social-media-arab-uprisings/.

Bryant, Miranda. 2021. "Spiked New York Times Column on Reporter's Exit Published by New York Post." *The Guardian*, February 12, sec. Media. https://www.theguardian.com/media/2021/feb/12/bret-stephens-new-york-post-publishes-donald-mcneil-new-york-times-column.

Buchanan, James M. 2000. *The Limits of Liberty: Between Anarchy and Leviathan*. Vol. 7, *The Collected Works of James M. Buchanan*. Indianapolis: Liberty Fund.

Burns, Eric. 2006. *Infamous Scribblers: The Founding Fathers and the Rowdy Beginnings of American Journalism*. 1st edition. New York: Public Affairs.

Bushman, Brad J., and Angela D. Stack. 1996. "Forbidden Fruit versus Tainted Fruit: Effects of Warning Labels on Attraction to Television Violence." *Journal of Experimental Psychology: Applied* 2 (3): 207–26. https://doi.org/10.1037/1076-898X.2.3.207.

Butler, Judith. 1998. "Ruled Out: Vocabularies of the Censor." In *Censorship and Silencing: Practices of Cultural Regulation*, edited by Robert Post, 247–60. Issues & Debates. Los Angeles: Getty Research Institute for the History of Art and the Humanities.

Candeub, Adam. 2020. "Bargaining for Free Speech: Common Carriage, Network Neutrality, and Section 230." *Yale Journal of Law and Technology* 22: 391–433.

Carl, Jeremy. 2017. "How to Break Silicon Valley's Anti-Free-Speech Monopoly." *National Review*, 2017. https://www.nationalreview.com/2017/08/silicon-valleys-anti-conservative-bias-solution-treat-major-tech-companies-utilities/.

Cass, Ronald A. 1987. "The Perils of Positive Thinking: Constitutional Interpretation and Negative First Amendment Theory Melville B. Nimmer Symposium." *UCLA Law Review* 34 (5 & 6): 1405–92.

CBS/AP. 2020. "'When the Looting Starts, the Shooting Starts': Trump Tweet Flagged by Twitter for 'Glorifying Violence.'" https://www.cbsnews.com/news/trump-minneapolis-protesters-thugs-flagged-twitter/.

Chartier, Gary. 2018. *An Ecological Theory of Free Expression*. Cham: Palgrave Macmillan.

Cherry, Myisha V. 2021. *The Case for Rage: Why Anger Is Essential to Anti-racist Struggle*. New York: Oxford University Press.

Chomsky, Noam. 1989. *Necessary Illusions: Thought Control in Democratic Societies*. Boston, MA: South End Press.

Citron, Danielle Keats. 2018. "Extremist Speech, Compelled Conformity, and Censorship Creep." *Notre Dame Law Review* 93 (3): 1035–72.

Citron, Danielle Keats, and Benjamin Wittes. 2017. "The Internet Will Not Break: Denying Bad Samaritans § 230 Immunity." *Fordham Law Review* 86 (3): 401–23.

"Civility In America 2019: Solutions for Tomorrow." 2019. Weber Shandwick. https://www.webershandwick.com/wp-content/uploads/2019/06/CivilityInAmerica2019SolutionsforTomorrow.pdf.

Clark, Russell D., III. 1994. "The Role of Censorship in Minority Influence." *European Journal of Social Psychology* 24 (3): 331–38. https://doi.org/10.1002/ejsp.2420240303.

Clemons, Eric K., and Nehal Madhani. 2010. "Regulation of Digital Businesses with Natural Monopolies or Third-Party Payment Business Models: Antitrust Lessons from the Analysis of Google." *Journal of Management Information Systems* 27 (3): 43–80. https://doi.org/10.2753/MIS0742-1222270303.

CNN. 2020. "READ: Trump's Executive Order Targeting Social Media Companies." CNN. May 28. https://www.cnn.com/2020/05/28/politics/read-social-media-executive-order/index.html.

Cohen, Andrew I., and Andrew J. Cohen. 2022. "The Possibility and Defensibility of Nonstate 'Censorship.'" In *New Directions in the Ethics and Politics of Speech*, edited by J. P. Messina, 13–31. Political Philosophy for the Real World. New York: Routledge.

Conway, Lucian Gideon, Amanda Salcido, Laura Janelle Gornick, Kate Ashley Bongard, Meghan A. Moran, and Chelsea Burfiend. 2009. "When Self-Censorship Norms Backfire: The Manufacturing of Positive Communication and Its Ironic Consequences for the Perceptions of Groups." *Basic and Applied Social Psychology* 31 (4): 335–47. https://doi.org/10.1080/01973530903317169.

Cooper, Brittney. 2017. "How Free Speech Works for White Academics." *The Chronicle of Higher Education* 64 (13). https://www.chronicle.com/article/how-free-speech-works-for-white-academics/.

Cooper, James C., and William E. Kovacic. 2011–2012. "Behavioral Economics and Its Meaning for Antitrust Agency Decision Making." *Journal of Law, Economics & Policy* 8 (4): 779–800. https://heinonline.org/HOL/P?h=hein.journals/jecoplcy8&i=795.

Cooper, Joel, Shane Blackman, and Kyle Keller. 2016. "Resistance to Persuasion." In *The Science of Attitudes*, edited by Cooper, Blackman, and Keller, 205–31. New York: Routledge. https://doi.org/10.4324/9781315717319-12.

Dal Bo, E. 2006. "Regulatory Capture: A Review." *Oxford Review of Economic Policy* 22 (2): 203–25. https://doi.org/10.1093/oxrep/grj013.

Damore, James. 2017. "Why I Was Fired by Google." *Wall Street Journal*, August 11, sec. Life. https://www.wsj.com/articles/why-i-was-fired-by-google-1502481290.

Dannin, Ellen. 2007. "Why At-Will Employment Is Bad for Employers and Just Cause Is Good for Them." *Labor Law Journal*, 58 (5): 5–16.

Darnton, Robert. 2014. *Censors at Work*. New York: W.W. Norton & Company.

Davis, Michael. 2010. "Why Journalism Is a Profession." In *Journalism Ethics: A Philosophical Approach*, edited by Christopher Meyers, 91–102. Practical and Professional Ethics Series. Oxford: Oxford University Press.

Daymont, Thomas N. 2001–2002. "Effects of Job Displacement on Post-Displacement Earnings, The." *Journal of Legal Economics* 11 (3): 39–52. https://heinonline.org/HOL/P?h=hein.journals/jole11&i=249.

DeGuerin, Mack. 2022. "Dozens of States Are Jumping on the Social Media Censorship Bandwagon." Gizmodo. July 25. https://gizmodo.com/social-media-censorship-faceb ook-twitter-shadow-ban-1849320395.

Diamantis, Mihailis. 2021. "Algorithms Acting Badly: A Solution from Corporate Law." *The George Washington Law Review* 89 (4): 801–56. https://www.gwlr.org/algorithms-acting-badly/.

Diaz, Jaclyn. 2022. "Florida's Governor Signs Controversial Law Opponents Dubbed 'Don't Say Gay.'" NPR. March 28. https://www.npr.org/2022/03/28/1089221657/dont-say-gay-florida-desantis.

Downs, Anthony. 1957. *An Economic Theory of Democracy*. New York: Harper & Row.

Dzenis, Sandra, and Filipe Nobre Faria. 2020. "Political Correctness: The Twofold Protection of Liberalism." *Philosophia* 48 (1): 95–114. https://doi.org/10.1007/s11 406-019-00094-4.

The Economist. 2019. "Google Rewards Reputable Reporting, Not Left-Wing Politics." May 27. https://www.economist.com/graphic-detail/2019/06/08/google-rewards-reputable-reporting-not-left-wing-politics?fbclid=IwAR3k59jaPjXKc4F0GfZxhLNEc Dbewv7o50C3CILy_K79lvLAy1CTt6E2BGo.

Eggers, Andrew C., Haritz Garro, and Justin Grimmer. 2021. "No Evidence for Systematic Voter Fraud: A Guide to Statistical Claims about the 2020 Election." *Proceedings of the National Academy of Sciences* 118 (45): e2103619118. https://doi.org/10.1073/pnas.210 3619118.

Elkins, Emily. 2020. "Poll: 62% of Americans Say They Have Political Views They're Afraid to Share." Cato Institute. https://www.cato.org/survey-reports/poll-62-americans-say-they-have-political-views-theyre-afraid-share.

Emerson, Thomas I. 1964. "Freedom of Association and Freedom of Expression." *The Yale Law Journal* 74 (1): 1–35. https://doi.org/10.2307/794804.

Epstein, Richard A. 1984. "In Defense of the Contract at Will." *The University of Chicago Law Review* 51 (4): 947. https://doi.org/10.2307/1599554.

"EU Poised to Impose Sweeping Social Media Regulation with Digital Services Act." 2022. *The* Reporters Committee for Freedom of the Press (blog). May 9. https://www.rcfp.org/eu-dsa-social-media-regulation/.

Fagan, Jeffrey, and Tracey L Meares. 2008. "Punishment, Deterrence and Social Control: The Paradox of Punishment in Minority Communities." *Ohio Journal of Criminal Law* 6: 173–229.

Fine, Sarah. 2017. "Freedom of Association Is Not the Answer." In *Disputed Moral Issues: A Reader*, 5th edition, edited by Mark Timmons, 318–28. New York: Oxford University Press.

Finkel, Jacob, and Luciana Herman. 2017. "Fake News & Misinformation Policy Practicum." Stanford Law and Policy Lab. Stanford Law School.

Fish, Stanley. 1994. *There's No Such Thing As Free Speech: And It's a Good Thing, Too.* Oxford; New York: Oxford University Press.

Fish, Stanley. 2013. "Academic Freedom against Itself: Boycotting Israeli Universities." In *Think Again!: Contrarian Reflections on Life, Culture, Politics, Religion, Law, and Education*, edited by Stanley Fish, 402–6. Princeton, NJ: Princeton University Press.

Fish, Stanley. 2019. *The First: How to Think about Hate Speech, Campus Speech, Religious Speech, Fake News, Post-Truth, and Donald Trump*. 1st edition. New York: Atria.

Flood, Brian. 2017. "Bloomberg Editor-in-Chief Spikes Positive Story about Fox Business (Exclusive)." https://www.thewrap.com/bloomberg-exec-spikes-positive-story-about-rival-fox-business/.

Flynn, Kerry. 2021. "Teen Vogue's New Editor out of a Job after Backlash over Old Tweets | CNN Business." CNN. March 18. https://www.cnn.com/2021/03/18/media/alexi-mccammond-teen-vogue-out/index.html.

Forestal, Jennifer, and Abraham Singer. 2020. "Social Media Ethics and the Politics of Information." *Business Ethics Journal Review*, 8 (6): 32–38.

Fricker, Miranda. 2011. *Epistemic Injustice: Power and the Ethics of Knowing*. Oxford: Oxford University Press.

Frye, Harrison. 2022. "The Problem of Public Shaming." *Journal of Political Philosophy* 30 (2): 188–208. https://doi.org/10.1111/jopp.12252.

Fung, Brian. 2021. "Parler Sues Amazon for Cutting Off Its Services." CNN Business. https://www.cnn.com/2021/01/11/tech/parler-amazon-lawsuit/index.html.

Ghaffary, Shirin. 2019. "Political Tension at Google Is Only Getting Worse." Vox. August 2. https://www.vox.com/recode/2019/8/2/20751822/google-employee-dissent-james-damore-cernekee-conservatives-bias.

Garrett, Brandon L. 2014. "The Constitutional Standing of Corporations." *University of Pennsylvania Law Review* 163: 70.

Garrett, R. Kelly, and Brian E. Weeks. 2013. "The Promise and Peril of Real-Time Corrections to Political Misperceptions." *Proceedings of the 2013 Conference on Computer Supported Cooperative Work—CSCW '13*, 1047. https://doi.org/10.1145/2441776.2441895.

Gastil, John. 2019. "Seeking a Mutuality of Tolerance: A Practical Defense of Civility in a Time of Political Warfare." In *A Crisis of Civility? Political Discourse and Its Discontents*, edited by Boatwright, Shaffer, Sobieraj, and Young, 161–75. New York: Routledge.

Gelfand, Michele. 2018. *Rule Makers, Rule Breakers: How Tight and Loose Cultures Wire Our World*. New York: Scribner.

Gentzkow, Matthew, and Jesse M. Shapiro. 2006. "Media Bias and Reputation." *Journal of Political Economy* 114 (2): 280–316. https://doi.org/10.1086/499414.

Gentzkow, Matthew, and Jesse M Shapiro. 2008. "Competition and Truth in the Market for News." *The Journal of Economic Perspectives* 22 (2): 133–54.

Gentzkow, Matthew, and Jesse M Shapiro. 2010. "What Drives Media Slant? Evidence From U.S. Daily Newspapers." *Econometrica* 78 (1): 35–71. https://doi.org/10.3982/ECTA7195.

Gentzkow, Matthew, Jesse M Shapiro, and Michael Sinkinson. 2011. "The Effect of Newspaper Entry and Exit on Electoral Politics." *American Economic Review* 101 (7): 2980–3018. https://doi.org/10.1257/aer.101.7.2980.

Gentzkow, Matthew, Jesse M. Shapiro, and Michael Sinkinson. 2014. "Competition and Ideological Diversity: Historical Evidence from US Newspapers." *American Economic Review* 104 (10): 3073–3114. https://doi.org/10.1257/aer.104.10.3073.

Gervais, Bryan T. 2014. "Following the News? Reception of Uncivil Partisan Media and the Use of Incivility in Political Expression." *Political Communication* 31 (4): 564–83. https://doi.org/10.1080/10584609.2013.852640.

Gervais, Bryan T. 2015. "Incivility Online: Affective and Behavioral Reactions to Uncivil Political Posts in a Web-Based Experiment." *Journal of Information Technology & Politics* 12 (2): 167–85. https://doi.org/10.1080/19331681.2014.997416.

Gift, Karen, and Thomas Gift. 2015. "Does Politics Influence Hiring? Evidence from a Randomized Experiment." *Political Behavior* 37 (3): 653–75. https://doi.org/10.1007/s11109-014-9286-0.

Gillespie, Tarleton. 2018. *Custodians of the Internet: Platforms, Content Moderation, and the Hidden Decisions That Shape Social Media.* New Haven, CT: Yale University Press.

Gillett, M. Tyler. 2021. "Ohio AG Seeks to Have Google Declared Public Utility." Jurist. https://www.jurist.org/news/2021/06/ohio-ag-seeks-to-have-google-declared-public-utility/.

Gläßel, Christian, and Katrin Paula. 2020. "Sometimes Less Is More: Censorship, News Falsification, and Disapproval in 1989 East Germany." *American Journal of Political Science* 64 (3): 682–98. https://doi.org/10.1111/ajps.12501.

"Google Search Is Dying." 2022. DKB (blog). https://dkb.io/post/google-search-is-dying.

Gorwa, Robert, Reuben Binns, and Christian Katzenbach. 2020. "Algorithmic Content Moderation: Technical and Political Challenges in the Automation of Platform Governance." *Big Data & Society* 7 (1): 205395171989794. https://doi.org/10.1177/2053951719897945.

Guess, Andrew, Jonathan Nagler, and Joshua Tucker. 2019. "Less Than You Think: Prevalence and Predictors of Fake News Dissemination on Facebook." *Science Advances* 5 (1): eaau4586. https://doi.org/10.1126/sciadv.aau4586.

Guggenberger, Nikolas. 2020. "Essential Platform Monopolies: Open Up, then Undo." ProMarket (blog). https://promarket.org/2020/12/07/essential-facilities-regulation-platform-monopolies-google-apple-facebook/.

Haidt, Jonathan. 2013. *The Righteous Mind: Why Good People Are Divided by Politics and Religion.* Illustrated edition. New York: Vintage.

Hallin, Daniel C. 1986. *The "Uncensored War": The Media and Vietnam.* New York: Oxford University Press.

Han, Soo-Hye, LeAnn M. Brazeal, and Natalie Pennington. 2018. "Is Civility Contagious? Examining the Impact of Modeling in Online Political Discussions." *Social Media + Society* 4 (3): 205630511879340. https://doi.org/10.1177/2056305118793404.

Harcourt, Mark, Maureen Hannay, and Helen Lam. 2013. "Distributive Justice, Employment-at-Will and Just-Cause Dismissal." *Journal of Business Ethics* 115 (2): 311–25. https://doi.org/10.1007/s10551-012-1400-9.

Harrold, Emily, dir. 2013. *Reporting on the Times: The New York Times and the Holocaust—Educational Version with Public Performance Rights.* New York: Filmakers Library.

Hasnas, John. 2013. "Teaching Business Ethics: The Principles Approach." *Journal of Business Ethics Education* 10: 275–304. http://www.pdcnet.org/oom/service?url_ver=Z39.88-2004&rft_val_fmt=&rft.imuse_id=jbee_2013_0010_0275_0304&svc_id=info:www.pdcnet.org/collection.

Hawkins, Stephen, Daniel Yudkin, Miriam Juan-Torres, and Tim Dixon. 2019. *Hidden Tribes: A Study of America's Polarized Landscape.* New York, NY: More in Common. https://hiddentribes.us/media/qfpekz4g/hidden_tribes_report.pdf.

Hayek, Friedrich A. von. 1996. *Individualism and Economic Order.* Paperback edition, [Nachdr.]. Chicago: University of Chicago Press.

Hemmer, Nicole. 2017. "From 'Faith in Facts' to 'Fair and Balanced': Conservative Media, Liberal Bias, and the Origins of Balance." In *Media Nation*, edited by Bruce J. Schulman and Julian E. Zelizer, 126–43. Philadelphia, PA: University of Pennsylvania Press. https://doi.org/10.9783/9780812293746-009.

Herbst, Susan. 2010. *Rude Democracy: Civility and Incivility in American Politics.* Philadelphia: Temple University Press.

Herman, Edward S., and Noam Chomsky. 2002. *Manufacturing Consent: The Political Economy of the Mass Media.* New York: Pantheon Books.

Hern, Alex. 2021. "Facebook Lifts Ban on Posts Claiming Covid-19 Was Man-Made." *The Guardian.* May 27. http://www.theguardian.com/technology/2021/may/27/facebook-lifts-ban-on-posts-claiming-covid-19-was-man-made.

Hobbes, Thomas. 1994. *Leviathan: With Selected Variants from the Latin Edition of 1668.* Edited by E. M. Curley. Indianapolis: Hackett Pub. Co.

Hobbs, William R., and Margaret E. Roberts. 2018. "How Sudden Censorship Can Increase Access to Information." *American Political Science Review* 112 (3): 621–36. https://doi.org/10.1017/S0003055418000084.

Horwitz, Jeff. 2021. "Facebook Says Its Rules Apply to All. Company Documents Reveal a Secret Elite That's Exempt." *Wall Street Journal*, September 13, sec. Tech. https://www.wsj.com/articles/facebook-files-xcheck-zuckerberg-elite-rules-11631541353.

Horwitz, Keach Hagey, and Jeff Horwitz. 2021. "Facebook's Internal Chat Boards Show Politics Often at Center of Decision Making." *Wall Street Journal*, October 24, sec. Tech. https://www.wsj.com/articles/facebook-politics-decision-making-documents-1163 5100195.

Horwitz, Paul. 2013. *First Amendment Institutions.* Cambridge, MA: Harvard University Press.

Howard, Jeffrey W. 2019. "Dangerous Speech." *Philosophy & Public Affairs* 47 (2): 208–54. https://doi.org/10.1111/papa.12145.

Huemer, Michael. forthcoming. "When to Suppress Speech." *Georgetown Journal of Law & Public Policy*, forthcoming.

Humboldt, Wilhelm von. 1993. *The Limits of State Action.* Translated by J. W. Burrow. Indianapolis: Liberty Fund.

Iyengar, Shanto. 2016. "*E Pluribus Pluribus*, or Divided We Stand." *Public Opinion Quarterly* 80 (S1): 219–24. https://doi.org/10.1093/poq/nfv084.

Iyengar, Shanto, Yphtach Lelkes, Matthew Levendusky, Neil Malhotra, and Sean J. Westwood. 2019. "The Origins and Consequences of Affective Polarization in the United States." *Annual Review of Political Science* 22 (1): 129–46. https://doi.org/10.1146/annurev-polisci-051117-073034.

Jacquet, Jennifer. 2016. *Is Shame Necessary? New Uses for an Old Tool.* 1st edition. New York: Vintage Books.

Jansen, Sue Curry, and Brian Martin. 2003. "Making Censorship Backfire." *Counterpoise* 7 (3): 5–15.

Jansen, Sue Curry, and Brian Martin. 2015. "The Streisand Effect and Censorship Backfire." *International Journal of Communication* 9: 656–71.

Johnson, Carolyn Y., Yasmeen Abutaleb, and Joel Achenbach. 2021. "CDC Study Shows Three-Fourths of People Infected in Massachusetts Coronavirus Outbreak Were Vaccinated but Few Required Hospitalization." *Washington Post*, August 6. https://www.washingtonpost.com/health/2021/07/30/provincetown-covid-outbreak-vaccinated/.

Joshi, Hrishikesh. 2021. *Why It's OK to Speak Your Mind.* New York: Routledge.

Joshi, Hrishikesh. 2022. "Taxation, Ideology, and Higher Education." In *New Directions in the Ethics and Politics of Speech*, edited by J. P. Messina, 61–78. Political Philosophy for the Real World. New York: Routledge.

Joshi, Hrishikesh. forthcoming. "The Epistemic Significance of Social Pressure." *Canadian Journal of Philosophy.* https://philarchive.org/rec/JOSTES-2.

Kelly, Keith J. 2021. "Teen Vogue Editor Resigns Amid Uproar over Offensive Tweets from College Days." *New York Post* (blog). March 18. https://nypost.com/2021/03/18/teen-vogue-editor-resigns-amid-uproar-over-offensive-tweets-from-college/.

Kendi, Ibram X. 2019. *How to Be an Antiracist.* 1st edition. New York: One World.

Kitcher, Philip. 1990. "The Division of Cognitive Labor." *The Journal of Philosophy* 87 (1): 5–22. https://doi.org/10.2307/2026796.

Klonick, Kate. 2018. "The New Governors: The People, Rules, and Processes Governing Online Speech." *Harvard Law Review* 131: 1598–1670.

Kosseff, Jeff. 2019. *The Twenty-Six Words That Created the Internet.* Ithaca, NY: Cornell University Press.

Landry, Alexander P., Elliott Ihm, Spencer Kwit, and Jonathan W. Schooler. 2021. "Metadehumanization Erodes Democratic Norms during the 2020 Presidential Election." *Analyses of Social Issues and Public Policy* 21 (1): 51–63. https://doi.org/10.1111/asap.12253.

Langton, Rae. 1993. "Speech Acts and Unspeakable Acts." *Philosophy & Public Affairs* 22 (4): 293–330. https://www.jstor.org/stable/2265469.

Leavitt, Kieran. 2021. "Canada Lays Out Major Plans to Target Illegal Content on Facebook, YouTube, Pornhub and Other Platforms." *Toronto Star.* https://www.thestar.com/news/canada/2021/07/29/canada-proposes-digital-safety-commissioner-to-keep-illegal-content-off-facebook-youtube-pornhub-and-other-platforms.html?utm_source=Twitter&utm_medium=SocialMedia&utm_campaign=Federalpolitics&utm_content=digitalsafety.

Lebovic, Sam. 2016. *Free Speech and Unfree News: The Paradox of Press Freedom in America.* Cambridge, MA: Harvard University Press.

Leiter, Brian. 2014. "The Case against Free Speech." *Sydney Law Review* 38 (4): 407–39. https://doi.org/10.2139/ssrn.2450866.

Leiter, Brian. 2022. "The Epistemology of the Internet and the Regulation of Speech in America." SSRN Scholarly Paper ID 3939948. Rochester, NY: Social Science Research Network. https://doi.org/10.2139/ssrn.3939948.

Leiter, Michael P., Heather K. Spence Laschinger, Arla Day, and Debra Gilin Oore. 2011. "The Impact of Civility Interventions on Employee Social Behavior, Distress, and Attitudes." *Journal of Applied Psychology* 96 (6): 1258–74. https://doi.org/10.1037/a0024442.

Levy, Jacob. 2015. *Rationalism, Pluralism, and Freedom.* Oxford; New York: Oxford University Press.

Levy, Neil. 2020. "Virtue Signaling Is Virtuous." *Synthese* 198: 9545–62. https://doi.org/10.1007/s11229-020-02653-9.

Lichtenberg, Judith. 1987. "Foundations and Limits of Freedom of the Press." *Philosophy & Public Affairs* 16 (4): 329–55. https://doi.org/10.1017/CBO9781139172271.005.

Lippmann, Walter. 2008. *Liberty and the News.* 1st Princeton paperback edition. The James Madison Library in American Politics. Princeton, NJ: Princeton University Press.

Loury, Glenn C. 1994. "Self-Censorship in Public Discourse: A Theory of 'Political Correctness' and Related Phenomena." *Rationality and Society* 6 (4): 428–61. https://doi.org/10.1177/1043463194006004002.

Lukianoff, Greg, and Jonathan Haidt. 2019. *The Coddling of the American Mind: How Good Intentions and Bad Ideas Are Setting up a Generation for Failure.* New York: Penguin Books.

MacKinnon, Catherine A. 1994. *Feminism Unmodified: Discourses on Life and Law.* Cambridge, MA: Harvard University Press.

Macnab, Aidan. 2021. "Lawyers React to Proposed Regulatory Framework for 'Harmful Online Content.'" https://www.canadianlawyermag.com/practice-areas/privacy-and-data/lawyers-react-to-proposed-regulatory-framework-for-harmful-online-content/358586.

Madison, James. 1822. "James Madison to W. T. Barry, August 4, 1822." *Library of Congress.* https://www.loc.gov/resource/mjm.20_0155_0159/?sp=1&st=text.

Mandavilli, Apoorva. 2021. "C.D.C. Internal Report Calls Delta Variant as Contagious as Chickenpox." *The New York Times*, July 30, sec. Health. https://www.nytimes.com/2021/07/30/health/covid-cdc-delta-masks.html.

Manne, Geoffrey A., and Joshua D. Wright. 2011. "Google and the Limits of Antitrust: The Case against the Case against Google." *Harvard Journal of Law & Public Policy* 34 (1): 171–244. https://heinonline.org/HOL/P?h=hein.journals/hjlpp34&i=177.

Manne, Geoffrey A., and Joshua D. Wright. 2012. "If Search Neutrality Is the Answer, What's the Question." *Columbia Business Law Review* 2012 (1): 151–239. https://heinonline.org/HOL/P?h=hein.journals/colb2012&i=153.

Marantz, Andrew. 2019. *Antisocial: Online Extremists, Techno-Utopians, and the Hijacking of the American Conversation.* New York: Viking.

Marcuse, Herbert. 1965. "Repressive Tolerance." In *A Critique of Pure Tolerance*, 1st edition, by Robert Paul Wolff, Barrington Moore, Jr., and Herbert Marcuse, 81–123. Boston, MA: Beacon Press.

Mays, Lisa. 2015. "The Consequences of Search Bias: How Application of the Essential Facilities Doctrine Remedies Google's Unrestricted Monopoly on Search in the United States and Europe." *George Washington Law Review* 83 (2): 721–60. https://heinonline.org/HOL/P?h=hein.journals/gwlr83&i=755.

McGowan, Mary Kate. 2009. "Oppressive Speech." *Australasian Journal of Philosophy* 87 (3): 389–407. https://doi.org/10.1080/00048400802370334.

McGowan, Mary Kate. 2014. "Sincerity Silencing." *Hypatia* 29 (2): 458–73. https://doi.org/10.1111/hypa.12034.

McGowan, Mary Kate. 2019. *Just Words: On Speech and Hidden Harm.* 1st edition. Oxford: Oxford University Press.

McGowan, Mary Kate, Alexandra Adelman, Sara Helmers, and Jacqueline Stolzenberg. 2011. "A Partial Defense of Illocutionary Silencing." *Hypatia* 26 (1): 132–49. https://doi.org/10.1111/j.1527-2001.2010.01122.x.

McKinnon, Catriona. 2016. "Should We Tolerate Climate Change Denial?" *Midwest Studies In Philosophy* 40 (1): 205–16. https://doi.org/10.1111/misp.12056.

McNeil Jr., Donald. "NYTimes Peru N-Word, Part Four: What Happened in Peru?" *Medium* (blog), March 12, 2021. https://donaldgmcneiljr1954.medium.com/nytimes-peru-n-word-part-four-what-happened-in-peru-2a641a9b5e83.

Meadows, Maxwell. 2015. "The Essential Facilities Doctrine in Information Economies: Illustrating Why the Antitrust Duty to Deal Is Still Necessary in the New Economy." *Fordham Intellectual Property, Media and Entertainment Law Journal* 25 (3): 795–830.

Messina, J. P. 2020. "Freedom of Expression and the Liberalism of Fear." *Philosophers' Imprint* 20 (34): 17.

Messina, J. P. 2022a. "Ethics in Conversation: Why Mere Civility is Not Enough." *Georgetown Journal of Law and Public Policy* 20 (S): 1033–54.

Messina, J. P. 2022b. "Legal Protections for Employer Speech: Narrower, if at All." *International Comparative Approaches to Free Speech and Open Inquiry (FSOI)*, edited by Luke Sheahan, 219–42. London, UK: Palgrave Macmillan.

Messina, J. P. 2022c. "Public Calls for Censorship as Bad Speech." *Journal of Free Speech Law*, 2 (1): 87–106.

Metaxa, Danaë, Joon Sung Park, James A. Landay, and Jeff Hancock. 2019. "Search Media and Elections: A Longitudinal Investigation of Political Search Results." *Proceedings of the ACM on Human-Computer Interaction—CSCW '3*, 1–17. https://doi.org/10.1145/3359231.

Meyers, Christopher, ed. 2010. *Journalism Ethics: A Philosophical Approach*. Practical and Professional Ethics Series. Oxford: Oxford University Press.

Meyers, Christopher. 2019. "Partisan News, the Myth of Objectivity, and the Standards of Responsible Journalism." In *Media Ethics, Free Speech, and the Requirements of Democracy*, 1st edition, edited by Carl Fox and Joe Saunders, 219–39. New York: Routledge. https://doi.org/10.4324/9780203702444.

Mill, John Stuart. 2003. *On Liberty*. Edited by David Bromwich, George Kateb, and Jean Bethke Elshtain. Rethinking the Western Tradition. New Haven, CT: Yale University Press.

Miller, Christopher. 2021. "Far-Right Militias Are Recruiting on Facebook, Report Finds." BuzzFeed News. https://www.buzzfeednews.com/article/christopherm51/far-right-militias-facebook-recruiting-report.

Miller, Erin. 2022. "Media Power Through Epistemic Funnels." *Georgetown Journal of Law and Public Policy* 20 (S): 873–902.

Miškolci, Jozef, Kováčová, Lucia, and Rigová, Edita. 2020. "Countering Hate Speech on Facebook: The Case of the Roma Minority in Slovakia." *Social Science Computer Review* 38 (2): 128–46. https://doi.org/10.1177/0894439318791786.

Moore-Berg, Samantha L., Lee-Or Ankori-Karlinsky, Boaz Hameiri, and Emile Bruneau. 2020. "Exaggerated Meta-perceptions Predict Intergroup Hostility between American Political Partisans." *Proceedings of the National Academy of Sciences* 117 (26): 14864–72. https://doi.org/10.1073/pnas.2001263117.

Mosleh, Mohsen, Cameron Martel, Dean Eckles, and David Rand. 2021. "Perverse Downstream Consequences of Debunking: Being Corrected by Another User for Posting False Political News Increases Subsequent Sharing of Low Quality, Partisan, and Toxic Content in a Twitter Field Experiment." *Proceedings of the 2021 CHI Conference on Human Factors in Computing Systems* edited by Yoshifumi Kitamura and Aaron Quigley. —CHI '21, 1–13. https://doi.org/10.1145/3411764.3445642.

Mounk, Yascha. 2020. "Stop Firing the Innocent." *The Atlantic*. June 27. https://www.theatlantic.com/ideas/archive/2020/06/stop-firing-innocent/613615/.

Muldoon, Ryan. 2018a. "Campus Speech, Diverse Perspectives, and the Distribution of Burdens." In *The Value and Limits of Academic Speech*, edited by Chris W. Surprenant and Donald Downs, 285–99. New York: Routledge.

Muldoon, Ryan. 2018b. "The Paradox of Diversity." *Georgetown Journal of Law & Public Policy* 16 (Special Issue): 807–20. https://heinonline.org/HOL/P?h=hein.journals/geojlap16&i=824.

Muldoon, Ryan. 2022. "Speech, Sorting, and Discovery." In *New Directions in the Ethics and Politics of Speech*, edited by J. P. Messina, 32–49. Political Philosophy for the Real World. New York: Routledge.

Mullen, Andrew, and Jeffery Klaehn. 2010. "The Herman-Chomsky Propaganda Model: A Critical Approach to Analysing Mass Media Behaviour." *Sociology Compass* 4 (4): 215–29. https://doi.org/10.1111/j.1751-9020.2010.00275.x.

Mutz, Diana C. 2007. "Effects of 'In-Your-Face' Television Discourse on Perceptions of a Legitimate Opposition." *American Political Science Review* 101 (4): 621–35. https://doi.org/10.1017/S000305540707044X.

Mutz, Diana C. 2015. *In-Your-Face Politics: The Consequences of Uncivil Media*. Princeton, NJ: Princeton University Press.

Mutz, Diana C., and Jeffery J. Mondak. 2006. "The Workplace as a Context for Cross-Cutting Political Discourse." *The Journal of Politics* 68 (1): 140–55. https://doi.org/10.1111/j.1468-2508.2006.00376.x.

Myers, Fraser. 2020. "Why Has Google Censored the Great Barrington Declaration?" https://www.spiked-online.com/2020/10/12/why-has-google-censored-the-great-barrington-declaration/.

Nadim, Marjan, and Audun Fladmoe. 2021. "Silencing Women? Gender and Online Harassment." *Social Science Computer Review* 39 (2): 245–58. https://doi.org/10.1177/0894439319865518.

Nai, Alessandro. 2013. "What Really Matters Is Which Camp Goes Dirty: Differential Effects of Negative Campaigning on Turnout During Swiss Federal Ballots." *European Journal of Political Research* 52 (1): 44–70. https://doi.org/10.1111/j.1475-6765.2012.02060.x.

Naylor, Brian. 2021. "Read Trump's Jan. 6 Speech, A Key Part Of Impeachment Trial." NPR. February 10, sec. Politics. https://www.npr.org/2021/02/10/966396848/read-trumps-jan-6-speech-a-key-part-of-impeachment-trial.

Nelson, Stephen. 2022. "CBS 'Confirms' Hunter Biden Laptop Is Real 769 Days after Post Broke Story." *New York Post*, November 21. https://nypost.com/2022/11/21/cbs-confirms-hunter-biden-laptop-is-real-769-days-after-post-broke-story/.

Nizer, Louis. 1968. *The Jury Returns: My Life in Court*. Denver, CO: Pocket.

Noble, Safiya Umoja. 2018. *Algorithms of Oppression: How Search Engines Reinforce Racism*. Illustrated edition. New York: NYU Press.

Norlock, Kathryn J. 2017. "Online Shaming." *Social Philosophy Today* 33: 187–97. https://doi.org/10.5840/socphiltoday201762343.

Norton, Helen. 2009. "Constraining Public Employee Speech: Government's Control of Its Workers Speech to Protect Its Own Expression." *Duke Law Journal* 59 (2): 1–68.

Nozick, Robert. 1974. *Anarchy, State, and Utopia*. New York: Basic Books.

Nussbaum, Emily. 2019. "CBS Censors 'The Good Fight' for a Musical Short About China." *The New Yorker*. https://www.newyorker.com/culture/culture-desk/cbs-censors-the-good-fight-for-a-musical-short-about-china.

"NY State Assembly Bill A7865a." 2021. NY State Senate. June 9. https://www.nysenate.gov/legislation/bills/2021/a7865/amendment/a.

Ott, Haley. 2022. "Teacher Jailed for Contempt of Court in Dispute over Misgendering Student." MSN. 2022. https://www.msn.com/en-us/news/crime/teacher-jailed-for-contempt-of-court-in-dispute-over-misgendering-student/ar-AA11x0e4.

Page, Scott, and Katherine Phillips. 2017. *The Diversity Bonus: How Great Teams Pay Off in the Knowledge Economy*. Edited by Earl Lewis and Nancy Cantor. Princeton, NJ: Princeton University Press.

Pasquale, Frank. 2008. "Asterisk Revisited: Debating a Right of Reply on Search Results." *Journal of Business and Technology Law* 3 (1): 61–85.

Pennycook, Gordon, Adam Bear, Evan T. Collins, and David G. Rand. 2020. "The Implied Truth Effect: Attaching Warnings to a Subset of Fake News Headlines Increases Perceived Accuracy of Headlines without Warnings." *Management Science* 66 (11): 4944–57. https://doi.org/10.1287/mnsc.2019.3478.

Pew Research. 2022. "Social Media and News Fact Sheet." *Pew Research Center's Journalism Project* (blog). Accessed November 20, 2022. https://www.pewresearch.org/journalism/fact-sheet/social-media-and-news-fact-sheet/.

Phillips, Katherine W., Katie A. Liljenquist, and Margaret A. Neale. 2009. "Is the Pain Worth the Gain? The Advantages and Liabilities of Agreeing with Socially Distinct Newcomers." *Personality and Social Psychology Bulletin* 35 (3): 336–50. https://doi.org/10.1177/0146167208328062.

Plato. 1997. "The Gorgias." In *Complete Works*, edited by John M. Cooper and D. S. Hutchinson, translated by Donald Zeyl, 791–869. Indianapolis: Hackett.

Porath, Christine L., Alexandra Gerbasi, and Sebastian L. Schorch. 2015. "The Effects of Civility on Advice, Leadership, and Performance." *Journal of Applied Psychology* 100 (5): 1527–41. https://doi.org/10.1037/apl0000016.

Posner, Richard A. 2019. *Antitrust Law*. 2nd edition. Chicago, IL: University of Chicago Press.

Powers, Kathleen E., and Dan Altman. 2022. "The Psychology of Coercion Failure: How Reactance Explains Resistance to Threats." *American Journal of Political Science* (June): ajps.12711. https://doi.org/10.1111/ajps.12711.

Pressman, Matthew. 2017. "Objectivity and Its Discontents: The Struggle for the Soul of American Journalism in the 1960s and 1970s." In *Media Nation*, edited by Bruce J. Schulman and Julian E. Zelizer, 96–113. Philadelphia, PA: University of Pennsylvania Press. https://doi.org/10.9783/9780812293746-007.

Pulitzer, Joseph. 1904. "The College of Journalism." *The North American Review* 178 (570): 641–80. https://www.jstor.org/stable/25119561.

Purnell, Newley. 2021. "India Accused of Censorship for Blocking Social Media Criticism amid Covid Surge." *Wall Street Journal*, April 26, sec. World. https://www.wsj.com/articles/india-accused-of-censorship-for-blocking-social-media-criticism-amid-covid-surge-11619435006.

Radin, Tara J., and Patricia H. Werhane. 2003. "Employment-at-Will, Employee Rights, and Future Directions for Employment." *Business Ethics Quarterly* 13 (2): 113–30. https://doi.org/10.5840/beq200313212.

Radzik, Linda. 2020. *The Ethics of Social Punishment: The Enforcement of Morality in Everyday Life*. Cambridge, UK; New York: Cambridge University Press.

Rasmussen, Katharina Berndt, and Nicolas Olsson Yaouzis. 2020. "#MeToo, Social Norms, and Sanctions." *Journal of Political Philosophy* 28 (3): 273–95. https://doi.org/https://doi.org/10.1111/jopp.12207.

Rauch, Jonathan. 2021. *The Constitution of Knowledge: A Defense of Truth*. Washington, DC: Brookings Institution Press.

Rid, Thomas. 2020. *Active Measures: The Secret History of Disinformation and Political Warfare*. New York: Farrar, Straus and Giroux.

Robinson, Charles. 2020. "In Light of George Floyd's Death, Ex-NFL Exec Admits What We Knew All Along: Protests Ended Colin Kaepernick's Career." Yahoo. https://www.yahoo.com/now/in-light-of-george-floyds-death-ex-nfl-exec-admits-what-we-knew-all-along-protests-ended-colin-kaepernicks-career-175616379.html.

Robinson, Nathan. 2020. "Facebook Has The Power To Repeal The First Amendment." *Current Affairs*. https://www.currentaffairs.org/2020/05/facebook-has-the-power-to-repeal-the-first-amendment.

Roese, Neal J., and Gerald N. Sande. 1993. "Backlash Effects in Attack Politics." *Journal of Applied Social Psychology* 23 (8): 632–53. https://doi.org/10.1111/j.1559-1816.1993.tb01106.x.

Rosenberg, Benjamin D., and Jason T. Siegel. 2018. "A 50-Year Review of Psychological Reactance Theory: Do Not Read This Article." *Motivation Science* 4 (4): 281–300. https://doi.org/10.1037/mot0000091.

Rosling, Hans, Ola Rosling, and Anna Rosling Rönnlund. 2018. *Factfulness: Ten Reasons We're Wrong about the World—and Why Things Are Better Than You Think*. 1st edition. New York: Flatiron Books.

Rudy, Jesse. 2002. "What They Don't Know Won't Hurt Them: Defending Employment-at-Will in Light of Findings That Employees Believe They Possess Just Cause Protection." *Berkeley Journal of Employment and Labor Law* 23 (2): 307–68. https://heinonline.org/HOL/P?h=hein.journals/berkjemp23&i=315.

Sachs, Jeffrey. 2021. "Supporters of Anti-Woke Laws Haven't Thought It Through." *Arc Digital* (blog). March 5. https://medium.com/arc-digital/supporters-of-anti-woke-laws-havent-thought-it-through-5a061cd24fca.

Saul, Derek, and Forbes Staff. 2022. "'Freedom Of Speech, but Not Freedom Of Reach': Musk Reinstates Kathy Griffin and Jordan Peterson Amid New Policy—but Not Trump Yet." https://www.msn.com/en-us/money/companies/freedom-of-speech-but-not-freedom-of-reach-musk-reinstates-kathy-griffin-and-jordan-peterson-amid-new-policy-e2-80-94-but-not-trump-yet/ar-AA14kucv.

Scanlon, T. M. 2011. "Why Not Base Free Speech on Autonomy or Democracy?" *Virginia Law Review* 97 (3): 541–48. https://www.jstor.org/stable/41261520.

Scanlon, Thomas. 1972. "A Theory of Freedom of Expression." *Philosophy & Public Affairs* 1 (2): 204–26. https://www.jstor.org/stable/2264971.

Schauer, Frederick. 1982. *Free Speech: A Philosophical Enquiry*. Cambridge, UK: Cambridge University Press.

Schauer, Frederick. 1998. "The Ontology of Censorship." In *Censorship and Silencing: Practices of Cultural Regulation*, edited by Robert Post, 147–68. Issues & Debates. Los Angeles: Getty Research Institute for the History of Art and the Humanities.

Schudson, Michael. 1978. *Discovering the News: A Social History of American Newspapers*. New York: Basic Books.

Scudder, Mary F. *Beyond Empathy and Inclusion: The Challenge of Listening in Democratic Deliberation*. New York, NY: Oxford University Press, 2020.

Seifert, Kevin, and Dan Graziano. 2018. "NFL Owners Pass New National Anthem Policy." ESPN.com. May 23. https://www.espn.com/nfl/story/_/id/23582533/nfl-owners-approve-new-national-anthem-policy.

Seldes, George. 1935. *Freedom of the Press*. Indianapolis: The Bobbs-Merrill Company.

Sheahan, Luke C. 2020. *Why Associations Matter: The Case for First Amendment Pluralism*. Lawrence: University Press of Kansas.

Shephard, Alex. 2021. "Don't Fire People for Dumb Tweets." *The New Republic*, January 22. https://newrepublic.com/article/161029/will-wilkinson-tweets-cancel-culture.

Sherman, Roger. 2008. *Market Regulation*. Hoboken, NJ: Prentice Hall.

Shmargad, Yotam, Kevin Coe, Kate Kenski, and Stephen A. Rains. 2022. "Social Norms and the Dynamics of Online Incivility." *Social Science Computer Review* 40 (3): 717–35. https://doi.org/10.1177/0894439320985527.

Siegel, Alexandra A., and Vivienne Badaan. 2020. "#No2Sectarianism: Experimental Approaches to Reducing Sectarian Hate Speech Online." *American Political Science Review* 114 (3): 837–55. https://doi.org/10.1017/S0003055420000283.

Simons, Josh, and Dipayan Ghosh. 2020. "Utilities for Democracy: Why and How the Algorithmic Infrastructure of Facebook and Google Must Be Regulated." *Foreign Policy at Brookings*, 1–28.

Singer, Jane B. 2010. "Norms and the Network: Journalistic Ethics in a Shared Media Space." In *Journalism Ethics: A Philosophical Approach*, edited by Christopher Meyers, 117–29. Practical and Professional Ethics Series. Oxford: Oxford University Press.

Slechten, Laura, Cédric Courtois, Lennert Coenen, and Bieke Zaman. 2022. "Adapting the Selective Exposure Perspective to Algorithmically Governed Platforms: The Case of Google Search." *Communication Research* 49 (8): 1039–65. https://doi.org/10.1177/00936502211012154.

Smith, Craig. 1999. "The Campaign to Repeal the Fairness Doctrine." *Rhetoric & Public Affairs* 2 (3): 481–505. https://doi.org/10.1353/rap.2010.0134.

Soley, Lawrence. 2002. *Censorship, Inc.: The Corporate Threat to Free Speech in the United States*. New York: Monthly Review Press.

Starr, Paul. 2005. *The Creation of the Media: Political Origins of Modern Communications*. New York: Basic Books.

Steindl, Christina, Eva Jonas, Sandra Sittenthaler, Eva Traut-Mattausch, and Jeff Greenberg. 2015. "Understanding Psychological Reactance: New Developments and Findings." *Zeitschrift Für Psychologie* 223 (4): 205–14. https://doi.org/10.1027/2151-2604/a000222.

Stigler, George J. 1971. "The Theory of Economic Regulation." *The Bell Journal of Economics and Management Science* 2 (1): 3. https://doi.org/10.2307/3003160.

Stout, Lynn A. 2012a. "The Problem of Corporate Purpose." *The Brookings Institution*, Governance Studies, no. 48: 1–14.

Stout, Lynn A. 2012b. *The Shareholder Value Myth: How Putting Shareholders First Harms Investors, Corporations, and the Public*. 1st edition. San Francisco: Berrett-Koehler.

Strossen, Nadine. 2018. *Hate: Why We Should Resist It with Free Speech, Not Censorship*. Inalienable Rights Series. New York: Oxford University Press.

Stroud, Natalie Jomini, Joshua M. Scacco, Ashley Muddiman, and Alexander L. Curry. 2015. "Changing Deliberative Norms on News Organizations' Facebook Sites." *Journal of Computer-Mediated Communication* 20 (2): 188–203. https://doi.org/10.1111/jcc4.12104.

Sunstein, Cass R. 2018. *#Republic: Divided Democracy in the Age of Social Media*. 1st paperback printing. Princeton, NJ; Oxford: Princeton University Press.

Sunstein, Cass R. 2021. *Liars: Falsehoods and Free Speech in an Age of Deception*. 1st edition. New York: Oxford University Press.

Schwaiger, Tobias M. 2020. "Wir dürfen die Kritik am Öffentlich-Rechtlichen Rundfunk nicht den Populisten überlassen." *Telepolis*. https://www.heise.de/tp/features/Wir-duerfen-die-Kritik-am-Oeffentlich-Rechtlichen-Rundfunk-nicht-den-Populisten-uebe rlassen-4886435.html.

Talisse, Robert B. 2019. *Overdoing Democracy: Why We Must Put Politics in Its Place*. New York: Oxford University Press.

Taylor, Robert S. 2017. *Exit Left: Markets and Mobility in Republican Thought*. 1st edition. Oxford: Oxford University Press.

Tepper, Jonathan. 2019. "Facebook and Google Must Be Regulated Now." The American Conservative. May 13. https://www.theamericanconservative.com/facebook-and-goo gle-must-be-regulated-now/.

The Associated Press. 2022. "EU Law Targets Big Tech over Hate Speech, Disinformation." NPR. April 23, sec. Technology. https://www.npr.org/2022/04/23/1094485542/eu-law-big-tech-hate-speech-disinformation.

"The Bill of Rights: A Transcription." 2015. National Archives. November 4. https://www.archives.gov/founding-docs/bill-of-rights-transcript.

The Editorial Board. 2021. "Opinion | Censorship Coordination Deepens." *Wall Street Journal*, July 16, sec. Opinion. https://www.wsj.com/articles/censorship-coordination-deepens-11626474643.

Thierer, Adam. 2013. "The Perils of Classifying Social Media Platforms as Public Utilities." *CommLaw Conspectus: Journal of Communications Law and Technology Policy* 21 (2): 249–97. https://scholarship.law.edu/commlaw/vol21/iss2/2.

Thomason, Krista K. 2018. *Naked: The Dark Side of Shame and Moral Life*. New York: Oxford University Press.

Thomason, Krista K. 2021. "The Moral Risks of Online Shaming." In *The Oxford Handbook of Digital Ethics*, edited by Carissa Véliz. 1–19. Oxford: Oxford University Press. https://doi.org/10.1093/oxfordhb/9780198857815.013.8.

Threet, Dan. 2018. "Mill's Social Pressure Puzzle:" *Social Theory and Practice* 44 (4): 539–65. http://www.pdcnet.org/oom/service?url_ver=Z39.88-2004&rft_val_fmt=&rft.imuse_id=soctheorpract_2018_0044_0004_0539_0565&svc_id=info:www.pdcnet.org/collection.

Tirole, Jean. 2017. *Economics for the Common Good*. Translated by Steven Rendall. Princeton, NJ: Princeton University Press.

Tosi, Justin, and Brandon Warmke. 2020. *Grandstanding: The Use and Abuse of Moral Talk*. New York, NY: Oxford University Press.

Tuccille, J. D. 2023. "Twitter Files Reveal Politicians, Officials Evading the Constitution's Restrictions." Reason.com. January 1. https://reason.com/2023/01/02/twitter-files-reveal-politicians-officials-evading-the-constitutions-restrictions/.

Tucker, Joshua, Andrew Guess, Pablo Barbera, Cristian Vaccari, Alexandra Siegel, Sergey Sanovich, Denis Stukal, and Brendan Nyhan. 2018. "Social Media, Political Polarization, and Political Disinformation: A Review of the Scientific Literature." The William and Flora Hewlett Foundation. https://www.ssrn.com/abstract=3144139.

Twitter. 2021. "Permanent Suspension of @realDonaldTrump." Twitter Blog. 2021. https://blog.twitter.com/en_us/topics/company/2020/suspension.

University of California. 1999. "Tools for Department Chairs and Deans: Tool: Recognizing Microaggressions and the Messages They Send." http://web.archive.org/web/20210730141212/https://diversity.ucsf.edu/sites/diversity.ucsf.edu/files/Tools%20for%20Department%20Chairs%20and%20Deans.pdf.

U.S. Department of Justice v. Google LLC. 2020. Case 1:20-cv-03010. "Complaint."

Volokh, Eugene. 2012. "Private Employees' Speech and Political Activity: Statutory Protection against Employer Retaliation." *Texas Review of Law and Politics* 16 (2): 42.

Volokh, Eugene. 2021. "What Cheap Speech Has Done: (Greater) Equality and Its Discontents." *UC Davis Law Review* 54: 2303–40.

Waldron, Jeremy. 1981. "A Right to Do Wrong." *Ethics*, 92 (1): 21–39.

Waldron, Jeremy. 2003. "Mill as a Critic of Culture and Society." In *On Liberty*, edited by David Bromwich and George Kateb, 224–46. New Haven, CT: Yale University Press.

Waldron, Jeremy. 2014. *The Harm in Hate Speech*. 1st paperback edition. Cambridge: Harvard University Press.

Waldron, Jeremy. 2020. "Debate: Taking Offense: A Reply." *Journal of Political Philosophy* 28 (3): 343–52. https://doi.org/https://doi.org/10.1111/jopp.12229.

Walker, David D., Danielle D. van Jaarsveld, and Daniel P. Skarlicki. 2017. "Sticks and Stones Can Break My Bones but Words Can Also Hurt Me: The Relationship between Customer Verbal Aggression and Employee Incivility." *Journal of Applied Psychology* 102 (2): 163–79. https://doi.org/10.1037/apl0000170.

Wall Street Journal. 2021. "The Facebook Files." October 1, sec. Tech. https://www.wsj.com/articles/the-facebook-files-11631713039.

Wasow, Omar. 2020. "Agenda Seeding: How 1960s Black Protests Moved Elites, Public Opinion and Voting." *American Political Science Review,* 3 (114): 638–59.

Weber, Patrick, Fabian Prochazka, and Wolfgang Schweiger. 2019. "Why User Comments Affect the Perceived Quality of Journalistic Content: The Role of Judgment Processes." *Journal of Media Psychology* 31 (1): 24–34. https://doi.org/10.1027/1864-1105/a000217.

White, Stuart. 1997. "Freedom of Association and the Right to Exclude." *Journal of Political Philosophy* 5 (4): 373–91. https://doi.org/https://doi.org/10.1111/1467-9760.00039.

Williams, Daniel. 2022. "The Marketplace of Rationalizations." *Economics and Philosophy* (March): 1–25. https://doi.org/10.1017/S0266267121000389.

Witt, Mariah. 2019. "Don't Google It: The European Union's Antitrust Parade ('Enforcement') against America's Tech Giants." *San Diego International Law Journal* 21 (1): 365–98. https://digital.sandiego.edu/ilj/vol21/iss1/12.

Woan, Tansy. 2013. "Searching for an Answer: Can Google Legally Manipulate Search Engine Results?" *University of Pennsylvania Journal of Business Law* 16: 294–331.

Woodruff, Betsy Swan, and Nicholas Wu. 2021. "Secret Service Warned Capitol Police about Violent Threats 1 Day Before Jan. 6." Politico. 2021. https://www.politico.com/news/2021/08/25/secret-service-warned-capitol-police-violent-threats-january-riot-506806.

Worchel, Stephen, and Susan E. Arnold. 1973. "The Effects of Censorship and Attractiveness of the Censor on Attitude Change." *Journal of Experimental Social Psychology* 9 (4): 365–77. https://doi.org/10.1016/0022-1031(73)90072-3.

Worsnip, Alex. 2018. "The Obligation to Diversify One's Sources: Against Epistemic Partisanship in the Consumption of News Media." In *Media Ethics, Free Speech, and the Requirements of Democracy,* edited by Carl Fox and Joe Saunders, 240–64. New York, NY: Routledge. https://doi.org/10.4324/9780203702444-14.

Wragg, Paul. 2015. "Free Speech Rights at Work: Resolving the Differences between Practice and Liberal Principle." *Industrial Law Journal* 44 (1): 1–28. https://doi.org/10.1093/indlaw/dwu031.

Wright, Ava Thomas. 2021. "Mill's Social Epistemic Rationale for the Freedom to Dispute Scientific Knowledge: Why We Must Put Up with Flat-Earthers." *Philosophers' Imprint* 21 (14): 1–14.

Wu, Tim. 2011a. "Is Filtering Censorship?: The Second Free Speech Tradition." In *Constitution 3.0,* edited by Jeffrey Rosen and Benjamin Wittes, 83–99. Washington, DC: Brookings Institution Press.

Wu, Tim. 2011b. *The Master Switch: The Rise and Fall of Information Empires.* 1st edition. New York: Vintage Books.

Wu, Tim. 2018. *The Curse of Bigness: Antitrust in the New Gilded Age.* New York: Columbia Global Reports.

Wyatt, Wendy N. 2010. "The Ethical Obligations of News Consumers." In *Journalism Ethics: A Philosophical Approach*, edited by Christopher Meyers, 283–95. Practical and Professional Ethics Series. Oxford: Oxford University Press.

Yglesias, Matthew. 2020. "The Real Stakes in the David Shor Saga." *Vox.* July 29. https://www.vox.com/2020/7/29/21340308/david-shor-omar-wasow-speech.

Zamalin, Alex. 2021. *Against Civility: The Hidden Racism in Our Obsession with Civility.* Boston, MA: Beacon Press.

Zelizer, Julian E. 2017. "How Washington Helped Create the Contemporary Media: Ending the Fairness Doctrine in 1987." In *Media Nation: The Political History of News in Modern America*, edited by Bruce J. Schulman, 176–89. Philadelphia, PA: University of Pennsylvania Press. https://doi.org/10.9783/9780812293746-012.

Index

For the benefit of digital users, indexed terms that span two pages (e.g., 52–53) may, on occasion, appear on only one of those pages.